THE COMPLETE
CANOEIST'S GUIDE

ALSO BY RAYMOND BRIDGE

The Complete Snow Camper's Guide
America's Backpacking Book
Freewheeling: The Bicycle Camping Book
Tourguide to the Rocky Mountain Wilderness
The Camper's Guide to Alaska, the Yukon,
and Northern British Columbia
Climbing: A Guide to Mountaineering
The Complete Guide to Kayaking

THE COMPLETE CANOEIST'S GUIDE

Raymond Bridge

CHARLES SCRIBNER'S SONS · NEW YORK

Library of Congress Cataloging in Publication Data
Bridge, Raymond.
  The complete canoeist's guide.
  Includes index.
  1. Canoes and canoeing. 2. White-water canoeing.
I. Title.
GV783.B65   797.1'22   77-27865
ISBN 0-684-15369-6

1 3 5 7 9 11 13 15 17 19 V/C 20 18 16 14 12 10 8 6 4 2

PRINTED IN THE UNITED STATES OF AMERICA

To MADDIE,

with thanks and appreciation

CONTENTS

THE COMPLETE
CANOEIST'S GUIDE

INTRODUCTION

Canoeing has passed through many phases during its long history in North America. The canoe was the primary means of transportation for many Indian tribes, who invented it when they needed a practical way to move about and to hunt throughout much of the North American continent. It is still the perfect wilderness vehicle for many regions. It can be paddled over small ponds a few inches deep and across large lakes with winds raising six-foot waves. It will negotiate small streams, large rivers, and winding rapids. It can be used to carry heavy loads, yet it is light enough to be carried across rough terrain by a single person. That is why it was a favorite of Chippewa Indians and of European traders, trappers and explorers. It is still a favorite of wilderness wanderers today.

Besides remaining the preferred craft on North American wilderness waterways through the centuries, the canoe has been in vogue as a fixture for summer camps and an acceptable means for courting couples to find time alone on a Sunday afternoon. It is still a popular craft for many family outings on local lakes and for fishermen who want light boats that can be used in nearly every kind of water.

Modern materials and modern tastes have, however, come up with uses for the canoe that its inventors would have studiously avoided. The canoe provides a means of accepting the challenge of turbulent white-water, and canoeists now run extremely difficult rapids for the fun of it. Paddlers will travel for hundreds of miles to reach a stretch

Canoeing can be many things: running white-water in remote canyons like this (ABOVE), far from civilization and help, or a family outing on a small lake in a city park (RIGHT).

of pounding water that the Indian and the trapper carefully carried their canoes around, partly because birch bark was more fragile than modern hulls and partly because life for wilderness dwellers had enough built-in adventure to obviate the need for extra thrills.

Canoeing was once a technique of wilderness travel, and it is to this day. Long backcountry trips by canoe are among the most satisfying adventures available to those weary of cities and traffic. The canoe is also still one of the finest ways to enjoy a nearby lake or river. Modern white-water paddling has added a new dimension to canoeing, however, and it has affected traditional uses of the canoe. Rapids are now often the attractions of a river instead of obstacles to be avoided on it. Wilderness rivers that would have been considered unnavigable in the past are often run for sport now. The strokes developed for use in white-water give new confidence and stability to other kinds of paddling. Specialized types of canoe have been developed for particular branches of the sport, whereas general-purpose boats have become tougher and more versatile with the use of new materials.

The attraction enjoyed most universally by canoeists is surely the simple joy of leisurely paddling in peaceful surroundings, but the sport comprises a multitude of other activities. The experience of running

white-water will be different, depending on whether it is run in open canoes, in boats modified by the addition of fabric covers to prevent their shipping water in large waves, or in specially designed white-water canoes that are mistaken by the uninitiated for kayaks. For more variety, one may run either alone or with a partner. The rapids run may be close to a highway or deep in the wilderness, with remoteness lending a host of additional difficulties and obstacles to the activity.

Races have been designed to test the virtuosity of the paddler, and competition is the main interest of many canoeists. There are races putting a premium on pure speed through flat or rough water and competitions demanding precise control of the boat, each with classes for various kinds of boats and combinations of canoeists. Racing has the great virtue of vastly improving technique, whether or not the competition in its own right has much attraction for the canoeist.

Some canoeists do all their paddling in white-water boats, devoting their attention to the big, turbulent rapids that can be run only in specialized craft. They may spend their vacations on big wilderness rivers that are famous for huge rapids or in training for races in Europe.

The majority of canoeists paddle in open boats, never entering the touchy white-water variety. In an open canoe one can have just as much of a thrill paddling much smaller rapids.

For most long wilderness treks, the traditional open canoe is the ideal craft. For comfort, load-carrying capacity, and ease of portaging it cannot be matched by the white-water boats. Some canoeists learn the old-timer's art of poling, the key to exploration upstream along small rivers and creeks. Like white-water paddling, poling has recently undergone a revolution in technique, and the modern canoe poler can work upstream through very tough rapids, provided the water is not too deep. He can work downstream as well, with fewer thrills but a lot more control than the paddler. Racing has begun to have the same effect of improving poling technique that it had a few years ago on paddling.

All these skills have greatly broadened the range of the original use of the canoe. The canoeist in the wilderness must still be far more conservative about running rapids or chancing big waves on a lake or ocean than a paddler close to the car, but practice on a body of water near the road can extend one's safety margin to include much rougher conditions, even in the backcountry.

This book is an introduction to modern canoeing for beginners and intermediate paddlers. It presents most of the information that someone interested in wilderness canoe travel or in white-water paddling needs to get started, as well as basics of paddling and safety for the novice who wants to go out and canoe on a lake in a city park. It does not discuss every specialized facet of the sport. There is no catalogue of rules for racing training or provisioning for expeditions, details that have been discussed elsewhere. I have tried to cover those aspects of canoeing that will interest the beginner and the intermediate paddler who wants to start doing river tours of several days' length or to get into unfamiliar paddling in white-water or big lakes. The dedicated beginning paddler can often learn in one season to paddle white-water that would not have been essayed a couple of decades ago by the toughest old-timer. This is not because one can become river-wise in a year but because current methods and equipment give us the advantage.

One emphasis in this book is on promoting modern camping techniques that have little impact on the land. Big fires, lean-tos made of cut poles, and the like have no place in most of the woods and wilderness areas frequented by canoeists these days. Even those going on long expeditions to remote wilderness rivers rarely visited by people will do most of their paddling nearer to home, and along more frequented waterways the paddler must consider those who will come after him. With a little care it is possible to make canoe trips without leaving any sign of one's passage, thus preserving the wilderness experience for those who follow. Such care is particularly important for paddlers, because they nearly always camp along the narrow and vulnerable banks of lakes and rivers.

No one can learn to paddle from a book, a point that the novice should keep repeating to himself or herself. Knowing how a stroke

Canoeing may also mean competitive paddling. Here a canoeist in a one-person white-water canoe does a reverse maneuver through a slalom gate.

should be made is not the same as being able to make it; a world of experience lies between. The only way to learn to be a good paddler is to get out and practice as often as possible with canoeists more experienced than yourself. The overconfident can get into trouble with a canoe, particularly on white-water or in deep wilderness. Recognition of water features and anticipation of problems is a matter of training. A few hours of instruction by experienced paddlers is worth days of reading, and the availability of experienced rescuers will enable the beginner to progress much faster than would otherwise be possible.

With all this said, however, a lot can be learned from books. They permit the beginner to profit from others' experience, to use practice periods to the greatest advantage, and sometimes to perceive where mistakes have been made. I hope this book will prove helpful to other paddlers.

I also hope that canoeists who read this book and learn to appreciate the rivers and other waterways of North America will make the effort to help preserve them. More than any other part of our remaining wilderness and open space, the rivers, streams, and lakes are threatened by the encroachments of civilization. Most of the great rivers south of the Canadian border have already been polluted, filled with trash, dammed, channeled, and diverted until they hardly bear any resemblance to the beautiful living entities they once were.

Rivers, streams, and lakes are particularly subject to abuse, for a number of reasons. They are an attractive place for the irresponsible to dump waste, as it is simply carried away, and the federal government has never bothered to enforce laws prohibiting the practice, which have been on the books for three-quarters of a century. Lakes are often abused in the same way, and although they are damaged more slowly, they may never recover. Many flood-control practices needlessly destroy all the life along a river in order to protect both the investments of developers who build houses in a floodway and the tenure of politicians who permit them to do so. Power dams and irrigation projects have far more legitimacy, but with most rivers dammed out of existence now, it is time to preserve those that remain for us.

Finally, the lovers of waterways themselves are a threat to many rivers and lakes. Since use is concentrated along vulnerable shorelines, poor camping practices and overuse can seriously degrade the local environment and destroy much of the beauty that campers come to enjoy. This is particularly true on dammed rivers that no longer have natural flooding to cleanse their shores. It is important to develop good practices oneself and to work for sound management by government agencies. On a more selfish note, those who love the wilderness experience and the adventures that can be had along white-water rivers have to concern themselves with the growth of large, commercially operated rafting trips. Some of the government trustees for the land, such as the National Park Service and the Forest Service, prefer to deal with bureaucracies like their own, and when the number of river travelers must be limited these agencies give preference to large commercial organizations and sometimes even to motorized travel.

Although our remaining wilderness cannot survive without our attention, the wilderness activities of river running and canoeing on lakes still offer their practitioners a greater sense of freedom and self-reliance than can be found almost anywhere else. Along the waterways of North America one can still find solitude, real companionship, beauty, adventure, and a sense of the power and majesty of the earth's great natural forces and of the order of the universe. Good paddling.

CHAPTER 1

THE CANOE

Canoeing is one of the most American of sports. Canoes were invented by the native Americans who inhabited lands now included in Canada and the United States before Europeans came to the continent. Much of the wilderness of North America was laced with rivers and lakes, which often formed a more convenient network for travel than trails on land. This was particularly true of the northern part of the continent, where the waterways form an almost continuous passage from east to west for a versatile boat with a shallow draft that can be carried over the short, intervening necks of land that separate one watershed from the next.

Canoes of one form or another have been invented by many peoples throughout the world. Depending on the materials available and the needs of the particular civilization that produced them, these canoes have had different characteristics and been suitable for different purposes. The canoe with which most Americans are familiar today is, however, a direct descendant of the ones used by a number of North American Indian tribes, and, except for changes in materials, it looks almost identical to those that were used by Ojibways, Malecites, and many other native American tribes.

The most famous of the Indian craft were the various designs of birchbark canoe, and justifiably so, since the combination of lightness and strength achieved in these boats was not surpassed until the last few decades. In fact, there are many canoes made today that still do not compare favorably with those built by the Indians.

The canoe is a double-ended, relatively narrow boat of shallow draft that normally is propelled with paddles or a pole. The Indian designs used a light frame covered with pieces of birch bark (where it was available) sewn together and sealed with pitch. A sixteen-foot birchbark canoe weighed between forty and sixty pounds. The birchbark canoe was made in a number of designs, depending on the tribe that built it and the function it was made to fulfill. Other types of canoes were made in North America, some covered with other types of bark where birch was unavailable, and some using skin coverings. Dugout canoes, particularly the great ocean-going canoes of the Pacific Northwest, were also made, but the birchbark canoe was the classic design that opened up the continent. It was tough, readily repaired, portable, and suitable for many kinds of paddling—the ideal wilderness craft.

The canoe is one of the most versatile and superbly maneuverable of all watercraft.

CANOE DESIGN

The wood frame covered with birch bark allowed the early boat builders a good deal of freedom in designing their canoes. Modern boat builders have even more freedom because of the nature of the materials available to them. It is interesting, however, that except for specialized white-water canoes, the hull shape of the canoe has not been significantly improved over the original Indian designs. Some canoe manufacturers could, in fact, use a few lessons from the native craftsmen who built canoes here five hundred years ago.

Any canoe is a compromise between a number of desirable attributes. A designer must trade carrying capacity for speed, or ease of paddling on flat water for maneuverability in rapids. The prospective buyer or canoe builder has to find a boat that comes closest to suiting his needs. A canoe may be nearly ideal for one kind of paddling and poor for another. Some canoes are not much good for any purpose.

THE STRUCTURE OF A CANOE

Length

Canoes range in size from little pack canoes ten feet long to great boats approaching thirty feet that can be used for carrying freight or at summer camp. Most open canoes fall between fifteen and eighteen and a half feet. Length affects the weight of the canoe, of course, but it affects other characteristics much more. For example, increasing the length of a canoe from sixteen to eighteen feet will often make a canoe weigh 20 percent more while increasing its carrying capacity 40 percent. Indeed, getting a longer canoe is generally the best way to obtain more load-carrying capacity with the least sacrifice of other desirable characteristics.

A longer canoe will weigh a little more and be able to carry a lot more than a shorter one, other things being equal. The longer boat will also be faster and track better, meaning it will tend to hold its course well in flat water and will bob about less in small waves. Long boats are generally easy to paddle in lakes and slow rivers, and they can be made narrow and very fast if desired.

Shorter canoes are more maneuverable and are thus a better choice when maneuverability is at a premium, as when choosing a boat for picking courses through mazes of rocks in white-water. A shorter boat is also less likely to plunge into big waves. However, a short canoe that is overloaded is neither easily maneuvered nor very buoyant; it is sluggish and slow.

Width

The widest part of a canoe is normally at the center, except in some specialized racing designs. In general, a wider canoe will carry a bit more, will be slower, and will have more inherent stability in calm water. Yet such a canoe may actually be harder to handle in rough water, where real stability depends on the actions of the paddlers. Width at various points along the length of the canoe is interdependent with the overall form of the hull and will be discussed below.

Depth

A deeper canoe can carry more weight without coming dangerously close to shipping water than can a shallower one. Depth is normally measured amidships, at the center of the canoe. It is important, however, that the depth be carried properly through the canoe, as will be shown below. Like the other factors mentioned, depth interacts with the rest of the canoe design. A narrow canoe, for example, may need to be deeper than a wide one so that the same height of canoe side will be sticking above the water after loading. The height of the side above the water at the lowest point, after loading, is called freeboard. Fewer than six inches of freeboard indicates that a canoe is dangerously overloaded, even in calm water.

Keel

A keel is a projection running lengthwise along the bottom of a boat. When canoe keels are used they are quite shallow, projecting

This fiberglass canoe has a shallow keel, a rounded ridge molded into the hull. It has some rocker, is fairly maneuverable, and is fairly swift in flat paddling.

perhaps an inch from the bottom of the hull. A *shoe keel* is a shallower, more rounded version intended to compromise between the characteristics of hulls with and without keels. *Bilge keels* are shorter keels placed on either side of the center one and running part of the length of the canoe. They formerly served partly to protect the hulls of canvas canoes against rocky bottoms and are rarely used in modern canoes.

A keel helps the canoe to track straight when it is being paddled on relatively flat water, reducing the effort required to make course corrections. When one is paddling across the path of the wind, a keel will slow the sideways slip of the hull in the water. In some circumstances the keel may also help protect the hull from rock damage. On the other hand, a keel reduces the maneuverability of the boat. Good tracking and good maneuverability are generally opposite ends of a spectrum along which the designer must compromise somewhere. Canoes intended mainly for lake paddling will normally be equipped with keels, whereas those designed for river canoeing, particularly if many

intricate rapids will be negotiated, will be keelless or have a shoe keel.
Because of the way aluminum canoes are constructed, they must be
made with at least a shoe keel.

Form

This term is generally used to refer to the overall shape of the canoe
hull as viewed from above or below. As mentioned, the hull of the
canoe will be symmetrical both from side to side and from bow to
stern, except in some specialized racing designs. Form may be quite
different, however, even between two canoes of the same length and
the same width amidships. The faster canoe will probably narrow rapidly toward the ends, making the bow and stern sharp and narrow.
When the bow parts the surface of the lake as it moves forward, the
water does not have to be pushed to the side as quickly by a sharply
angled bow. If, for example, the canoe is ten inches wide at the waterline at a point three feet behind the bow, the water on either side
has to be pushed out five inches as the canoe goes three feet forward.
If the canoe is twenty inches wide at that point, the water must be
pushed twice as far for the same progress. Less acceleration of the
water requires less energy. Paddling will be more efficient because
canoeists will be able to take their strokes closer to the centerline of
the boat, since the sides of the canoe near the normal paddling positions will not project so far. Such a canoe will have less volume than
one that is full at the ends, and it will thus have less load-carrying capacity. The narrow ends will tend to cut through waves rather than riding over them, making the canoe faster and easier to handle in small
waves but more easily swamped in large ones.

Sheer

Sheer is the upward curve of the hull, viewed from the side, toward
the bow and stern. The shape of the sheer line or gunwale line is important to the margin of safety that the canoe has in rough water and to
its handling in the wind. The bow and stern need to curve upward, of
course, so that water will not be shipped over them when the canoe is

plunging into a wave or is overtaken by a following wave. Exaggerated high sterns and bows, which have occasionally been fashionable, serve no useful function, however, and they catch the wind badly, making the canoe difficult to handle whenever a breeze comes up and impossible with a strong blow.

For the height of the bow or stern to be effective in keeping out water when the canoe is bobbing in the waves, the sheer line must begin curving up quickly from amidships rather than remaining flat for many feet and then sweeping rapidly up near the end. A canoe whose sheer rises rapidly near the bow will ship water just behind the curve whenever the bow dives through a wave, so that the higher bow serves no purpose except as a wind catcher. The best shape of the sheer line is one that rises at a fairly steady rate from amidships to a relatively low bow and stern.

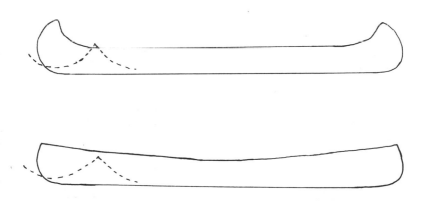

Two canoes with identical lower hull shapes and depths amidships, but with different sheer lines. TOP. This canoe has a higher bow and stern, which will catch the wind badly, but because this height is not carried back toward the center, waves will easily swamp the boat, as the dotted line shows. BOTTOM. This canoe has a lower bow and stern, but the height is carried well back toward the center, so the craft can handle larger waves even though it will be less affected by wind.

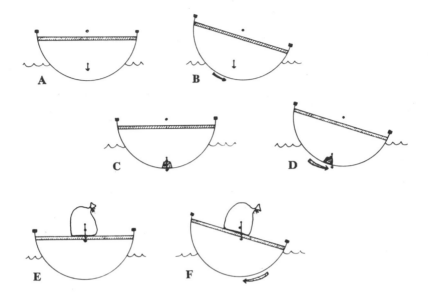

The relationship between the roll center, center of gravity, and stability of a boat. A round hull, shown here for simplicity, will tend to roll around the center of the circle, in this case right at the level of the gunwales.

A. The boat is floating at rest on the water. Gravity pulls on the whole hull as though pulling at the center of gravity, shown by the point at the tail of the arrow. When the center of gravity is below the roll center, as here, the boat tends to stay in the same position.

B. If the boat is tilted to one side, the center of gravity is raised slightly and the pull of the earth tugs it down toward its original position, exerting a force on the hull that tends to turn it upright again.

C. When weight is loaded in the bottom of the boat, the center of gravity is lowered and the total weight increases.

D. Tipping the boat with the weight moves the lowered center farther, so the resultant force turning the hull back upright is larger.

E. If weight is loaded high so the center of gravity is raised, the boat becomes less stable. Here a large weight that has been loaded onto the thwarts is heavy enough actually to raise the center of gravity *above* the roll center. Even a slight tip of the hull brings about the situation shown in **F,** where gravity pulling down at the center tends to roll the boat over.

Cross-Sectional Shape

The curve of the hull down to the waterline and below is among the most important design features of a canoe and is related to all the others. In fact, the designer is quite likely to mix cross-sectional shapes, trying to achieve the desired handling characteristics by moving from one curve near the center to another nearer the ends.

Cross-sectional shape has a major influence on the stability of a boat hull. Among the several factors that influence stability, the first is the relative positions of the roll center of the hull and the center of gravity of the boat. The roll center (longitudinal axis) is the line around which the hull will tend to turn if it is pushed over by some force. In the illustration a semicircular hull is shown because its roll center is so easily seen; it is simply the center of the circle, of which the hull is a part. In this case the roll center is in the middle of the boat, right at the level of the gunwales. The center of gravity of the empty hull is directly below the roll center. When the boat tips, as in B, the center of gravity is lifted slightly, which will tend to roll the hull back into position, though not very quickly because it has only been lifted slightly. In c the hull has been loaded with more weight below the center of gravity, lowering the overall center of gravity. The hull will now tend to return to equilibrium more quickly. In E the hull has been loaded above the roll center, raising the center of gravity of the whole system above it. With a slight tip, gravity then turns the boat farther over rather than rights it. The boat will then be stable upside down.

In considering hull stability, it is important to note that canoes are not always paddled in an upright position. The canoe may tilt while riding waves, or the paddler may deliberately lean to one side for various reasons. As we shall see, some canoes that are very stable in flat water lose their stability suddenly when they lean beyond a certain point, whereas in rough water and in the hands of a good paddler seemingly tippy canoes may actually be more stable. It is also worth noting that much rough water stability is achieved with proper paddling techniques, the canoeist reaching out to brace against the water so that again stability is not always as simple as it seems. A boat that is virtually impossible to tip over in flat water may be dangerous in rough water, even in the hands of an expert. Many flat-bottom rowboats are very stable on the quiet waters of a pond but would quickly swamp in waves that can be easily handled in a canoe.

A round bottom results in a very tippy canoe because the only resistance offered to tipping comes from raising the center of gravity slightly. However, the round bottom does not reach any point (short of shipping water) where it becomes more unstable, so in rough water it is easy to lean and return it to its original position. This is also a fast hull shape. Narrow canoes with relatively round bottoms and no keel are often preferred by good paddlers, particularly for white-water. Such designs are tricky and may be treacherous except in the hands of an expert.

A flat bottom is quite stable in its normal position because to tip it the same distance as a round bottom the center of gravity must be lifted higher, as shown. Once the boat is tipped over a certain amount, however, it becomes quite unstable and can be flipped very suddenly. The difficulty in leaning the boat at a moderate angle can also be inconvenient in some rough water circumstances.

The flat-bottom boat generally floats quite high in the water, particularly if fullness is carried well into the ends, so that it is less likely to run aground in shallow water. It will tend to have a larger load-carrying capacity than a round-bottom boat of the same depth because it will draw less water with a given load.

A **V** bottom is very fast and directionally quite stable, since the bottom acts like a keel, even if no actual keel is present. It is very tippy, even more so than a round bottom, but it tends to become more stable as it rolls, the opposite of a flat bottom. In fact, when turned partway over on its side, it in effect becomes a flat-bottom craft.

Tumblehome

Tumblehome is the curving back of the side of a canoe at the top, where the widest section is lower down near the waterline. A modest

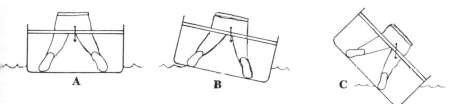

Flat-bottom boats are widely believed to be very stable and are often adver tised as such. This is only partly true, and in rough water a flat-bottom boat may be very unstable.

A. A canoeist kneeling in a flat-bottom canoe. The dot shows the combined center of gravity of the paddler and the boat, with the arrow representing the force of gravity.

B. When the canoe is tipped slightly, the force of gravity tends to bring the hull rapidly back upright, making for stability.

C. When the boat is tipped far over, however, as it will frequently be in rough water, the hull is in quite an unstable position. With a bit more tipping, gravity will capsize the canoe rather than right it again. Such a wide hull will be forced over into similar positions in waves, as they exert a great deal of tipping force on the large, flat bottom.

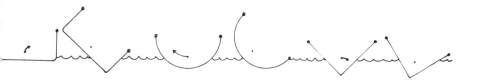

Comparisons of the stability of three hull shapes. The first drawing in each pair shows the hull at rest, its center of gravity, and an arrow showing the di rection the center must travel to reach the position on the right. Lifting the center of gravity is the same as lifting the boat and requires work. The flat bottom is initially very stable, because the center of gravity must be lifted straight up, but the farther it tips, the easier it is to tip farther. The round bottom is initially fairly easy to tip, but the farther it is rolled, the more work is required to increase the tip. The **V**-bottom is initially unstable, because the center of gravity at first moves down, but it too becomes progressively more stable. It is most tippy when upright and less so as it is tilted over. Practical canoe bottoms use combinations of these shapes.

amount of tumblehome is desirable, particularly in a wide canoe, because it allows the canoeist to paddle a little closer to the hull, resulting in increased efficiency. Excessive tumblehome allows waves breaking against the side of the canoe to slosh in. A fiberglass or ABS (Acrylonitrile-butadiene-styrene, a heat-formed plastic laminate) canoe that has the hull molded in one piece often has little or no tumblehome so that it can be more easily removed from the mold.

Rocker

The rocker of a canoe is the upward curvature toward the ends of the bottom of the hull. If a canoe is set upright on a flat surface, the keel or centerline of an unrockered boat will lie flat through the length of the boat, until the points where the ends start to curve up. A rockered boat will begin to curve up much nearer the center. Canoes should never curve downward from the middle toward the ends.

A canoe with a great deal of rocker is very maneuverable, tracks rather poorly, and is not very fast. A boat with no rocker is fast, tracks better, and is harder to turn.

Different canoe designs mix the elements just discussed, together with other, more subtle ones, in proportions to achieve the desired

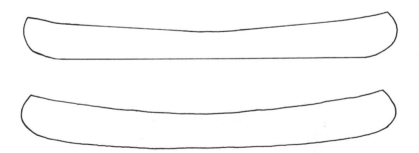

TOP. A canoe with a straight, or unrockered, keel line. BOTTOM. A canoe with a good deal of rocker; the keel line rises toward the bow and the stern.

handling characteristics. The newcomer must try to choose a boat that is well designed and that suits his or her needs.

Paddlers who want a stable boat with a good load capacity for recreational use on lakes and easy rivers would probably select a relatively wide canoe, perhaps thirty-six inches at the center in a sixteen-foot model, with the width carried toward the ends, giving a full bow and stern. The bottom would be fairly flat in the center, becoming more rounded toward the ends. The canoe would have a keel and little if any rocker. A typical depth at the center would be twelve inches.

One modification of this sort of canoe is to make it more maneuverable and capable of carrying good loads while being able to navigate rough water. Depth can be increased somewhat, perhaps to fourteen inches in the sixteen-foot model, the keel can be removed for maneuverability, and a little rocker introduced. This type of canoe, often known as a Prospector model, is a wilderness workhorse.

A different direction might be taken to make the canoe maneuverable in white-water but still very fast in lakes, at the expense of its load-carrying capacity and stability for the novice. The keel can be left off and the moderate rocker left on, though the bottom is rounded a good deal and the whole canoe is slimmed down, perhaps to thirty-four inches in a sixteen-foot model. Depth will probably be one foot at the center. This type of boat, a joy to paddle for the proficient canoeist, is often known as a Cruiser model.

For a canoe designed specifically for running white-water, the length will first be reduced to the minimum that will support the loads expected; fifteen-foot models are very popular among white-water paddlers, although longer boats may be necessary for extended trips. A canoe designed for white-water will be keelless or have a shoe keel if it is aluminum, will have considerable rocker, and may be a bit deeper than the average.

These examples give some indication of the features you should look for in a canoe. Every paddler seeks the ideal compromise, the boat that will do everything well, but you will find yours only by carefully examining the kind of paddling that you really intend to do

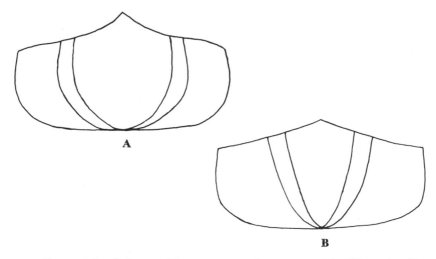

Cross-sectional shapes of three seventeen-foot canoes with different handling qualities. The outside curve shows the widest cross section, which is amidships in all these canoes. The middle curve indicates the cross section four feet from each end of the canoe, the smallest curve, the one two feet from each end. All these canoes are unrockered. The cross sections all curve down to the same depth.

A. This is a commonly found type of canoe. The bottom is fairly flat, and the fullness is carried well out toward the ends. This canoe will have the largest carrying capacity of the three, will float high, and turn easily. The wide bows will lift well in waves. If the canoe is being paddled forward, the water being displaced by the hull must be pushed out of the way rapidly to accommodate the wide bow. If the canoe is being paddled 2½ miles per hour, the water on the surface has to be moved over at a rate of almost a foot per second. The paddlers of the other two boats shown need to accelerate the displaced water only about half as fast, so less effort is required to paddle them. Note that **A** has a fair amount of tumblehome.

B. This canoe is about as broad and flat at the midsection as **A,** so it will be nearly as stable on flat water. The ends are much narrower, though, so capacity will be reduced, whereas tracking and speed will be improved. Displaced water does not have to be pushed out of the way as rapidly for the canoe to go at a given speed, so less paddling effort is required. The bow or stern will not rise as well on waves, but the flaring about the waterline increases flotation as the end cuts into a wave, somewhat reducing the tendency to dive.

and then measuring that against different canoes. Avoid the common mistake of buying a canoe that is perfectly suited for boating that you wish you could do but won't.

MATERIALS

Wood-and-Canvas

For many years the best approximation to the birchbark craft was the wood-and-canvas canoe. This was a noble craft, even though it fell a bit short of the original, and it provided the standard against which other materials and methods of construction were measured for many years. It was strong, durable, fairly light for its strength, and could be repaired with what seemed reasonable labor at the time.

Wood-and-canvas canoes are made with ribs running crossways around the curve of the hull from one gunwale to the other. Planking running the length of the canoe is fastened to the outside of these ribs

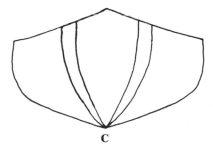

C

C. The narrow midsection, sharp entry lines, and slight **V** even in the midsection of this canoe will make it very fast. The **V** will also make it track very well. It will have much less carrying capacity than either of the other canoes and will require more effort or better technique to turn. (Leaning a canoe over on its side effectively introduces rocker and is one method of turning a canoe like this one rapidly.) A canoe such as this is a joy to paddle and is often preferred by those willing to take the time to learn to paddle well. The fine entry lines will make the bow and stern tend to dive into big waves easily, but the decreased stability of the hull will make it easier for skilled paddlers to ride such waves sideways or quartering.

and then covered with canvas. The wood is varnished and the canvas painted to seal the boat. Such canoes are quiet, beautiful, and a joy to paddle. They also require considerable maintenance and are less durable than canoes properly made of modern materials. They have become very expensive because of labor costs.

In judging the weight of a wood-and-canvas canoe, it is important to remember that water will be absorbed even by a properly maintained boat, so that its practical weight, while in use, is likely to be at least 10 percent more than the weight of the craft when it left the factory.

In general, except for the dedicated paddler who is willing to put up with a good deal of extra expense and trouble for his or her aesthetic bias, wood-and-canvas has become obsolete as a method of canoe construction. As compensation we have tougher and lighter canoes made from modern materials.

Aluminum

Aluminum is now the standard canoe material. Grumman, the largest canoe manufacturer, makes only aluminum boats, the introduction of which a number of years ago ushered in the modern age in canoeing. Aluminum has a number of major advantages as a material for building boats. It is light, strong, and waterproof and can be pressed into the shape of a canoe so that the skin and structure become one unit, requiring only seaming and reinforcement to complete the hull, a process far simpler than wood-and-canvas construction. A well-made aluminum canoe is very tough and is a fine boat for rough wilderness travel or white-water paddling, capable of surviving collisions with rocks and general abuse of the kind that sent many a wood-and-canvas boat to an early grave. It requires essentially no maintenance; an aluminum craft will last a lifetime if you avoid wrapping it around a boulder or allowing it to fall off your car on the highway. It may even survive one of these calamities.

Aesthetically, few would find the aluminum canoe as pleasant as the craft it replaced. Even when painted it retains its undeniably metallic look, and its tinny clatter when struck with a paddle is hollow and annoying. It is hot and shiny when the sun is beating down and cold when the water is chilly. Since aluminum is heavier than water, special flotation chambers must be built into metal canoes to prevent them from sinking should they capsize. These chambers must usually be put in the ends of the canoe, requiring in turn that the ends have large volume.

Aluminum canoes have to be pressed in forms that require very expensive tooling, so their production is confined to large manufacturers. For the same reason, once a design has gone into production, the maker will not be inclined to make changes.

On the other hand, uniformity of quality and strength is easy to achieve with aluminum, and defects are likely to be readily apparent. Economies of scale allow an excellent canoe to be made relatively cheaply, more so than a comparable canoe made of other materials by a large manufacturer.

Fiberglass

This term is commonly used to describe constructions using a lamination of a number of layers of some kind of synthetic cloth put in a mold and saturated with a plastic resin that then hardens. The correct term for a laminate using fiberglass cloth is *fiberglass-reinforced plastic,* but *fiberglass* is used loosely even to describe laminates that have different reinforcements.

Fiberglass is relatively easy to work with on a small scale, so many fiberglass canoes have been made by small manufacturers and amateur builders. This has many advantages. Excellent boats can sometimes be obtained cheaply, and experimentation with design is much more feasible with fiberglass than with aluminum. The material itself imposes less restriction on shape than other materials do. Unfortunately, fiberglass is so easy to use that many incompetent builders and designers have made canoes that are heavy, brittle, and often atrociously conceived, giving the material a bad name.

A good builder can make very light, strong canoes using fiberglass. Since quality control and materials are of critical importance in making a good canoe, one is very dependent on the maker, probably more with a fiberglass canoe than an aluminum one, where more of the quality (or lack of it) in the construction may be visible to the naked eye.

A good fiberglass canoe is more flexible than an aluminum one, and within limits it will bounce back after collisions with rocks. It is less likely to catch on sharp rocks, although it will scratch more easily and will generally show the scratches more. It is easier to repair than aluminum, especially when major damage has occurred, but the materials are messier and require control of heat and moisture in the repair area.

There is far more choice among designs in fiberglass than aluminum, although finding the design you want may not be so simple. Fiberglass canoes are much quieter than aluminum ones and less subject to annoying extremes of temperature, but the average low- or medium-priced fiberglass boat will probably be heavier than a comparable aluminum one.

Thermoplastics

Another way to make a canoe, which requires a good deal of investment, is by forming it in a mold from a plastic material at high temperatures. The main material of this type currently being used in canoe building is ABS (Acrylonitrile-butadiene-styrene) in a combination laminate with vinyl and foam. A sheet of the material is heated and pulled into a mold by vacuum to shape it into a canoe. Those manufacturers who have worked out the initial problems with this material have managed to make extremely tough and light canoes with it. It is fortunate that the material is so durable, since repairs are difficult.

FINISHING FEATURES

Attached to the hull are a number of other features important to the paddler. Depending on the type of construction, these may be an integral part of the construction of the hull or may be easily removable or readily modified. Thwarts (described below) in a wood-and-canvas canoe, for example, were easily removed, so the purchaser was not wedded to the particular thwart placement that was in the boat when it was purchased. The same is true of some modern canoes, but others have thwarts that are difficult or impossible to change. The canoeist should give a good deal of consideration to these secondary features.

Flotation

Wood, birchbark, and wood-and-canvas canoes will float, even if they are filled completely with water. A wood-and-canvas canoe will float even if it is filled with water, and if it turns over it will float even higher upside down, because of the air trapped underneath the inverted hull. Most modern canoe hulls would sink to the bottom when filled with water if they were not provided with separate flotation, since aluminum and fiberglass laminates are both denser than water.

Most commonly, the ends of the canoe are closed off to form flotation chambers, the amount of flotation provided being determined by the volume of the enclosed space. One concern of the canoeist should be whether these chambers are simply filled with air, in which case they will be effective only as long as they are watertight, or whether they enclose blocks of closed-cell foam, so that they will retain their usefulness even if a leak is sprung.

ABS canoes incorporate flotation material in the laminate; thus the basic material is buoyant, like wood. Some fiberglass canoes have also had foam included in some parts of the laminate. Additional flotation may be placed to good effect in other parts of the canoe; for example, along the sides.

Most modern canoes are designed to be self-righting, as the major flotation is put in the ends of the boat. This sounds wonderful, but it is actually of questionable value, since an overturned canoe traps lots of air and floats a good deal higher than when that same canoe turns itself back over and fills with water in the process. In white-water, this will mean that the canoe will be floating down the river very low, filled with a ton or so of water, which ensures that it will have a hard time surviving any crashes against rocks. An upside-down canoe can be thrown upright by an experienced boater so that little water is left inside, provided no duffel is tied in it. Since there is no real problem in turning a canoe upright from the water, the self-righting feature may be more negative than positive. Its one real advantage is that the lower-floating canoe that has righted itself will not be blown away from a swimmer as quickly on a windy lake.

It is important to recognize the limitations of any of these kinds of flotation. Any canoe that simply uses buoyant material in the hull or has a couple of small flotation chambers will be "unsinkable," but the canoeist should understand that it can still be swamped just as readily in a heavy sea or in white-water. A canoe full of water weighs a tremendous amount, and if it is swept into a rocky shore by waves or carried into a boulder in the river it is likely to be destroyed. For this reason, white-water paddlers often add other flotation to their canoes, a subject discussed more in Chapter 11.

Decks

The bow and stern decks or plates generally form part of the flotation compartments. They are also important structurally, since they form triangular braces that set the angles of the sides of the canoe. In canoes used for white-water, the decks are sometimes extended farther toward the center of the canoe, and the rear edge of the bow deck may be curved up and forward to prevent waves breaking over the bow from carrying on into the boat too easily. Some open canoes are modeled after covered white-water boats, with the decks extending over in a continuous curve from the hull so that the center of the boat is like one large cockpit big enough for both paddlers. Since this type of craft is more akin to true white-water canoes, it will be discussed with them.

Stiffeners

A hull thick enough to be rigid without any supports at all would be unnecessarily heavy in most cases, so even aluminum and fiberglass canoes have various kinds of stiffeners. A keel, if the canoe has one, acts as a lengthwise stiffener. If a canoe does not have a keel, an interior ridge like an upside-down keel may be added. Similar parallel ridges may be installed on either side. Complete or partial ribs may be used. Whatever stiffeners are used must be firmly attached to the hull or they will tear out later on. In an aluminum canoe, stiffeners that are not riveted with enough rivets of the right type may pull loose. In a fiberglass canoe a weak stiffener may break, one that is not solidly laminated may pull loose, or one badly chosen may cause the surrounding material to flex in too sharp a zone, resulting in a break in the hull.

Seats

Normally, two seats are installed in a canoe, one quite close to the rear of the boat for the stern paddler and one far enough back from the bow to accommodate the bow paddler. (Since the bow paddler is situated between the seat and the bow, whereas the stern paddler is in front of the stern, the bow seat is much farther from the end of the canoe than is the stern seat.)

The seats should be high enough so that when one kneels in front of them and uses the edge of the seat to support the buttocks, the feet fit underneath easily. People with big feet often have difficulty getting them under low seats, and since one paddles from a kneeling position most frequently in big waves or white-water, getting the feet stuck during an upset could be a safety hazard. Within this constraint, the seats should be placed as low as possible, so that the center of gravity of a seated paddler is also as low as feasible.

Some paddlers prefer to dispense with seats altogether, replacing them with thwarts, which serve perfectly well as supports for kneeling paddlers. Thwarts are narrow braces extending between the gunwales, whereas seats are wider and are generally installed lower in the canoe. For ordinary cruising, however, it is often pleasant to paddle from the seated position for relief, and most canoeists prefer to have seats. Since they normally are used to contribute rigidity to the structure of the canoe, they must be replaced with equally effective thwarts if they are removed. The only really persuasive reason for removing a seat is the safety consideration just mentioned. No seats should be included for passengers, however; they should sit in the bottom of the boat. Paddlers are controlling the boat's balance, and a passenger sitting high in the canoe can throw off the balance unawares, without having a paddle to make corrections.

Thwarts

Thwarts are included partly to hold the canoe in its proper shape. In combination with the two sides, each forms a triangle, thus lending rigidity to the structure of the hull. They also serve as partial supports for kneeling paddlers, relieving strain on the knees and giving additional contact with the canoe. A kneeling paddler with his buttocks supported by a thwart is in a strong position to drive the canoe forward or brace on the paddle. This, the most stable and strongest paddling position, is preferred both in difficult situations and simply for covering the miles in cruising. Seats, being wider, are less versatile than thwarts, so only two seats are normally installed in a canoe, whereas thwarts can be placed at other possible paddling positions. The beginner should note that it is not always desirable to paddle from the same position in the canoe.

The center thwart is also often used to portage the canoe; that is, to carry it between lakes, around rapids, and between the car and the water. Some conflict often arises in thwart placement for this reason. When paddling a canoe solo, it is normally best to paddle from a position near the center of the canoe or just behind the center. A paddler using a center thwart for support will be kneeling a foot or so in front of the center of the boat, which is too far forward for effective control. Thus, those who paddle alone a good deal often prefer this thwart to be placed from twelve to fourteen inches behind the true center of the canoe. However, the thwart is then too far off from the balance position to be used conveniently for portaging.

Those who do not expect to do much solo paddling can solve this problem easily by leaving the thwart at the center, where most manufacturers put it. For occasional solo paddling one can either kneel at the proper position or turn the canoe around and paddle from the back edge of the bow seat, although this position is usually a bit too far back.

Various other solutions can be arranged. For example, you can install two thwarts twenty-eight inches apart with a removable portaging arrangement that fits between. If you want such a system, however, it is important to see whether it could be installed on a particular canoe without major effort. Some canoes are not constructed in a way that makes the center thwart movable.

CHOOSING A CANOE

Many of the factors involved in choosing a canoe have already been discussed. The prospective purchaser needs first to consider his or her needs and budget and decide whether to buy a new boat or search for a secondhand one. The uses to which the canoe will be put and the amount of weight it will be carrying are the first and most important questions that have to be answered.

The experienced canoeist ought to have a fairly good idea of the kind of paddling for which the canoe will be used. The novice needs to make a realistic evaluation; before you go out and buy the latest lightweight marvel for white-water, consider for a moment the sort of canoeing you will really be doing in the next couple of years. Canoes designed to handle raging white-water really well are generally recalcitrant and rather cranky on lakes, particularly in the hands of a novice paddler. This is a price well worth paying for the canoeist who really needs the agility in rough water, but it is merely a nuisance to those who do not. Competent paddlers can handle moderate rapids perfectly well in a good lake canoe. Versatility is the greatest virtue of the canoe and it should not be sacrificed lightly for a very specialized boat, either a touchy craft designed for competition or a stable barge that is almost as wide as it is long.

It is worth taking a careful look at a standard recreational canoe to get an idea of the design against which others can be measured, so as to be able to judge better their strengths and weaknesses. The Grumman standard aluminum canoe is one of the most popular. Old Town Carletons or Chippewyans are good examples in fiberglass and ABS.

If most of your travel is likely to be on lakes and easy rivers, a canoe with a keel is probably more suitable. If, on the other hand, you expect to do a fair amount of white-water paddling and want to take your canoeing a bit more seriously and develop good paddling technique, you are more likely to enjoy a canoe with no keel or a shoe keel.

Pay careful attention to the capacity of the canoe. Capacities claimed by manufacturers are sometimes imaginative and probably will give you a good basis for comparison only within one canoe maker's line. Remember that carrying capacity is a function of length (most important); width amidships; the degree to which the width is carried out toward the ends; depth amidships; and, for rough water, a correct sheer line, so that the side near the bow will not plunge underwater even when plenty of freeboard is left. When you are given figures on carrying capacity, ask how much freeboard is left at that loading and remember that six inches of freeboard is a bare minimum, even on flat water. There are no miracles to be had in the capacity of a canoe, because capacity is determined not by the materials with which the boat is made, but by the amount of water weighing the same as the extra load. A longer or wider canoe will not have to sink as much to displace the same volume of water. The only other variable is the weight of the canoe itself, and although light weight is a great advantage in other ways, it has negligible effect on carrying capacity. The difference in carrying capacity between a sixty-pound and an eighty-pound canoe of the same design can be only twenty pounds.

Fifteen feet is a minimum length for general use, and this length is often chosen for white-water, but there will be little carrying capacity beyond two paddlers and a minimum amount of gear. A fifteen-foot canoe may be adequate for a solo paddler on long trips, but it doesn't have much reserve for two. It will be totally inadequate for a

A number of types of canoes preparing to start an easy river run. At the right in the water are two aluminum canoes built for general use. The two canoes farther left are faster designs that are more responsive to skilled paddlers. The white boat on the shore is an 18½-foot cruising canoe, made of fiberglass, designed for marathon racing. It is great to paddle, but skill is needed to turn it rapidly.

family of four in most situations. The seventeen-foot canoe is a good all-around length for most purposes. It has considerably larger carrying capacity than the fifteen-footer, both in roominess and in terms of the load it will carry comfortably and safely. With careful choice of equipment and food, two people can easily head off on a wilderness trip of six weeks on a rough river with a seventeen-footer; a family of four can make jaunts of a week or two with no problem; and yet a well-designed seventeen-foot canoe can be handled well by one person. An eighteen-foot canoe has enough carrying capacity for most normal uses and begins to approach the comfortable and graceful handling limit of one or two people in tight maneuvering on both the water and the portage trail. The most versatile canoe is sixteen and a half to seventeen and a half feet long, which is not to say you should not buy a canoe longer or shorter than that, but if you do you should have good reasons in mind.

This discussion of length must be tempered by considerations brought up earlier. A fast, sensitive round-bottomed boat with a narrow waist seventeen feet long cannot be expected to carry a husband and wife, their two children, the family Saint Bernard, and camping gear for a week without groaning under the load. The whole design of the boat must be considered.

ALUMINUM CANOES

As a general rule, an aluminum canoe will not be quite as good a performer as a high quality fiberglass or ABS model, but it will be tougher and lighter than fiberglass boats of intermediate quality. The question of which material will provide the better bargain is difficult to answer, partly because prices change rapidly but also because transportation is a large percentage of the price of a canoe. Where various canoe makers are located and where you buy the boat will have a great effect on the price of any kind of canoe.

Aluminum canoes are often a good choice for general canoeing. Designs tend to be fairly standardized, which is a disadvantage for those who want a compromise between design features different from the one that nearly all aluminum models represent, but this can be an advantage for the shopper confused by a dozen different conflicting claims about the ideal canoe. The compromise represented in the standard aluminum canoe is a fairly good one for most beginners and many experts: a stable, rugged boat with a great deal of load-carrying capacity, fair speed, and a reasonable price tag. All the lengths of aluminum canoe from the same manufacturer are made with basically the same dies, lengthened in the middle, so their behavior will be what you would expect with length alone added or subtracted. The longer ones track better, whereas the short ones tend to be wide for their length, particularly at the bows, and they will consequently be a bit sluggish in flat water.

Aluminum canoes are generally held together with rivets. It is a real advantage if these do not protrude but are flush with the skin so that they will be less easily damaged by scraping against rocks. Construction should be from a tough aluminum alloy that provides good rigidity but is not excessively brittle. (The most durable alloy used for canoes is 6061.) After it is formed, the hull should be treated to a hardness of T-6. Heat treating involves heating a metal after it is shaped and then cooling it at a rate that will produce the desired hardness. T-3, at which the metal starts, is too soft and ductile for a finished canoe. Excessive tempering would produce a canoe that was too brittle. Proper tempering attains the optimum balance between malleability and tensile strength.

Push hard on the thwarts and seats of the canoe. They should be sturdy, and so should the fastenings. If you can't stand gently on the center thwart, which is supposed to support the canoe over many a bouncing portage, then it isn't strong enough. If the salesperson doesn't want you to try it, he doesn't have much confidence in the product; search elsewhere. Study the spacing of the rivets holding the canoe together and compare this with other canoes. A closer rivet pattern makes for a stronger hull. The stem should be substantial where it joins the keel, since that is the usual collision point when you hit a rock. Kick the hull a bit and push hard on the sides; any canoe should be able to put up with minor indignities without complaint.

Unless you plan to use your canoe strictly for travel on lakes, a shoe keel is preferable to the regular T-keel and is well worth the extra money. (A T-keel is simply a standard keel on an aluminum canoe, so-called because of the shape of the metal piece used. The two halves of the canoe are riveted to the crosspiece of a T-shaped length of aluminum, with the upright forming the keel.) It will markedly improve river maneuverability without harming performance on flat water too much. If you are buying a second-hand boat at a good price, you need not reject it because of the keel, but recognize that the T-keel makes it less agile.

The normal thickness of the skin of aluminum canoes is .05 inch, and this should probably be your choice, since it has proved a good compromise between weight and durability. Lightweight models, with the thickness cut down to between .03 and .04 inch, can have 20 percent shaved off the weight, but they require more care in handling and are not particularly well suited to white-water use. In fact, manufacturers will not generally provide shoe keels on lightweight models because they do not feel that the canoes will stand up to banging against rocks. A good canoeist can take lightweight models through fairly rough rapids, and if many portages are planned, they are often worth the sacrifice in durability. For wilderness use, however, most experienced canoeists prefer the standard model. Lightweight ones need extra reinforcement with ribs to achieve rigidity comparable to standard models, making a well-designed lightweight more expensive than the standard, despite the fact that less metal is used.

Wide, short canoes with sponsons (big flotation bumpers running along under the gunwales) on the sides are more stable in flat water but are inefficient to paddle and less stable in rough water than a narrower boat in the hands of a competent canoeist. The big flat bottom causes the boat to slide down the face of a wave, burying the lower gunwale in the next rise. Rowboats are stable on flat water, too, but they do not have the versatility of a canoe in the hands of someone willing to learn how to use one. Sponsons, formed in the sides of the canoe by pressing the aluminum out into a long, wide ridge on each side, do not interfere with paddling as much, but they do catch the current in white-water, making them more useful for the lake fisherman than for the wilderness canoeist.

There are many minor details in outfitting the canoe that can be readily modified later, but they may give an indication of the thought put into the craft by the manufacturer. Minimum flotation standards are now established by a trade association, but additional flotation will be appreciated by the canoeist. The hardware for attaching painters (lines or ropes running to the bow and stern) should be sturdy and firmly attached to the boat just above its normal waterline when loaded. When these attachments are at the highest points on the bow and stern, they allow currents to pull the hull out from under the pulling line when the canoe is being towed or lined through a rapid. If the seats are contoured, they should have drain holes to let out puddles formed by rain or spray. A comfortable portaging yoke (see pages 55–56) in the center of the canoe is a real help.

FIBERGLASS CANOES

Canoes made from laminates of resin reinforced by fiberglass or synthetics include many of the best and worst boats on the market today. Fiberglass canoes can be designed and produced in small quantities, a fact that attracts some of the best canoe makers, who design boats for good paddlers, not just for the lowest common denominator. It also attracts makers of other fiberglass products who give the same consideration to the manufacture of canoes that they do to the portable outhouses they make for construction companies. Small manufacturers of fiberglass canoes are often the best, when they care about craftsmanship and quality. Larger makers have a major advantage in the manufacture of aluminum canoes and to a lesser degree in the making of ABS ones, but the competent garage builder of fiberglass canoes can often turn out a better product than the large maker—and at a lower price.

The difficulty for the buyer is, of course, deciding whether he has found a craftsman or a shyster. Design, overall craftsmanship, and discussion will tell you a great deal. Ask what the layup of the canoe is. (The layup is the specific combination of reinforcing cloths that make up the laminate.) Any small builder and most honest salespeople will be happy to tell you. Less knowledgeable clerks may not know but should be willing to find out. A few large manufacturers may regard this information as a trade secret.

The worst way to make a fiberglass boat is with a "spray-up" machine, which squirts a mixture of resin and chopped glass fibers into the mold, making a very heavy, brittle boat. Weight is one give-away that this technique has been used. A sprayed-up boat that is also light will be so weak that it will be destroyed in its first brush with a rock. A good healthy kick may even do the job. Get the seller's permission and then try one. Turn the boat on its side and lean fairly hard on the hull; it should give and then spring back. The amount of give will be dependent on the weight and durability of the boat, but a very flexible hull will not stand up to much rough treatment in an open canoe. As the hull is deflected with reasonable pressure, it should give without crackling, which would indicate brittleness without strength.

Cloth reinforcement can be either woven or mat. Mat cloth is made by simply pressing relatively short glass fibers together into a sheet, rather like felt, whereas woven cloth is formed of continuous fibers woven together just as most cloth is. Cloth is chosen by a manufacturer for its weight, the weaving pattern, the finish on the fibers (which must be compatible with the resin system used), and the material.

Mat is undesirable for building canoes because it is not as strong as woven cloth and it absorbs so much resin, making for a heavy, brittle boat. It may be used by good builders for some accessory purposes such as attaching seats or stiffening the bottom, but it is poor for the main layup. Look at both the interior and the exterior of the hull. You should be able to see the pattern of the cloth. If the regular warp-and-woof pattern of woven cloth shows through, then at least the inner and outer layers of the layup are of woven cloth. If, on the other hand, you can see a network of random fibers, either mat or spray-up has been used.

The standard construction for fiberglass canoes is with conventional fiberglass (E-glass) and polyester resin. Layers of the glass are laid in the mold and saturated with the resin. Sometimes material like nylon or polyester cloth is used as part of the laminate. Such materials help to hold damaged areas together and prevent total breakage, but when they are not used well they may cause delamination problems—two of the layers of cloth in the hull may begin to pull apart. Stronger boats can be made if epoxy resins are used instead of polyester, but since epoxies are more expensive and harder to work with, they will also be more costly. The new vinyl ester resins combine many of the advantages of epoxies and polyesters, but they are still not being used by commercial builders. A stronger type of fiberglass (S-glass) may be used with epoxy by a sophisticated builder to make still stronger boats.

Best of all, in terms of lightness and strength, are canoes built with epoxy resin and a synthetic material called Kevlar, a Dupont trademark, or with a combination of Kevlar and S-glass.

A fiberglass boat or one made with synthetics is only as good as the builder, however, regardless of the materials used. The best and most expensive materials have to be correctly matched and used or they will be weaker than conventional ones. Whichever materials are picked, the ideal for the builder is to saturate the cloth completely, using as little resin as possible. If air pockets are left, the laminate will be very weak at those points, but any excess resin beyond the amount required will simply make the boat heavier and more brittle, not stronger. The outside of a canoe is normally covered with a colored coat of resin that has been put on the mold first for cosmetic purposes, although this "gel coat" is easily scratched and does not contribute to the strength of the canoe. Look at the inside of the hull. If the hardened resin has formed pools in the bottom, they will result in unnecessary weight and brittleness. Large amounts of pooling indicate sloppy workmanship. If, on the other hand, the weaves of the cloth show through in a whitish pattern, the resin has been squeezed out too much on the surface. This will result both in a weaker boat and in a problem with itchy bits of fiberglass getting into your skin for as long as you own the boat. Unfortunately, a paint job can conceal this "resin-starved" condition; it will solve the itching problem but not the reduction in strength.

A well-made fiberglass canoe constructed with conventional materials is a bit lighter than an aluminum one of generally comparable strength and about the same weight as an ABS craft. One utilizing Kevlar and epoxy will weigh one-third less. The particular advantages of fiberglass have been discussed already: the range of available designs (including high-performance models), ease of repair, little tendency to catch on rocks, and reduced noise and thermal problems. It should also be noted that damage to a fiberglass boat tends to be isolated to the area that received the impact, whereas denting often extends damage in an aluminum boat.

Like most hull materials, fiberglass is not self-supporting in the weight and thickness used for canoe making. A keel, usually rounded, may be molded in, providing additional rigidity. Check to be sure that such reinforcements are not placed where the knees would go when one is assuming the most common paddling positions; if they are, custom-made pads will have to be made to correct the problem. The upper structure of decks, gunwales, thwarts, and seats should be sturdily attached and should hold the form of the canoe rigidly.

As with aluminum canoes, flotation chambers should contain closed-cell foam flotation, not sealed air chambers alone, so that the boat will float even if the bow or stern is damaged. Any attachments directly to the inside of the hull of a fiberglass canoe, such as seat brackets, should be glassed in; that is, the areas to which they are attached must be sanded, and resin-saturated cloth should be applied to make the bond.

ABS CANOES

Canoes made from ABS are very strong and durable and will slide off rocks even better than fiberglass boats. It is very hard for ABS hulls to fail in collisions, although resistance to abrasion is less good. The material is fairly flexible so that when it hits a rock it will give, bounce, and slide off. This great durability is the major attraction of an ABS canoe, although the material is also quiet, insulates well, and is inherently buoyant once it has been heated and molded. Once damage has been sustained, however, it is likely to be massive and quite difficult to repair.

An ABS canoe will weigh about the same as a comparable boat of aluminum or standard fiberglass construction. As with other materials, design is affected somewhat by the characteristics of ABS and the method of construction. It is difficult, for example, to pull the laminate into sharp edges in a mold, so edges on ABS boats are normally quite rounded. Since the material is pulled into the mold in a single piece, the hull is seamless and keelless.

The laminate in an ABS boat is of uniform thickness throughout.

Look carefully along the outside of the hull from many angles to be sure there are no waves or concavities in the laminate. Various materials are used for the gunwales, thwarts, and seats. Rigid vinyl gunwales are perhaps the most common, but wood and aluminum are also used successfully. As with canoes made from other materials, the upper structure must be rigid and firmly attached to the hull, since it holds the shape of the hull.

ABS canoes are generally somewhat more expensive than comparable aluminum or fiberglass boats, but they are cheaper than canoes of Kevlar, epoxy, and S-glass.

WOOD-STRIP-AND-FIBERGLASS CANOES

This type of construction is unusual, but it is responsible for the most beautiful canoes being made today. They involve much handwork, so they are quite expensive unless you build your own. Also, the beauty of these canoes and the investment in money or time that they call for would probably inhibit most paddlers from taking them on risky white-water runs, though they are quite strong. (*Risky* is, of course, a term that could have a wide variety of meanings to different canoeists, depending on attitudes and skill.) This type of boat is probably not a beginner's boat, except for those who plan to stick to lake paddling.

Wood-strip canoes were made many years ago by a laborious process of individually fitting together strips, usually of cedar, to form a canoe that would be watertight when varnished. They are somewhat easier to build today, using a clever fitting technique and hand-held power tools to seal the boat with layers of clear resin and fiberglass. Details on this method of canoe building are found in David Hazen's *The Stripper's Guide to Canoe Building* (Montana Books, 1974).

CHAPTER 2

CANOEING EQUIPMENT

PADDLES

The paddle is second only to the canoe itself in importance to the canoeist; it is an extension of both his limbs and his personality. With a paddle the canoeist can reach out and brace on the water to correct situations where balance is difficult, push the canoe rapidly through calm water, or slow its progress in swift currents. Without either a paddle or a pole he is relatively helpless, at the mercy of wind and wave. The paddle is so important to the canoeist that its selection deserves a great deal of care; it will become an old friend or a much cursed foe, depending on its quality and suitability for the purpose it is intended to fill.

STRUCTURE

Because the paddle is such a cherished item of the canoeist's equipment, arguments over the merits of various subtle differences in shape and material are part of the stock of campfire discussions along lakes and rivers. Many of these controversies concern subtle differences in the feel of paddles and are therefore of little concern to the beginner.

Length

This dimension is probably the one most worried about by novices, yet it is one of the least critical factors. Fashions and preferences as to length vary a good deal, partly because different conditions make varying lengths advantageous. Individual paddling styles, physique, and habit also influence choice. A taller person naturally prefers a slightly longer paddle, and a person with longer arms can handle a longer one without difficulty. In deep water a longer paddle is best, but in shallow places, particularly in rapids, a shorter paddle is less awkward. A paddle that reaches to about one's chin is a good length to start with. Experienced canoeists often use longer paddles in the stern than in the bow because the stern paddler is in a position higher above the water.

Grip

The most important feature of the grip is that it be comfortable for long periods of paddling. It should fit the hand perfectly. The "pear" grip, probably the most popular shape for general paddling, fits the hand naturally and allows variations in the grip. Most white-water paddlers and racers prefer a modified **T**-grip, which allows a very firm hold on the paddle and accurate control of the blade angle.

Two of the many types of paddle grips. LEFT. The conventional pear grip, which is comfortable to use and very suitable for cruising. RIGHT. A modified T-grip, which allows the paddle to be held firmly and gives excellent control over blade angle. This type of grip and variations of it are particularly popular among white-water paddlers. Individual comfort should be a primary consideration in choosing a grip.

Blade Size

Preferences vary a good deal depending on both strength and style of the paddler. A larger blade permits great power to be put into a stroke when it is wanted and anchors the paddle more firmly in place when it is used as a pivot or a brace in the water. Many paddlers prefer to get their power by stroking more quickly with a smaller blade, however. The area gained by adding width makes the paddle tricky to recover underwater or to use as a rudder; adding length is useless and awkward when the water is not deep enough to use the full length. Shape also influences area, since a paddle that is square on the bottom and has the width carried up nearly to the joint with the shaft will have much more area than one with a blade of the same length and maximum width but with a curved bottom and a width gradually tapering toward the shaft. Blades that are narrower than 7 inches at the widest point are considered too small by most experienced paddlers, and even powerful paddlers who like large blades consider 8¾ inches or 9 inches wide enough. Most experienced canoeists like blades of 7½ or 8 inches for general paddling. Blades longer than 26 inches are rarely used except for certain types of competition, and even this length is a bit long for general use when shallow water may often be encountered. Lengths between 22 and 25 inches are perhaps most common, with blades as short as 19 or 20 inches chosen by some who paddle a great deal in shallow rapids.

Blade Shape

The influence of length and width, which are related to shape, has been discussed. Materials are also important, as they influence the shape of the blade in various ways. Unreinforced wooden paddles should have the lower edge rounded. This distributes wear evenly and makes it less likely that the blade will split if a lower corner is caught. Unreinforced fiberglass blades are also rounded somewhat, at least at the corners, to reduce wear and stress at pointed corners. For white-water paddling especially, it is often convenient to have square corners that will hold well against rocks when the paddle is used for poling upstream or warding off boulders. These uses are practical only with a paddle reinforced with a metal strip along the bottom. The inward curve of the blade at the top where it meets the shaft is less critical, although shorter blades need to turn more sharply to maintain a reasonable blade area.

MATERIALS

Wood Paddles

These include both the worst and some of the best canoe paddles generally available. In the first category are the department-store variety of heavy, weak, and unresponsive wooden paddles. The worst of these are often painted to hide imperfections in the wood. The blades are generally thick, giving an illusion of strength, while they are unnecessarily weighty.

Laminated wood paddles, the blades of which are covered with a layer of fiberglass. These particular paddles have short shafts and wide blades, which makes them suitable for paddling in shallow water. The canoe is designed for fast going on flat water, so the sides are rather low. The molded seat is comfortable, and there are foot braces fiberglassed into the bottom for more positive control when paddling in a sitting position. This style of seat, with foot braces, is standard in canoes made for marathon racing.

Traditional paddles made from single pieces of wood were standard until a few years ago, and a well-made one is still a pleasure to paddle with, but their usefulness has dwindled. It is difficult to produce a really fine paddle from a single piece of wood because a rare grain pattern is needed. Normally the grain in a board, even when it is fairly good, will veer to one side; the resulting paddle is weak or likely to warp in that spot. Most of the better quality paddles made from a single piece of wood come from ash or spruce. Spruce is lighter and makes a pleasant paddle to use that is also quite strong for its weight, but it is soft, so it is easily damaged by rocks. Ash is somewhat heavier and tougher. Maple, also used fairly commonly, is stronger and heavier still; it is also more subject to warping and cracking. In any case, the shape of the paddle and the pattern of the grain are more important than the type of wood used. For strength and proper grip the shaft should be oval, with the long axis running perpendicular to the plane of the blade. The grain should run straight through the shaft, since the shaft must withstand all the stress of the paddle strokes, regardless of the care taken to avoid hitting rocks or catching the paddle among roots. The grip should be comfortable, and the paddle should have some spring when force is exerted in the center of the shaft. (If the person selling you the paddle is worried about the paddle breaking under the application of reasonable force, you should be too.) The thickness of the shaft should carry well into the blade, to avoid a weak spot at the junction, or "throat." The blade should taper off toward the edges and the tip to a thickness of a quarter of an inch or so. A rounded blade end is generally best on an unreinforced paddle, since it wears more evenly and is less likely to split in rough use. The balance of the paddle should be good, with the balance point about where the lower hand normally grips, so that the paddle can be turned with minimum effort during each stroke.

The best wooden paddles are normally made with laminated wood. Lamination techniques are not new, but modern waterproof glues have made them simpler and more effective. Laminating a number of pieces of wood together eliminates the difficulty in finding longer pieces of wood with the correct grain, since shorter and thinner pieces can be used. Warping and splitting are far less of a problem with correctly made laminated paddles, since grains can be crossed to prevent these difficulties. Proper selection of wood can also combine the advantages of various kinds while minimizing their disadvantages. High quality laminated paddles tend to be rather expensive, so most beginners should probably choose one of the more rugged and economical synthetic materials for a first paddle, unless only deep-water canoeing is anticipated. Fine laminated models are undoubtedly the most beautiful paddles made, however, and are coveted by many paddlers. For quality and selection of woods, one is largely dependent on the craftsmanship of the maker, which, fortunately, is fairly apparent when the paddle is inspected.

Many paddles today are made with laminated wood combined with some layers of fiberglass or other synthetics. Proper use of such materials can improve the strength and durability of laminated wood paddles without a loss in looks or feel. A number of techniques can be used, some of the more common being laminating a fiberglass strip into the shaft, gluing glass rovings (strands) around the lower edge of the blade, and laying glass over the surface of the blade and throat of the paddle, layers that become transparent after they are saturated with resin.

Fiberglass-Bladed Paddles

These have become the most common type for white-water and wilderness use because when properly made they are very strong, lightweight, and not too expensive. By *fiberglass* we mean resin reinforced with glass or synthetic cloth. Even more than with a canoe, the quality of a fiberglass paddle will depend on the skill of the builder, the exact materials and construction method used, and good design. Blades built with epoxy resins are normally stronger than those made with polyester resins, but a good builder can do a better job with polyesters than a mediocre one can with epoxies. New resin systems appear every year, however, so generalizations are difficult.

Both weight and strength are critical in a paddle, so it is important to saturate the cloth with the smallest amount of resin possible. More resin than necessary adds weight and decreases strength, but too little weakens the blade even more. Pressure molds are often used to squeeze out excess resin, but air is sometimes trapped by the process. Pinholes or a visible surface of cloth are bad signs on a paddle blade.

The most common fiberglass construction results simply in a thin blade made only of cloth and resin. A few manufacturers gain thickness by using a foam core; this is a good idea if it is well done, since it achieves the necessary thickness with minimum cloth and resin and closely approximates the buoyancy of a wood paddle.

Shafts for fiberglass paddles can be of wood, aluminum tubing, fiberglass, or a combination. Wood has a pleasant feel for moderate use, but it is not as strong as the other materials. Aluminum tubing, generally coated with some kind of plastic, is the most common shaft material. It is very strong if bends and crimps are not too sharp, but it is sometimes difficult to get a good bond with the blade. Most commonly, the tubing extends most or all of the way down the blade, gradually flattening as it nears the tip. Some manufacturers use this construction and then fiberglass the whole shaft so that no weak joint develops from uneven expansion between the two materials in heat and cold. Others prefer to use fiberglass pole-vaulting shaft material for the paddle shaft, whereas still others use a foam core with fiberglass or synthetic covering for both paddle blade and shaft.

Synthetic paddles should float, preferably even if the shaft breaks; this would require foam in aluminum shafts. A paddle that will not float is too easy to lose in an upset.

The paddle should be coated smoothly enough to be easy on the hands, wet or dry, for a full day of paddling. Even the smoothest surface will be hard on untoughened hands, and a rougher shaft will be impossible.

Other Plastics

Such other plastics as thermoplastics like ABS and injection-molded structural foams are used for paddle blades. Shafts may be from any of the materials used with fiberglass. ABS is probably the most common material used. Some of the paddles fashioned from it are quite strong and make excellent, inexpensive spares. ABS-bladed paddles have not gained general acceptance for normal use, partly because of aesthetics and partly because the original designs were not as strong as they should have been.

CARE OF PADDLES

Most broken paddles suffer their fate on shore, not in the water. Paddles carelessly left where they can be stepped on or driven over with a car are the most frequent victims. The best solution is to form the habit of always putting paddles in a safe place.

Wooden paddles need occasional maintenance to prevent rotting, splitting, or warping. Those who don't want to be bothered should choose paddles made from synthetic materials. The wooden blade has to be protected with good marine varnish, which should be touched up whenever spots become worn through to prevent water being absorbed, thus making the paddle heavier and more prone to rotting and splitting. Rivet holes on metal protectors for wood paddles should be sealed to prevent water from seeping into them and rotting the wood. Some paddlers varnish wood shafts as well, whereas some prefer to sand the wood bare and then soak it periodically with boiled linseed oil. The edge of a blade that receives heavy wear can be protected with a few rovings of fiberglass applied with resin. Vinyl tape is often used to protect the lower part of the shaft where it rubs against the gunwale in stern paddling.

Wooden paddles, particularly wet hardwood ones, should not be left out where the hot sun may split them. Maple is particularly prone to splitting, a tendency that can be reduced by sanding varnish off the blade and soaking it well with boiled linseed oil. Wooden paddles and those with wooden shafts should also be protected from porcupines in camp; the salt from perspiring hands is a treat for these animals, and they will be happy to chew through a paddle shaft to get it.

The various synthetic paddles require little maintenance. Fiberglass-reinforced polyester will deform if heated too much, so polyester blades should not be left in contact with a car roof or a rock in the hot sun. The same precaution applies to thermoplastics like ABS.

LIFE PRESERVERS

Whether life preservers are needed for lake canoeing depends on the particular circumstances. Anyone who is not a swimmer certainly should be wearing a life vest at all times in a canoe, although it would be best to have the person learn to swim first. It is foolish to have a whole boatload of nonswimmers in a canoe, with or without life jackets. A good swimmer with lifesaving experience may reasonably take a nonswimmer out in easy water, provided the nonswimmer is wearing a life vest.

Experienced canoeists who are strong swimmers have little need of life preservers for lake canoeing in reasonably warm water. It is important to note, however, that various government agencies often require that life-preserving devices be on board. In any case, the serious paddler will wear a life preserver for more difficult paddling, particularly in white-water.

Life preservers are absolutely essential for safe white-water paddling. Even the strongest swimmer, caught in a white-water capsize, will be buffeted around and carried where the water wants to take him. Real effort may allow him to swim into an eddy, but only if he does not need to concentrate on keeping his head out of water. In really turbulent rapids the water has so much air beat into it in places that one will float to the surface only part of the time even with a life vest. Without one, survival becomes largely a matter of luck. Unless you enjoy taking completely unnecessary risks, get a good life preserver and wear it in any white-water canoeing.

Similarly, cold water presents hazards that are hard to appreciate until they have been experienced. The body's warmth and ability to function are sapped with incredible rapidity. A swimmer can be rendered helpless in a couple of minutes by cold water, regardless of his strength or swimming ability. A life jacket alone may not be adequate insurance against cold-water spills, but it should be considered the minimum safety margin in many circumstances.

Even on flat water, the inexperienced canoeist can come to grief without a life preserver, whether or not he is a good swimmer, if he manages to fall out of his canoe while a good breeze is blowing. Unless the boat or painter is caught in the hand immediately, the wind can start moving the canoe across the water at a rate considerably faster than anyone can swim. If one is far from shore and such a mishap occurs, the lack of a life preserver may be sorely regretted.

Life preservers for canoeing should be of the vest or yoke type, which easily keeps the wearer afloat and is comfortable enough so that it will be worn. Ideally, a vest should float an unconscious victim faceup in the water with the nose and mouth well above the surface. This capability is often sacrificed for comfort and ease of movement, however. Many types of life preserver that supposedly will turn an unconscious victim faceup do not in fact do so, or do so only with some people. Individual physiology is important in this respect, and one can only be sure by experimenting with a particular life preserver in the water. At a minimum, however, the flotation should be placed in such a way that the swimmer will need to exert little effort to keep his head out of water. The flotation should be high on the body and there should be more in the front than the back, lest the wearer be turned facedown. The flotation belts designed for water skiers, for example, are inadequate for most canoeing purposes.

A life preserver for canoeing should not restrict paddling movements or be so cumbersome as to be annoying. It is all too likely that such jackets will not be worn when needed. Durability is worth considering, also. Covers made of cotton tend to rot fairly quickly, and nylon is preferred. The standard yokes and vests, with flotation made from kapok inside plastic bags, are vulnerable to damage, particularly with the usual thin gauge of plastic. Once the bags are punctured or popped, any extended time in the water will begin to soak the kapok, and then either the jacket or the flotation has to be replaced. The thickness of the plastic casing (which is not visible from outside) is normally only eight gauge; twelve or sixteen gauge is far sturdier. Anything you buy in a standard discount house or department store will be eight gauge, so don't bother to ask; most clerks won't know anyway. Only some specialty houses carry the heavier duty vests. Whichever kind you have, this type of preserver has to be handled with care. Don't sit on the jacket; you'll pop the bags. Avoid snagging the jacket and risking punctures.

For use on lakes and on moderate white-water the conventional bib-type preserver with flotation in front of the chest and a yoke continued around the neck and behind the head is quite adequate. This type of life preserver is also relatively inexpensive. Jackets with panels of closed-cell foam or with a number of oblong pieces of such foam stitched in tubes between layers of nylon are generally preferred by people who canoe a lot, though they are more expensive. They provide flotation in the same general range as the yokes. In really heavy white-water, not generally paddled in open canoes, many paddlers prefer a larger vest, providing around thirty pounds of flotation, or they wear two of the lighter jackets.

WET SUITS

Wet suits are garments made from neoprene foam that provide insulation by retaining a trapped layer of warmed water near the body, excluding the penetration of cold water. They are not needed for most canoeing, but they provide an important safety margin in severe conditions. The general safety rule is to wear a wet suit when there is a danger of capsizing and when water temperatures are below 50°F.

Some canoeing accessories. LEFT. A short-sleeved wet suit top. These suits are vital for safety whenever there is a chance of capsizing in cold water. On the wet suit top is a pair of boating shoes (running or tennis sneakers old enough to have plenty of holes). Shoes should normally be worn to protect the feet from sharp rocks or broken glass. CENTER. An inexpensive yoke type life preserver and a pair of short wet-suit pants. RIGHT. A more expensive and comfortable life preserver that uses closed-cell foam for flotation.

Normal clothing gives the body only minimal protection in case of immersion. Since cold water saps the body of warmth very rapidly in case of a ducking, and cold air above is likely to finish the job, a wet suit becomes an essential item of equipment whenever there is a risk of capsizing in very cold water. For serious white-water paddling, a wet suit should be worn if the water is even moderately cold.

For canoeing the most commonly used wet suits are made from ⅛-inch foam, although more protective suits of ³/₁₆-inch material are available. A set of "Farmer John" pants extending up over the torso and a top with a crotch strap provides a versatile combination, since they can be worn separately in moderate conditions. When worn together they make a double layer of insulation over the trunk, which is the part of the body most in need of protection.

FOOTWEAR

Preferences for canoeing footwear vary with personal taste and with the conditions in which one normally canoes. Those who do much lake canoeing with many portages may be primarily concerned with having shoes that are comfortable for walking, since with care the footgear can often be kept dry, provided that the portage trails themselves are not marshy. Those encountering river portages on rugged ground sometimes prefer lug-soled hiking boots that allow good traction when climbing dirt banks or edging on small footholds.

Many wilderness canoeists like rubber-bottom boots for a good combination of comfort and protection from the typical wet slogging of many landings, launchings, and portage trails. The connoisseur's alternative is a pair of high-topped moccasins with low rubbers to go over them.

The most common river footwear, however, is the lowly sneaker. The older and more full of holes it is, the better suited it is for river wear, since if the holes are large enough and sufficiently numerous, the water runs out almost as fast as it runs in. For cold weather wear, a pair of sneakers a size too large fits nicely over a pair of socks made from wet suit material. High-top sneakers are preferable, since they cannot be readily sucked off the feet by either turbulent white-water or mud on a portage trail. A pair of light hiking boots or camp shoes can be carried separately for long walks or dry feet.

It is important to avoid stiff shoes if they have a tendency to catch under the seat of the canoe, as they might trap the wearer. This is a particular hazard for a big-footed bow paddler in white-water because the bow seat is normally lower than the stern.

Slick soles on many types of footwear may be a problem on wet rocks, aluminum, or plastic. A few pieces of the self-adhesive sandpaperlike tape used to provide traction along the edges of stairs can be put on the bottoms of shoes if this is a problem, or soles can be made of felt, outdoor carpeting, or wet suit material and glued to the bottom of the shoes with contact cement.

KNEE PADS

Although there is no reason for paddlers to kneel all the time, kneeling is one of the better paddling positions, and padding gives the knees considerably more comfort. Pads can be made from a number of materials, perhaps the most popular being strap-on gardener's kneeling pads. Some prefer foam or sawdust sealed in rubber or plastic pouches. Pieces of closed-cell foam or shaped cups of ethafoam can be glued onto the canoe at the normal paddling positions to avoid both the danger of loss and the inconvenience of having the pads strapped to the knees.

THIGH STRAPS

For white-water canoeing, thigh straps provide a good deal of extra control for the paddler. Some purists eschew them, maintaining that they are not sporting. For many, however, the ease with which the paddler can hold himself rigidly in the canoe with thigh straps is desirable. After all, if one wants an extra handicap one can always paddle the rapid backward.

Properly installed thigh straps hold the paddler in the boat only as long as muscle tension is maintained, so there is no real danger of trapping him. The straps simply provide a means of holding onto the hull with the legs. The installation of thigh straps is discussed in Chapter 12.

PORTAGE YOKES

Techniques for portaging canoes are as varied as the crafts themselves, and discussion of them brings up the same sort of lively disagreement. Probably the most comfortable arrangement is a yoke shaped to fit the neck and shoulders that either replaces the center thwart or fastens quickly in the center spot if there is no center thwart. Such yokes are traditionally carved from wood or molded in fiberglass. The ideal yoke of this type must fit the user, however, and one that is comfortable for someone with big, burly shoulders may not be so for a person with a slight build.

Special yokes with angled, padded platforms are more easily made and have a more universal fit, though not so good a one as a properly carved or molded yoke that is well mated to the individual. Another defect is that they must be carried separately, since the platforms interfere with the use of the thwart.

A light and inexpensive alternative is a pair of pads that tie onto the central thwart. The simplicity makes up for the slight sacrifice in comfort, particularly for those who do not expect many long portages.

Techniques for portaging with and without yokes are discussed in Chapters 3 and 5.

POLES

Poling is generally the best way of ascending rapid streams and small rivers, the alternatives often being portaging, lining, or pushing the canoe upstream while walking in the riverbed. The pole can also be the most effective means of controlling downstream progress and propelling the canoe through shallow water.

Poles were traditionally cut beside the river when needed, although a metal shoe to put on the bottom for better grip and wear might be carried. (Shoes are made in a number of sizes and shapes, ranging from a metal cap to fit over the pole, with a simple spike to grip the bottom, to duck-billed arrangements that open when pushed into the mucky floor of a marsh. Shoes with long, narrow rods attached are still sometimes used to permit fast poling upstream in shallow water.) Modern poling experts have worked a revolution in technique during the last few years using lightweight aluminum poles that are stronger than wood ones, less prone to nasty, jagged breaks, and adaptable to many techniques that were impossible with the heavier wood poles. Light weight is far more critical in poles than paddles because of their length. An extra few ounces in the blade of a paddle is only slightly noticeable, since the extra weight is only a short distance from the point of rotation. The same few ounces added to the end of a pole require far more energy to swing around because of the distance from the arms exerting the force. A stick five feet long and weighing ten pounds takes less effort to swing back and forth than one of half that weight that is fifteen feet long.

A pole has to be strong enough so that pushing against it cannot break it. It should have some flex under a solid push, but it should immediately spring back straight when pressure is released. The ends should be plugged tight so that it will float if dropped. Twelve feet is about the right length for a pole. Instructions for making one can be found in Chapter 12.

CHAPTER 3

GETTING TO THE WATER

CARRYING THE CANOE

The beginner often has more of a problem getting the canoe to the water than paddling it once it is there. The average canoe is a fairly awkward object to handle ashore, even for an experienced person. Attaining a modicum of grace in manipulating one takes a little practice. This is not just because of weight. A moderately strong person can shoulder and carry a seventy-five-pound pack for some distance, whereas a seventy-five-pound canoe may prove quite recalcitrant. It is bulky, the shape is strange, and most of its surface is deliberately smoothed and rounded so as to provide no hold.

Handling the canoe with two people is relatively simple. With one person at each end, the team not only has the advantage of twice the strength but also has a lot more control because of their strategic placement. Minor errors in judging balance points are less likely to prove disastrous. The only real obstacle to overcome is that of communication. Until the two have become a team unified from handling many canoes together, it is important that nothing be done without previously warning the partner. Do not assume that the person on the other end of the canoe understands what you are about to do and will coordinate his actions with yours. Such an assumption is likely to begin your education on the subtleties of canoeing teamwork on an unfortunate note. Two people can carry a canoe in many obvious ways. Each can put an end on one shoulder, with the canoe either rightside up or upside down. With an overturned canoe, the front person can carry the bow on his shoulder and watch the path while the rear person carries the stern seat on his shoulders, stabilizing the boat and following the leader's feet. The upright canoe can be carried by grabbing the undersides of the decks, grab loops, or other projections near the ends, depending on the structure of the particular canoe.

Whenever possible, use two people to put the canoe on a car top or take it off again, since this maneuver is always awkward to accomplish alone. It is pointless to struggle alone with the canoe when help is available, particularly if the boat is heavier than average or you are weaker.

Still, there are a number of good reasons for learning to handle the canoe alone, even if you do not paddle solo. Aside from the convenience of being able to load the canoe or move it down to the lake while your companion is busy with something else, it is often actually easier to carry a canoe alone than it is with someone else. For example, on a rough trail two people reaching rough spots at different times, with the ground rising for one and falling for the other, often have an awkward job of carrying. If there are not too many branches interfering at the height of the head and shoulders, one person can often carry the canoe balanced on his shoulders quite easily along the same trail.

The first step in learning to carry a canoe alone is to be sure that the weight is reasonable for you and to get the knack of balancing the canoe and walking around with it. For short distances, at least, actually carrying the canoe is not very hard. The most difficult problems involve getting the craft on your shoulders and off again. This can be done easily by having another person raise the bow end of the overturned canoe as high as is necessary for you to get under the center thwart or yoke. To do this your partner should first lift the bow above his or her head and then work the canoe down as far as necessary with one upraised arm holding up each gunwale. Get under the center thwart so that your shoulders are settled, using a jacket for a pad if necessary. Put one hand forward on each gunwale, then lift, gradually taking the whole weight of the boat. As with all heavy loads, do the lifting with your legs as much as possible. Walk around a bit to get the feel of the canoe. A slight downward pressure with the arms holds the boat in balance. The stern will normally drop of its own accord when pressure is released, because the stern seat is farther from the center. The canoe is usually carried with the bow up at an angle for visibility. To put the canoe down, reverse the procedure.

The simplest way to move the canoe short distances when you are alone is simply to pull up on the near gunwale from amidships (assuming the canoe is resting rightside up on the ground) until the hull is resting on your thigh or hip. However, since this carry relies completely on arm and grip strength, it is not practical for any distance.

To get the canoe onto your shoulders when you are working alone, start at the bow end with the canoe resting in a normal position on the ground. Stand in front of the bow, facing the canoe, and pick up that end with both hands, one on each gunwale. After you are standing upright, continue to pull the bow up and rotate the canoe to an upside-down position over your head as you turn around to face away from the canoe. This is not difficult, since more than half the weight of the boat is resting on the stern, which is still on the ground. You are now standing under the bow, holding it over your head with both arms. Work your way backward, holding the boat over your head by the gunwales and moving your hands down the gunwales a little at a time until you come to the center of the boat. Settle the canoe on your shoulders and you are ready for the carry. Reversing the method lets the canoe down.

The technique just described is the simplest and safest way of getting a canoe on your shoulders by yourself. It is tedious, hard work for the arms, and sometimes a little rough on the stern end of the boat, but there is little danger of dropping the canoe or throwing your back out of joint. This should be the method used if you have any doubts about your ability to raise the canoe up, particularly if you are small or the canoe is very heavy. Most experienced canoeists prefer, however, to lift the canoe with a rolling motion from amidships, which brings the canoe directly onto the shoulders. The method is not difficult or strenuous once learned, but it can be a tricky skill to acquire, particularly for individuals who are not very strong. Proper execution requires the whole lift to be done in one smooth motion so that the canoe is thrown up partly by the trunk muscles and the legs, without relying heavily on arm strength. Timidity or poor aim, though, can result in the canoe hanging on the arms as a dead weight, halfway up on its journey to the shoulders, a very awkward position from which it is easy to drop the canoe. Practice on a soft lawn where a mishap will not damage the boat. If you don't want to gamble on doing the lift correctly the first time, have a friend stand at each end of the boat, ready to grab it if you are unsuccessful, particularly if you are learning the technique with someone else's hand-crafted cedar canoe.

Stand beside the canoe amidships while the boat is resting on its bottom on the ground. Pull up with both hands on the gunwale near you, lifting up the side until the hull rests on your thighs. Reach across the inside of the canoe with the hand closest to the bow, assuming that you wish to carry the canoe bow-forward. Beginners have a tendency to reach across with the wrong hand and end up facing in the opposite direction from the one they intended. Grasp the center thwart as far over as possible, gripping it with the thumb toward the inside of the canoe. Shift the second hand from the gunwale to the near end of the thwart, also in a direction so that the thumb is closer to the inside of the canoe. In a single motion pull up with both hands, raise the upper part of your body, and roll the canoe up on your thighs, tossing it up over your head and turning underneath it so that the thwart or yoke settles onto your shoulders. A little extra push can often be given with one leg, depending somewhat on the width and shape of the canoe. The motion is not really complicated and comes fairly naturally if you go at it energetically.

For carrying a canoe short distances, there is no real need for special equipment or rigging. You can portage on the center thwart, using a piece of clothing for a pad, if you feel the need for it. More elaborate methods for portaging are discussed in Chapter 5.

CARTOPPING

Few of us are fortunate enough to have canoeable streams within walking distance of the backyard, so we must generally carry the canoe to the starting point for the trip on top of the car. Most boaters prefer to do this on a roof rack of some kind, although it is quite feasible to tie a single canoe on a car roof using either a blanket for padding or cushions that snap onto the gunwales of the canoe.

Whether the canoe is carried by one person or several, it is a good deal more convenient to load and unload it with at least two. The procedure for putting the canoe on a rack or roof alone is not complex: one merely slides it gingerly in the appropriate direction until the weight is transferred. But the procedure is awkward, especially for short people, and wood gunwales and the finish of the roof may be scuffed a little. If the car is low enough, it is best to slide the canoe on from the side; if not, work from the back. It is much easier, though, to have one person at each end of the canoe, permitting it to be lifted onto or off the rack with no trouble.

If you have a garage or a carport with the proper dimensions, it is easy to install a pulley arrangement to lift the canoe off the rack and store it hanging from the rafters. Loading the canoe is then simplified, since you have only to lower the boat from the ceiling.

When a canoe is tied to the top of a car, it is absolutely essential that it be secured so that it would be impossible for it to come loose. Many people seem to have difficulty realizing how much force can be exerted on a canoe by the combination of wind and the air drag of high-speed driving. Remember how much pressure the air exerts on your arm when you stick it out the window while driving your car at highway speeds and then think how much bigger the canoe is than your arm. The forces involved are quite large, and head winds, side winds, and turbulence from nearby trailer trucks can multiply them.

A good bracket for a roof rack, made of cast aluminum alloy with a quick-release cam-action lever. A two-by-four is bolted on to hold the canoe. The most important feature is that the gutter clamp is held in by a screw so that it cannot slip off and release the rack. Even so, the canoe must be tied to the bumpers as well as the rack for safety.

A canoe can be tied onto the top of a car either on a rack for convenience or directly on the roof, using gunwale blocks or old blankets for padding. It must be tied so that it can't shift or release if one line fails. The webbing used here pulls at the stern from both sides, so the boat cannot move to either side. Another line (not visible) goes up to a seat to prevent the canoe from moving forward.

Consider the consequences of a seventy-five-pound canoe atop a car traveling at fifty miles an hour going through the windshield of a car coming the other way at the same speed. Keep this in mind every time you tie your canoe down to the car and you will do a much better job of it. Carelessness is inexcusable; sloppy tie-downs might cost the paddler his canoe, but they could easily kill another person who did not agree to the risk.

The canoe has to be tied down so as to prevent both sideways and lengthways motion. It should also be secured so that the breakage or release of any one element in the system would not permit the canoe to come off. Thus, simply tying the boat down to a roof rack is dangerous; if the rack works loose, the whole combination will go bouncing down the road, still securely fastened together.

If the roof rack is really sturdy, a good way to tie the canoe down is to lash it securely front and back to the rack, then guy it (see below) to the front and back of the vehicle. The two crossbars of the rack should be as far apart as possible without sacrificing security of attachment, and the center of the canoe should be roughly midway between them. Blocks fastened to the crossbars outside the gunwales or notches in the crossbars make it easier to lash the canoe so that it will not move from side to side.

To guy the end of the canoe nearest the front of the car, tie the line to one side of the bumper or a nearby part of the car's frame, run it up and back to a convenient point on the canoe, tie it there, then run it down to the bumper or frame on the other side of the car. A **V** is formed in this way that helps to secure the canoe against sideways motion. If the end of the canoe protrudes past the front bumper, tie the rope to a sturdy seat or thwart so that the line is pulling forward on the canoe. If the thwarts are not strong enough, run the line around the thwart, then over the canoe.

The tie points on the car must be selected for solidity and padded wherever the line runs over a sharp edge. The most convenient arrangement is to install an eyebolt with a quarter-inch shaft or a cleat to each end of the bumper, making sure first that the bumper is sound.

The best tie points on the canoe will vary depending both on the way it is made and on the size of the car. Guy the rear in the same way, but with the lines going forward from the bumper so that tension pulls back on the canoe.

If no roof rack is used or if the rack is inadequately secured, tie a line tightly to each side of the center thwart and to a point on the car frame, to the post between the car windows, or through the windows to the other side. All these tie-downs should be done with heavy rope, rubber rope, or good quality shock cords. Cotton or plastic clothesline and cheap shock cords are not suitable.

LAUNCHING A CANOE

Getting the canoe into the water is simple enough, although a bad site may require some wading or awkward carrying. Descending a steep bank may be the biggest problem. Where the shoreline is reasonably manageable, two people can stand on opposite sides of the canoe grasping the gunwales and run it into the water hand-over-hand. As the bow goes into the water it will float. Keep at least half the hull on shore until you are ready to board; if there are waves, don't put the canoe in the water at all until you are ready to get in.

You should be cautious about pushing the canoe over subsurface rocks or stepping into it if there are sharp rocks an inch below the hull. However, as long as there are a few inches of unobstructed depth the boat can be worked out into the water until just the stern remains ashore. The bow paddler then walks down the center of the canoe and takes his place while the stern person steadies the canoe. Once the bow canoeist is in position, the stern paddler can usually push the canoe into the water, put one foot in, and push off with the other while steadying himself with his hands on the gunwales. If the bottom is shallow or irregular, the stern person may have to wade out, pushing the canoe until there is enough depth. This may frequently be necessary when launching into waves. If the bottom is very shallow, both paddlers may have to wade for a while.

When putting a canoe into the water alone, it is usually simplest to pick it up by one gunwale and lower the far side into the water first, so that the canoe is left floating parallel to shore. One end can then be swung out into the water. It is preferable to push the stern end out and climb into the canoe with the bow still on shore. When the canoeist moves to the stern end, the bow is raised clear and the canoe can easily be paddled out backward.

When launching from a dock and from some shorelines it is more convenient to hold the canoe parallel to the platform while one paddler at a time enters. Canoes are really quite stable, and there is no great trick to boarding or disembarking, as long as you keep the weight fairly well centered in the boat, either by stepping near the centerline or by holding both gunwales and putting your weight on your hands.

Before stepping into a canoe from a muddy shore, it is usually a good idea to dip each shoe sole in the water to wash off mud and grit. One should be particularly careful to take this precaution on entering a wooden or wood-and-canvas canoe. The varnished surface in these canoes is the only protection against water absorption, and gritty shoes can quickly mar the varnish.

LANDING

Landing is generally the reverse of the procedure for launching. Most commonly, the bow is brought into shore and the bow paddler steps out. The bow then rises, and the bow person pulls the canoe in farther before the stern paddler walks the length of the boat to disembark. During difficult landings the bow paddler may have to get out in waist-deep water to pull the boat in.

POSITIONS WITHIN THE CANOE

Much controversy has somehow been generated over the matter of sitting in a canoe. Kneeling is generally a more stable and powerful paddling position than sitting, so it is preferred by most experienced paddlers for white-water or fighting a wind across a lake. Sitting is also a comfortable position, however, and there is no reason not to alternate, particularly on long trips. Work on feeling at home in your canoe from a number of positions. Try paddling while sitting in the seats, but learn to paddle from a kneeling position as well. It is most comfortable if one kneels on a pad or pads with the knees spread wide and the buttocks resting on the forward edge of a seat or thwart. Learn also to paddle while kneeling without support, as it is often important to paddle from a particular position in a canoe, whether a seat or thwart is placed there or not.

While learning to paddle, get into the kneeling position whenever you are trying any maneuvers requiring tricky balance or whenever the canoe feels unstable to you. This position will give you the extra control of the hull you need and will lower your center of gravity. Avoid sitting on thwarts, but if you have seats in the boat the idea that sitting is dangerous during routine paddling is nonsense.

CHAPTER 4

LEARNING TO PADDLE

Practice is the key to learning how to handle a canoe, regardless of whether one has a teacher, learns with another beginner, or works alone. It takes time to develop the strength, feel for the paddle, coordination, and understanding of the dynamics of the canoe moving through the water that are required for efficient paddling and control of the boat. For tandem paddling one must add comprehension of the roles of bow and stern paddlers and the ability to synchronize with the other person.

The fastest way to develop the basic paddling technique is to be taught by someone who is both a good canoeist and a good teacher. If you are fortunate enough to have such a friend or to join a club with experienced members who are willing to teach you, then you will follow the method that they think best. Most commonly, the beginner paddles in the bow of the canoe first, learning the forward and backward strokes without steering, while the teacher corrects errors from the stern. Later, other bow strokes will be learned and the student may paddle on a few trips before taking the stern.

For beginners who must teach themselves, there are many advantages to taking the canoe out solo a few times before trying to coordinate with a partner. It is more difficult to paddle a canoe alone, but a great deal can be learned in this way because the single paddler must perform the roles of both bow and stern persons. When one is paddling solo, there is no question about whose strokes are causing a par-

By paddling solo one can quickly learn the way that strokes before and behind the centerline affect the boat's movement. The kneeling position is the most stable, so it is a good one to start with. The canoe is turned around so that the bow seat is at the rear and the paddler can sit on it if he wishes, although the optimum position for an unladen boat is just to the rear of the center thwart, where this canoeist is paddling. He is beginning a forward stroke with a little inward draw to help keep the canoe on a straight track.

Directional instability. Because the stern and bow of the canoe normally have the same shape, the moving canoe will turn more and more as soon as it turns a little to one side unless the paddler does something to correct the course. The canoe in the drawing starts in position 1, moving to the right. The paddler takes a stroke on the right side of the canoe, turning it slightly to the left while driving forward.

As the canoe moves into position 2, the drag of the water on the bow is no longer evenly distributed on both sides. It pushes on the right side of the bow, slowing it and pushing it to the left. The stern, encountering no drag from the water, moves forward and pivots around the dragging bow, moving out to the right. The turn thus becomes sharper and sharper. The tendency is increased if the bow is trimmed heavy, so that it drags more in the water.

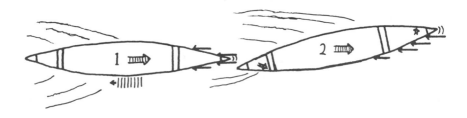

ticular effect. One can learn much quickly, although the experience may be a bit frustrating at first. There is also no one else to become impatient with when the canoe goes in a circle instead of the intended straight line.

WHICH SIDE SHOULD YOU PADDLE ON?

With a normal canoe paddle, each person paddles on only one side of the canoe. (A few canoeists prefer to paddle with a long double-bladed paddle like an elongated kayak paddle, particularly when paddling alone. Such paddles trade off some power, efficiency, and stability in the wind to avoid the single-bladed paddler's need to make course corrections.) A canoeist using a single-bladed paddle may change sides on occasion for relief or for specific advantage in white-water (about which more in Chapter 9), but constant switching back and forth for course correction is the mark of the raw neophyte. A competent canoeist can paddle on either side of the canoe and accomplish all normal maneuvering without switching the paddle from side to side.

It is important for the beginner to concentrate eventually on ambidexterity in paddling. It is a bad habit to develop a strong side at the expense of a weak one. At the beginning, however, there is no harm in concentrating on learning the basic strokes on one side first, developing the ability to maneuver the canoe properly without switching the paddle over, and then beginning work on the other side. Begin with whichever side seems more natural, but once you have achieved reasonable facility on that side, concentrate on the other until it feels just as natural. After this it is important to practice each new skill on both sides, spending more time on the weak side than the strong one.

When a canoe is paddled by a team of two, the person in the bow paddles on one side and the person in the stern on the other. Again, it makes little difference which position is used at the beginning. The goal is for both paddlers eventually to be equally proficient on either side and in either end of the boat.

PADDLING

A canoe is normally propelled with paddles that are held in the hands of the canoeists, not attached to the canoe at all. Oars, sails, and poles are used occasionally with canoes, but paddling is the most fundamental skill in canoeing. (Poling is discussed in Chapter 8.)

The paddle consists of a wide blade designed to resist movement through the water in a direction perpendicular to its surface, although it will slip edgeways easily. A blade is attached to a shaft, which serves as a handle for the paddler to hold and as a lever through which force can be applied to the blade from the grip at the top of the shaft.

The paddler grips the canoe in several ways with the lower part of the body so that he or she can push it in the desired direction, obtaining purchase to exert force by pushing the paddle blade against the water. Most of the paddling force is transmitted in this way through the canoeist's body, but leverage of the paddle shaft directly against the gunwale of the canoe is used to some degree.

In the most basic type of paddling, propelling the canoe straight ahead in flat water and through still air, the canoeist simply has to keep the canoe headed on a straight line and to push enough water backward with the paddle to overcome the friction of the water that tends to slow the boat. Achieving forward momentum is simple enough, but a beginner soon finds that keeping the canoe headed in a straight line is not always as easy as it looks.

Even though the force exerted against the water is transmitted to the canoe through the paddler's body, the canoeist cannot simply cancel out rotational forces; any paddle stroke taken straight along the line of travel will have a rotational effect unless it is directly on the keel line of the canoe. Since a normal paddle stroke has to be made at the side of the canoe some distance away from the keel line, it will tend to turn the canoe to an extent that depends on the design of the boat, the distance of the paddle from the keel line, the power of the stroke, and the paddler's position in the canoe. The reason that a twosome paddles on opposite sides of the canoe is to allow the rotational forces of the two strokes to cancel each other out partially.

When paddling alone, you should normally be positioned just a little behind the center of the canoe. There are many variations of this position (discussed later), but a fairly level trim is normally desirable. In an empty canoe this requires the paddler to be fairly close to the center, yet good control requires that the canoeist be able to reach fairly far back from there.

The exact position is not critical and may later be varied, but the beginner should start with a kneeling stance, which is stable, gives good control of the boat, and can be assumed without a seat or thwart if one is not available in the right position. Most canoes have a thwart placed in the center for portaging, and the single paddler should kneel behind this. Large canoes may have an extra thwart placed behind the center one for convenience in solo paddling. With small craft it may be possible to reverse directions and use the back end of the bow seat, but the beginner should choose a spot just behind the center thwart and ignore the seats in order to get the most advantageous position.

A standard canoe is too wide for comfortable paddling from a centered position near the middle of the canoe, so kneel a little to one side, as shown in the illustration on page 75, starting with whichever side feels most natural. The canoe will tilt somewhat toward the side on which you are kneeling, but this is not a problem.

THE MOVING CANOE

Before practicing normal forward paddling, the beginner must understand several things about the dynamics of a canoe moving forward in flat water. Assume for the moment that the canoe is trimmed evenly with the paddler(s) aboard, with the stern and bow riding at the same height in the water. If the canoe is propelled straight ahead it will move directly forward and not turn to either side, but if it begins to turn even slightly in either direction because of a paddle stroke off to the side or for some other reason, the turn will increase rapidly unless something is done to stop it. The standard canoe in normal trim is directionally unstable in forward or backward motion, because any turn is amplified.

The reason the canoe tends to turn more and more once it starts is related to the shape of the hull, as shown in the drawing. The keel alone will not increase a turn; it merely sends the canoe off along the new course determined by the original turning action, since the force exerted by the water through which the hull is moving balances exactly at the two ends. This would not be true if the keel were only at one end of the boat or were larger at one end; more directionally stable craft have more keel at the stern. The action of the water against the rest of the hull does not balance, however.

If the canoe is moving forward and begins to turn right, much more surface area is quickly presented to the water on the left side of the bow. This tends to push the bow farther to the right and also to slow it down so that the stern begins to sideslip around to the left as the bow is pushed right. The force on the bow is not balanced by another force against the stern, because the left side of the stern curves back the other way. The bow actually sideslips too, but not nearly as much as the stern.

This directional instability of a canoe is not an undesirable feature— it is what makes the canoe such a maneuverable craft—but the beginner is likely to find it frustrating because considerable practice is required to make the canoe go where the paddler wants. The finesse required will depend on the design of the boat. A long, narrow canoe with a V-shaped hull or keel will travel in a straight line fairly readily, but it is hard to maneuver. The flatter-bottomed, keelless short canoe will turn easily whether that is wanted or not.

One consequence of the canoe's turning characteristics is that most maneuvering and course corrections should be made nearer the stern of the canoe, assuming forward motion. If the bow begins to swing to the right, a correction can be made at the stern that pushes the rear of the canoe to the right also, thereby bringing the boat back into line. If instead one tries to pull the bow to the left, the sideslip that is already occurring increases, but it is very difficult to force the bow to sideslip faster than the stern and bring the boat back into line. There are exceptions, but in general steering is done toward the stern of the canoe when paddling single; if the boat is being paddled by two people, the stern paddler will have primary responsibility for steering. The roles are reversed with the direction of travel so that in back paddling, steering is done from the bow.

TYPES OF STROKES

FORWARD STROKES

The Bow, or Forward, Stroke

The main motion of the forward stroke should be parallel to the keel line, since that line points in the direction of forward travel. For a straight forward stroke, extend the paddle as far forward as possible consistent with good balance and a fairly erect position. Plunge the blade into the water so that it can be pulled straight back parallel to the keel line and as close to the hull as possible. Thus, a stroke taken at the center of the boat would start a little out from the hull, pass by the wide point at the center, nearly touching the gunwale, and finish a little out from the hull. If taken farther toward the stern, the stroke would begin next to the canoe side and move away as the hull curves. Nearer the bow, the stroke would start farther away and approach the gunwale at the end of the stroke; this is in fact exactly the stroke the bow paddler normally uses in a canoe being paddled by two people.

Whether one is paddling with this straight forward stroke or one of the variations discussed below, it is important to make the whole motion as efficient as possible. During a long day's paddling, one may take tens of thousands of forward strokes, so each one should put minimum strain on the body and move the canoe as far as possible in the direction of travel.

The more nearly vertical the blade is in the water, the more efficient

Beginning a regular forward or bow stroke, the paddler is kneeling a little to the right of center. The shaft goes practically straight down into the water to make the stroke efficient and keep the paddle as close to the side of the canoe as possible, thereby minimizing the tendency of the stroke to turn the canoe.

A paddler in a closed canoe drives forward in white-water. Note that the canoeist's arms are fairly straight, and rotation of the shoulders and trunk will drive the paddle back.

the stroke will be. When the blade slants forward or back while power is being applied to the paddle, some force is being exerted downward or upward on the water, and in a forward stroke, this is wasted energy. It is impossible to have the paddle dead vertical through the whole power phase of the stroke, but one should aim for this.

Much of the power of the stroke should come from the muscles of the trunk, back, and shoulders. Try to learn to put your body into each stroke rather than relying on arm strength, which is limited. As you extend the paddle forward, rotate the shoulders away from the paddling side and during the stroke turn them back toward it. Much of the power of the stroke should come from this rotation. Some of the force comes from the upper arm pushing forward on the grip of the paddle. Only a little comes from the lower arm, which acts mainly as a fulcrum through which the force is transmitted from the upper shaft to the blade.

To recover the paddle for the next stroke, pull it up smartly from the water as soon as the power phase is complete. Turn the blade so it is nearly parallel to the surface of the water and, keeping it horizontal and close to the surface of the water, swing it in an arc back to the starting point. The blade is thus slicing through the air rather than pushing on it. This turning of the blade, called feathering, greatly increases efficiency when paddling against the wind.

The J-Stroke and Its Variations

The J-stroke. This modification of the straight forward stroke is used by the single paddler or, in a twosome, the stern person when the canoe is paddled straight forward in flat water. Some version of the J-stroke is used constantly during most paddling by a single canoeist or by the stern member of a team, so it is in many ways the most fundamental of all strokes. Until it is mastered, the beginner will find himself making constant course corrections while trying to paddle in a straight line. Because of the asymmetry of propulsion with single paddles and the canoe's directional instability, a small correcting movement has to be incorporated into each stroke to prevent the canoe from starting to turn significantly. Remember that once a turn is well started it will tend to increase as long as the canoe is moving because the stern will start to sideslip out around the bow.

The **J**-stroke is a normal forward stroke with a hook at the end to make the necessary turning correction. As the paddle reaches the hips during the power phase of the stroke, turn the upper hand holding the grip ninety degrees so that the thumb moves away from your face. Then push the upper hand away from the paddling side, using the lower hand and the gunwale for a pivot so that the blade pushes water out from the canoe, making the necessary correction in course.

The **J**-stroke will be difficult to perform smoothly at first, but it will become quite smooth with practice. When first learning it, don't try to put a lot of power into the stroke; concentrate instead on form and on keeping the canoe headed straight without a lot of wiggling. Start to put your muscles into the stroke after it begins to feel smooth.

The **J**-stroke is important to master because it gives a great deal of

The last phase of a **J**-stroke. The paddler has just rotated the paddle by turning the hand on the grip counterclockwise (as viewed from above) and is pushing the blade out to correct for the turning action of the forward stroke. The gunwale may or may not be used as a fulcrum. Here the canoeist is paddling from a kneeling position but is using the bow seat as a rest to support some of his weight.

power and control, allowing a considerable turn to the paddling side when necessary. It is heavily relied on in white-water paddling, although on flat water many paddlers use variations.

The pitch stroke. This technique uses an angling of the paddle during the stroke to put sideways force on the stern of the canoe rather than having a separate phase at the end of the stroke. Make a normal forward stroke, except that during the second half of the stroke rotate the grip about forty-five degrees, turning the upper hand gradually, with the thumb moving away from the face so that the paddle blade is pushing against the water at an angle. As with the J-stroke, brace the paddle shaft with the lower hand, often using the gunwale as an aid.

Both the J and pitch strokes can be used with a good deal of variation in sideways force; the ideal is to need as little as possible. In general, a paddler sitting near the stern will need less corrective force because his basic stroke will be closer to the centerline of the canoe and will thus exert less turning force that needs correction. The single paddler near the center of the canoe needs to use a more exaggerated J or pitch stroke for two reasons: the beam is wider, so the stroke is farther from the centerline, and corrective movements are not as close to the stern, so they are less effective.

Many paddlers actually use combinations of the J and pitch strokes, pitching the paddle somewhat in the last part of the stroke and adding a bit of a J at the end when needed. As you progress, you will develop your own variation that is most comfortable for you. Be sure, however, to have a really powerful J-stroke available when it is needed for sharp course correction.

Other variations use the resistance of the paddle blade in the water as it is recovered to make minor course corrections. The lower hand is used as a pivot, perhaps moving out slightly from the side of the canoe while the upper hand drops over toward the off-paddle side. The blade is thus lifted from the water well out from the side of the canoe, and the resistance of the water against it tends to turn the canoe much more than resistance closer to the boat. The angle of the paddle is adjusted for more or less resistance. This technique is useful only for minor course corrections, as otherwise it slows the canoe's forward motion too much.

The solo paddler near the center of the boat often uses a bit of diagonal draw in the first part of the forward stroke, combined with a small **J** at the end. (The draw is described on pages 86–88.) The two combine to keep the canoe almost straight on course throughout the forward stroke.

The stern pry. This stroke is often used in combination with the forward stroke in white-water paddling when a strong course correction is needed. It can be practiced after the **J** and pitch strokes are mastered. Take a straight forward stroke and then quickly rotate the paddle ninety degrees in the water, with the thumb of the grip hand turning toward the face rather than away from it as in the other two strokes. Then pry the paddle away from the boat, using the hull and gunwale for leverage. This is not a smooth stroke for normal forward paddling. For more details on the pry, see the description of it on pages 88–93.

A stern pry used at the end of a forward stroke. The position of the paddle looks the same as the **J**-stroke at first glance, but a comparison with the preceding photograph will show that the grip hand has rotated in the opposite direction, the thumb moving up and toward the face rather than down and away, and the off-side arm can pull hard on the paddle, levering the blade out with the gunwale as a fulcrum.

BACK PADDLING

Proficiency in paddling the canoe backward is at least as important as in normal forward movement. It enables canoeists to stop or slow forward motion while they survey a possible course through a river rapid or in pounding surf. It provides the means for maneuvering across a river to a better channel, an eddy, or a landing spot. If worse comes to worst, it will at least soften the blow in an unavoidable collision with an obstacle, perhaps saving one from capsizing or stoving a hole in the boat.

A good deal of practice in back paddling is generally required before the canoe will go where you want it to, partly because the motion is somewhat less natural but mainly because it is difficult to sense the nuances of a course while looking over one's shoulder. The back paddling stroke is essentially the reverse of the forward stroke. Reach back with the hand on the paddling side and plant the paddle near the hull at or a little behind the hip; push forward with the lower hand while pulling with the upper, keeping the shaft as close to vertical as possible, and withdraw the paddle about where it is planted for the forward stroke.

Begin by aiming for control with the back stroke, increasing tempo and power as your ability to determine the direction of travel improves. Remember that when the canoe is traveling backward, steering corrections will be difficult to make toward the stern, just as they are difficult at the bow in forward movement. The single paddler should put a **J** in his back stroke as he ends it, toward the bow end of the boat. The bow paddler will make the **J**s for a tandem crew that is back paddling.

OTHER STROKES TO CONTROL A CANOE

There are a number of ways to turn a canoe or change its course, each having a particular use, and the beginner should aim to master a large number of strokes eventually. It is best to learn them as separate actions, although in paddling, one stroke will blend into another smoothly, and strokes are often mixtures of techniques that may be separately labeled here.

Rudder Strokes

The most obvious method of redirecting a canoe is to steer it when it is moving through the water, using the paddle somewhat like a rudder. This type of action relies on the motion of the canoe, the paddler, and the paddle over the water to create water resistance to the angled blade and to turn the canoe in the desired direction. There are a number of strokes of this type, but they share the characteristic of being useful, in most situations, mainly for slight course corrections because they use up the canoe's momentum, becoming less and less effective as they are prolonged.

Rudder-type strokes are more versatile in their action than might be apparent at first glance. A rudder held amidships will tend to drive the whole canoe over in the direction in which it leads, without turning the ends. If the canoeist paddling near the center of the boat wants to use a rudder to move toward the paddling side, he normally holds the paddle out from the side by rotating the upper body toward the paddling side and leaning out as far as is safe. So far this stroke is like the draw, discussed on pages 86–88, but in the rudder the blade is angled away from the line of travel at an appropriate angle up to about forty-five degrees. If, on the other hand, the canoeist wants to move away from the paddling side, he braces the paddle against the side of the boat, as in a pry, with the leading edge of the paddle angled in. In the first case additional movement can always be managed by moving into a draw, and in the second case a pushover or pry can follow. These same techniques can be used by the bow and stern paddlers in combination to move the canoe over somewhat. To move toward the bow paddler's side when the canoe is going forward, the bow paddler uses the draw-like rudder angled in and braced against the gunwale or hull. To move toward the stern's paddling side, the methods are reversed.

In the bow a rudder is often useful for initiating a turn and starting the stern sideslipping or for making a small course correction. For these purposes the rudder is most effective when held fairly far forward. For a turn toward the paddling side, the lower arm (the one on the paddling side) is stretched straight forward and out, holding the shaft out at the angle desired for the rudder. This can be done in several ways, depending on the canoe, on the angle, and on individual strength and style. The upper arm may be held high so that the body can lean on it (as in a draw), or both arms may be lowered so that the paddling-side hand or forearm can be braced against the gunwale for support. For a turn away from the paddling side, the paddle can simply be reached well forward and braced against the gunwale.

Either a rudder trailing out to the stern or one reached out toward the bow may be used by a single paddler positioned amidships. This is the method used instinctively by many beginners to correct direction after a forward stroke. It is generally far less effective than the **J** or pitch stroke, but it is sometimes useful when paddling through weeds, pulling up to a landing, or in similar situations.

Holding the paddle blade at an angle in the water is often useful for making minor course corrections when the canoe is moving at a reasonable speed with respect to the water. Such techniques may also be helpful to initiate movements that are finished with other strokes or to complete other, vigorous strokes. Remember that all rudders are inherently less effective than the appropriate draw or pry. A rudder is a passive stroke; a draw or pry, an active one.

Unfortunately, the nomenclature for the various rudder strokes is not consistent. One person's rudder is another's cut or stationary draw. The important points are that the blade may be angled either away from the hull or toward it and that such strokes can be made in the center of the boat or toward the bow or stern.

Sweep Strokes

Probably the most common way to turn, sweep strokes swing the paddle blade out in an arc as far from the hull as possible, turning the canoe in the direction opposite from the rotation of the paddle. Unlike rudder strokes, sweeps are active strokes and do not rely on the motion of the canoe relative to the water to produce a turning effect. They can be used whether the canoe is moving through the water or not and, unlike rudder strokes, can be used to turn the canoe through a wide angle, even in close quarters.

Sweep strokes are basic in learning to maneuver a canoe. They work particularly well in solo paddling, since the paddling position well out from the centerline is an advantage for once. The solo paddler sitting near the center of the canoe will use a full 180-degree sweep, whereas paddlers at the bow and stern normally use only a 90-degree partial sweep, depending on circumstances and the length of the canoe.

The forward sweep. This stroke turns the canoe away from the paddling side. The canoeist leans slightly forward, reaching as far forward as he comfortably can, for maximum leverage. One hand grasps the shaft and the off-side hand braces the grip lightly and acts as a pivot. The blade should slice into the water near the surface and be kept near it through the whole sweep. The blade should be put in the water as far forward as possible without overbalancing and should start as close to the hull as possible. The power face of the blade starts by being oriented straight out from the side of the canoe. (The power face of the paddle is the one that pushes on the water in the normal forward stroke.)

To do a forward sweep, swing the paddle around in a half-circle as far out from the side of the canoe as possible, keeping the arm on the paddle side fairly straight and using the off-side hand as a pivot throughout. The paddle is withdrawn after it travels back to the side of the canoe to the rear of the paddler. If the canoe needs to be turned only a short way, the complete sweep may not be used. If it needs to be turned farther, the paddle is feathered and recovered, with the grip hand still low, and the stroke is repeated. In practicing, the beginner should see how many strokes are needed to turn the boat completely while it stays in one place in the lake. The angle possible with each stroke will vary with the canoe and paddle: with a short slalom boat the canoe can be turned completely around with three strokes, but with a longer canoe with some keel more will be required.

The reverse sweep. This sweep follows the same motion as the forward one, except that the arc is started from the stern and the paddle is swung around toward the bow. The canoe turns toward the paddling side. As with the forward sweep, the action of the reverse sweep can be shortened or repeated, depending on the amount one wishes to turn.

Sweeps are useful for turning the canoe in cramped situations, particularly when it is moving slowly or not at all. A certain amount of sweep is also often incorporated into the forward stroke when paddling at an angle to wind or waves, in order to maintain a steady course. Practice sweeps, both forward and reverse, on both sides of the canoe each time you go out until you master them thoroughly.

In tandem paddling, the bow paddler normally uses only the first half of the forward sweep, beginning at the bow and continuing

Here a reverse sweep is being used to slow the forward-moving canoe and turn it to the paddler's right. The arc starts from the stern and sweeps out around forward, with the blade near the surface of the water. A forward sweep on the same side would reverse the motion and turn the canoe to the paddler's left.

around only until the paddle is perpendicular to the hull. The reverse sweep is less frequently useful in the bow, but when used it is started with the paddle straight out from the hull and traces a forward arc to the bow. The stern paddler uses the other half of the semicircles, beginning the forward sweep straight out from the hull and sweeping to the stern. The more useful reverse sweep starts at the stern and pushes in a forward arc until the paddle sticks straight out from the hull, at which point the stroke is repeated if necessary. To turn away from the bow's paddling side, the bow paddler does a forward sweep (as far as the perpendicular) and the stern paddler simultaneously does a reverse sweep (also as far as the straight-out position). If sweeps are to be used by a tandem crew to turn toward the bow paddling side, the bow paddler uses his half of the reverse sweep while the stern uses half of the forward one.

Sideways Motion

A number of strokes are used to move the canoe or one end of it sideways through the water. The draw stroke, in which the paddler reaches out as far as possible with the blade and pulls the boat toward the paddle, is the most important of these strokes. The pry, which pushes in the opposite direction from the draw, is another. These may be used to move the canoe sideways when it is sitting still on the water, to avoid an obstacle that is just ahead of the moving boat, or for similar purposes. These strokes, when applied at either end of the boat, are also used to turn the canoe. Two paddlers at opposite ends of the canoe drawing or prying in opposite directions can turn a canoe quickly and with great power.

It is important to remember that the paddle blade acts on and is resisted by the water it is in, whereas the hull is affected by the water in which it is floating. When paddling on a quiet lake, the canoeist will generally find that his boat and paddle have the same velocity relative to the water. In more complicated paddling, this is not necessarily the case. In a fast river the canoe may have its own momentum in one direction, the water under the bow may be flowing in another direction with that under the stern in the opposite way, and the current into which the paddle is plunged may be going in still another. Such complicated currents are not always even in the horizontal plane, sometimes welling up or sucking down instead. The experienced river paddler uses such crosscurrents to his advantage in maneuvering the canoe, reaching over with the paddle to catch a current that will spin the canoe around in the desired direction or using the pressure of the current against one side of the bow to shoot the boat across a channel. Such techniques will be discussed later, but the beginner should understand that the movements of the boat are a result of all the forces acting on it. You will begin to become an accomplished paddler when you start to learn to use these forces to help maneuver the canoe rather than fighting against them with main strength.

The Draw

Modern white-water canoeing technique is based largely on refinements of the draw stroke, which allows the canoeist to lean most of his weight on the paddle and reach far out to catch a current while at the same time increasing the stability of his position.

The beginner should start work on the draw stroke early, but one cannot expect to master it until one has reached a high degree of paddling proficiency. To perform this stroke, hold the paddle in the normal position, rotate the upper body toward the paddling side, and, leaning out as far as possible without losing balance, extend the paddle straight out away from the hull to catch the water well away from the canoe. The upper arm should be high and fully extended; the lower arm should reach out quite far. The paddle should be nearly vertical, and for a straight draw the face of the blade should run parallel to the keel line. After the blade is completely in the water, draw the paddle toward the canoe and flick it back out of the water just as it reaches the side.

Once the draw is developed enough to have some real power, the withdrawal of the blade becomes critical. If it is pulled out of the water too soon, much of the potential force of the technique is lost,

A draw stroke to move the canoe toward the paddling side. It may not always be desirable to lean as far out to begin the stroke, since the maximum force on the canoe is gained during the stage when the paddle is dead vertical, but it is important to practice the draw enough to gain real confidence in it, so that one actually leans on the paddle. Note that here the canoeist has most of his weight resting on the paddle and the water. The technique can later be used to stabilize the boat as well as move it.

but if the paddler is a little late and the hull overrides the paddle, the strength of the stroke and the rhythm of paddling will certainly be disturbed, and the canoeist may be thrown off-balance so badly that he capsizes. The aim of the novice should be to maintain full power until just before the hull and paddle come together, then to slice the paddle quickly out of the water for another draw or a different stroke. Rapid withdrawal is aided if the hand on the paddle side is used mainly as a pivot while the upper hand drops down toward the bow, thus rotating the blade up out of the water.

When the draw is made directly out from the center of the canoe, the whole boat is pulled sideways over the water. If it is made a little to the bow or stern, the whole canoe will be drawn over, but the end in which the stroke is made will move farther, so that the stroke has the effect of turning the canoe. If the members of a tandem crew paddling on opposite sides of a canoe each execute a draw stroke at their own ends, the canoe will pivot on its center. There are many other combinations and uses for the draw, but we first need to discuss its counterpart, the pry.

The Pry

The draw is used to move the hull or one end of it toward the paddling side. Prying strokes move the canoe or the end the paddler is in away from the paddling side, so the pry is the necessary complement of the draw for the paddler using a single blade. A pry is used by a single paddler amidships to move the canoe sideways in the water away from the paddling side or used by a paddler at either end of the canoe to move that end away from the paddling side.

The original version of the pry was the pushover stroke, which is a good one for the beginner to learn first as an introduction to the pry.

The pry is used to move the canoe, or one end of the canoe, away from the paddling side. It is not quite as powerful as the draw, but more importantly, the paddler cannot lean on the prying paddle. It is a very effective stroke, however. Begin with the blade somewhat under the hull and the plane of the blade parallel with the keel line. Hold the shaft against the gunwale with the paddling-side hand.

Pull the shaft back with the grip hand, levering the blade away from the canoe. Continue only until the shaft makes about a thirty-degree angle with the water; continuing the stroke will rock the side of the canoe down.

A quick underwater recovery is most effective when the pry is to be repeated. Rotate the paddle ninety degrees and rapidly slice the blade back to the starting position. Quick, powerful, short strokes are the most effective means of prying.

Insert the paddle close beside the canoe with the shaft vertical, thumb of the upper hand oriented toward your face and the blade parallel to the keel line. This is usually done by slicing the blade down into the water from the direction of the stern. The elbow of the lower arm should be tucked in by the paddle-side hip and the upper arm should be held high. Push the paddle out strongly from the hull, pushing against the water with the outside face of the paddle. The lower arm pushes while the upper arm pulls, using the lower hand as a pivot point. Push out as far as you can without sacrificing good power, but avoid stretching the lower arm far out while continuing leverage with the upper, which will merely tend to capsize the boat toward the paddling side. Recovery can be made toward the stern or, if another stroke is to be taken, an underwater recovery may be more effective. (Underwater recovery is discussed below.)

The pushover is not as strong a stroke as the draw, which is true mainly because the draw has a righting action on the paddler and the canoe, an effect discussed in more detail in Chapter 7 in connection with braces. At this stage we have to note only that the paddler can actually lean against the draw while pulling, enabling him to put his whole body into the stroke without fear of capsizing. The pushover stroke does not have this effect, so the paddler is forced to avoid overbalancing and cannot put as much power into the stroke.

With the advent of stronger canoes the pushover was made more powerful by beginning it with a pry off the hull of the canoe. The pry should not be used with fragile canoes or paddles. If you happen to have a fine veneer canoe designed strictly for lake use and a delicate lightweight wood paddle, stick to the pushover. However, with the more durable equipment designed for white-water use the pry will do no damage and will give a far more powerful stroke.

Begin the pry as you would the pushover, but slip the blade somewhat under the hull, with the shaft actually tilting out from the canoe and the lower shaft touching the side. Move your lower hand up the shaft a few inches to clear the gunwale. The paddle is also a little forward of its position in the pushover, near the knee rather than the

The pry can be used toward the bow or the stern by either the appropriate member of a team or the solo paddler to turn that end of the canoe away from the paddling side. Here a solo paddler is doing a stern pry, executed like the regular one except that the paddle is angled back toward the rear of the canoe.

A pry toward the bow end of the canoe by a solo paddler. Often preferred to accomplish the same purpose is the crossbow draw, illustrated on page 98.

hip. Now pull the shaft inward, levering water out from under the hull and pushing the hull across the surface of the water. Don't apply too much power until you have the feel of the stroke, since it is easy to capsize when first practicing this stroke. As you gain confidence, develop the pry into the powerful stroke it can be, starting the stroke well under the hull and pulling hard on the shaft with both arms. The pry can be finished with a pushover, but it is most effective if it is not continued out very far. Instead, recover and repeat the stroke. Underwater recovery is most effective with this stroke. At the end of the pry, rotate the paddle ninety degrees with the upper hand by turning the grip hand so that the thumb turns away from the face, slip the paddle edgeways through the water to its initial position, rotate it back again, and repeat the pry. The pry is most effective using short, powerful strokes with a rapid recovery.

Practice the pry extensively. It is useful only after you have achieved really effective control. The paddler who is not confident with it will be reluctant to use it when the boat is moving quickly or the water is rough, for fear of capsizing the canoe.

For the single canoeist, the pry can be used to move the boat di-

A moving canoe can be steered by using the paddle as a rudder, although this method slows the canoe and is not as positive a way of turning as sweeps, draws, and pries. Here the paddle is being held at an angle to turn the canoe to the left.

rectly over or to move one end more than the other if it is applied off the center. It is also used in a number of combination strokes discussed below. For a tandem team the combination of the pry and draw allows a canoe to be turned rapidly around its center in either direction or to be moved sideways to either right or left, whether the canoe is moving or not.

Avoid using the pry in shallow water or in a place where a subsurface rock would be likely to catch the paddle, since it is easy to capsize the boat or break the paddle when the blade catches during a strong pry.

Sculling

Sculling is a continuous stroke made at the side by sweeping the paddle back and forth with the blade always kept at a climbing angle. It can be used in all the ways that a draw stroke can, but it has the additional advantage of not requiring a recovery. At the end of each backward and each forward movement in the stroke the grip hand simply rotates the blade to the proper angle for moving back in the opposite direction, and the new phase begins almost immediately. Sculling takes some effort to master, but it is extremely useful. It is also excellent practice for the novice because to use it effectively one must learn to lean on the paddle and must develop an exact feeling for the angle of the blade.

Before trying to learn the proper form for sculling, the beginner should develop an understanding of the paddle's movement and a feel for the angle of the blade. Put the blade in the water beside the hip and parallel to the keel, with the arm holding the grip raised high. The upper part of the paddling-side arm should be close to the body and the forearm should be nearly perpendicular to it. Now turn the paddle about thirty degrees with the grip hand, with the thumb coming toward the face while rotating the leading edge of the paddle blade away from the hull, and move the blade toward the bow about eighteen inches, tracing a line parallel to the keel. At the end of this movement, rotate the paddle sixty degrees in the opposite direction as the thumb turns

Sculling. The sculling stroke has an effect much like the draw, except that it is continuous. The motion of the canoe to the side can be seen here from the ripples. The paddler has angled the forward edge of the paddle blade out from the hull and is beginning to sweep it forward.

The paddle has reached the far forward position and the paddler has just turned the blade so that the rear edge is angled out from the hull. He will now sweep the paddle back.

Here the blade is being turned for a backward sweep after completing the forward one.

The blade being turned for the forward sweep after making a backward one.

away from the face, until the rear edge of the blade is angled out thirty degrees. Sweep the paddle back past the hip about eighteen inches, making a backward sweep of three feet. Rotate the paddle so that the leading edge angles away from the canoe and sweep it forward again. Continue this motion back and forth without trying to put any real power into it or move the paddle rapidly until you have good control of the blade angle and path of the sweep. Sculling will move the canoe sideways; if you are positioned near the center, it should move directly to the side.

As you begin to gain confidence in sculling, put more power into it, without losing control of the direction of pull. Eventually you should be able to lean on the paddle while sculling, acquiring increased power and stability. Sculling at either end of the canoe has the effect of pulling that end over in the water just as the draw stroke does. Sculling can be combined with other strokes in the same way the draw stroke can. Its main advantage is that it is continuous, without the short, unbalanced recovery time of the draw stroke. On the other hand, one cannot move the canoe over quite so fast with a scull as with a draw.

As with the draw, it is possible for the paddler to support most of his weight on the sculling paddle. Here the paddle is midway in a stroke, moving forward.

Be sure to practice the scull equally on both sides of the canoe. It is a particularly good stroke to use while working for ambidexterity.

The sculling action can be reversed (pushing the blade back and forth with the leading edge angled toward the hull instead of away from it) to produce a *sculling pushover* or *sculling pry,* the former if all the force is transmitted through the arms and the latter if the shaft rests against the gunwale to transmit the force. These strokes are well worth practicing to gain extra paddle control, but they are far less useful than the *sculling draw* described above, since draw strokes allow the paddler to lean on the paddle, and this lean can be continuous while sculling. Since one cannot lean much on a pushover or pry stroke, there is less value in making them continuous at the expense of some power.

The Cross-Bow Draw

The cross-bow draw is an important turning stroke, especially for white-water canoeing, and is also sometimes useful on shallow flat water. It is used to turn the bow of the canoe toward the bow or solo paddler's off side. Its function is thus exactly the same as the pry.

To perform the cross-bow draw, keep your grip on the paddle the same, but throw it over to the other side of the canoe, pointing the blade forward at an angle and dropping it into the water like a rudder pointing to the front as far out as you can reach without overbalancing. If the canoe is moving rapidly or the water into which the paddle is placed is moving the other way, the stroke has a strong action even without your drawing the blade toward the canoe. In fact, unless you are careful, you are likely to fall over a few times during practice. The cross-bow draw can be used to move the end of the canoe over even when it is stationary by pulling in on the paddle, but it is most effective when the canoe is moving.

It is worthwhile to develop both a good pry and a reliable cross-bow draw. Each has some special advantages, though individual paddlers are likely to rely on one more than the other. The pry is more powerful, doesn't require that you cross the paddle over, and can be blended

Beginning a cross-bow draw, a useful method for the solo or bow paddler to turn the canoe away from the side he or she is paddling on. A normal grip is retained on the paddle as the blade is thrown over to the opposite side of the canoe and dropped into the water at an angle. The canoe is here moving forward, but if the draw were being used to catch an opposing current in a river it would not be extended as far.

The paddle is dropped into the water and drawn back in toward the hull. More balance is required than in a regular draw because the canoeist cannot brace on the paddle, but since the blade is close to the surface, in shallow water this stroke is preferred to the pry.

into other strokes. In shallow water, however, especially in rocky rivers, it is easy to catch the blade on a rock. The result is often a capsize or a broken paddle. The cross-bow draw is not braced against the hull, so this danger is not present, and it is a shallow stroke as well. It is also very useful for catching an eddy in a river, a technique that is discussed in Chapter 7.

COMBINING STROKES

It was pointed out earlier that many strokes used by the canoeist in practice are not pure examples of one of the movements just described but rather are combinations of two or more. It is important for the novice to learn the strokes in their basic forms because otherwise he is likely to develop sloppy habits at the beginning. Thus, practice the draw stroke near the center of the boat first and pull straight in toward the hull. If you are making a mistake in the angle of either the blade or the stroke it will be quickly apparent because the canoe will move at an angle instead of straight over.

Once the basic strokes are mastered, the paddler can begin to use them in various ways to maneuver the canoe. Several combination strokes have already been discussed in the section on forward paddling, during which the solo or stern paddler changes the angle of his paddling at the end of the stroke to correct the course taken by the canoe.

The draw, pry, and sculling strokes are often combined with normal forward or backward ones to produce intermediate results. For example, the *diagonal draw* is a combination of the straight forward stroke and the draw. The paddler reaches ahead and out from the hull, then takes a stroke that travels back and toward the canoe. If used by the solo paddler amidships, this stroke will move the canoe forward and toward the paddling side. Used by both the bow and stern paddlers of a tandem crew, diagonal draws will move the boat forward while turning it a good deal toward the bow's paddling side, as will a diagonal draw at the bow and a forward quarter sweep at the stern.

When paddling solo near the center of the canoe, it is common to use a slight diagonal draw at the beginning of the forward stroke and finish off with a **J** or pitch stroke. Because the distance from the paddle to the keel is greater when paddling near the middle of the boat, the tendency of the canoe to swerve is greater, particularly if it is a very maneuverable design. The slight diagonal draw at the beginning of the stroke makes the course correction more continuous so that the canoe follows a straighter course. In effect, the canoeist paddles at the bow end of the craft during the first part of the stroke and at the stern end during the latter.

A more exaggerated version of this stroke is the *C-stroke,* which can be used to turn the canoe toward the paddling side or to fight a current or a crosswind. The paddler begins with a strong diagonal draw made as far as possible, continues with a forward stroke amidships, and finishes with a strong **J** toward the stern. For an even more pronounced turning effect, the paddle can be turned ninety degrees at the end of the stroke for a stern pry.

The *figure-8 stroke* is a variation of sculling often used by solo paddlers amidships. It begins with a draw stroke somewhat forward or backward of the center of the canoe. As the paddle approaches the hull, the canoeist should turn the blade somewhat and scull outward past the center so that the blade comes into position for another draw on the other side of the center of the craft. At the end of this draw, scull out to the original position and repeat the whole sequence. By varying the size of the two draws nearer opposite ends of the canoe, the paddler has precise control of the orientation of the boat during lateral movement.

PADDLING TANDEM

The art of paddling tandem is one of achieving complete coordination between two individuals at opposite ends of the boat. This requires a good deal of practice but, once developed, it will enable two paddlers to handle a canoe with incomparable ease and grace. The solo paddler is always busy, particularly when a great deal of maneuvering is required, since he must handle both ends of the canoe and do it from a position of limited leverage. A tandem team has each member placed where he is in the optimum position to move one end of the boat around, yet where each can achieve the maximum forward thrust when that is wanted.

In normal flat-water paddling, the person paddling in the bow sets the tempo, since the stern paddler can see what is being done and match strokes more easily than if the roles were the other way around. The tempo should be regular, and both paddlers should be able to sustain it for long periods. It can be speeded up if there is some need to sprint, but a steady rhythm should be the rule for canoe paddling. When both paddlers are beginning, the bow person must remember that the stern has to use a more complicated stroke and should set the pace accordingly. The stern has the main responsibility for steering and thus for choosing a course. The role, again, is a natural one because the course is most easily controlled from the stern

The key to effective control of a canoe is teamwork, which is generally achieved by mutual confidence and understanding. If the bow paddler suddenly sees an obstacle from the superior forward vantage point, he should pull the bow over in whichever direction seems best, using a draw or pry if much movement is needed, a rudder if less is required, or hard back paddling if maneuvering will not avoid a collision. The stern does not need to wait to ask questions; he must follow the action of the bow and find out why later. If the bow pries, the stern draws, and vice versa. If the bow uses a rudder, the stern is brought around behind the bow, perhaps with either a stationary or an active draw or pry, depending on how much movement is needed.

Either paddler can call for a necessary action: "back," for example, but in general such decisions are left to the stern in flat-water paddling, unless the bow paddler sees an obstruction that calls for immediate action. Commands are rarely necessary, particularly as the canoeists become better coordinated, but at first some system of signals is helpful, and it should be agreed on in advance so that there is no chance of misunderstanding. One possibility is for the bow to call out the stroke that the stern should make, as, for example, "Draw left!" I prefer a system that simply calls for telling the other paddler what the result should be: "Right, hard!" means that the other paddler should move his end of the boat over to the right as fast as possible. A stern canoeist paddling on the right might use a draw; if paddling on the left he might use a pry. There seems to be less delay and little room for misunderstanding with this system, but the most important point is that both paddlers know and understand the commands to be used.

The two canoeists should be paddling on opposite sides of the canoe, of course, and, as with solo paddling, they should not change sides too often. When some relief is wanted by either paddler, he or she can call for a switch, to be made by both canoeists simultaneously at the beginning of the next stroke.

CHAPTER 5

LAKE CANOEING

Lakes are the best places to begin learning how to canoe, since the novice there does not have to contend with problems of seemingly hostile currents. Still, although on a calm day lake canoeing represents the simplest and most peaceful side of canoeing, windy conditions can change the character of the paddling drastically. To become a competent lake canoeist, the beginner needs to learn to portage the canoe, to pack it properly, and to paddle effectively. He must learn to trim the canoe properly for different circumstances, to shift the placement of baggage and passengers so he can use the wind and waves to assist in at least part of the paddling and steering effort. He must learn to find his way, anticipate possible weather hazards, and handle weather problems that catch him unawares.

The most fundamental skill for enjoyable and effective canoeing on lakes is a smooth cruising stroke that can be maintained with little or no rest for hours at a time. Whether one is canoeing alone or with a partner, an efficient cruising stroke is important for covering distances. The good lake canoeist rests during every stroke. Muscles alternately contract and relax in the paddling cycle, and the periodic relaxation of all the muscles involved in the paddle stroke permits the boater to paddle all day long with only a few rests. Stamina also plays a part, of course, and the beginner will generally have to work up to the level of endurance required for long days of paddling. Regardless of the strength of his arms, shoulders, and trunk, however, one's muscles will soon start to ache if they are kept tense through the entire stroke.

This relaxation of the paddling muscles is one of the important things for the novice to be conscious of as soon as he masters the basic strokes. Fortunately, there is no great mystery about the mistakes one is making. If the shoulder muscles are becoming tired, tense, and sore after an hour's paddling, it is a good indication that they are not being relaxed during the recovery portion of the stroke.

Pacing is another feature of the cruising stroke that is learned largely from experience. The new paddler has to learn to gauge how long a particular rhythm can be kept up. If plans for a trip call for paddling eight hours a day, one must learn not to start off in the morning at a rate that can be sustained for only four hours.

During normal lake paddling, the natural division of labor for two people paddling together is for the bow person to set the pace, with the stern following the bow's lead. The responsibility for steering and setting a course rests with the stern. The roles are natural because reversing them creates a lot of difficulty: the bow paddler cannot see the stern without twisting around, so it is virtually impossible for him to coordinate the paddling rhythm by following the stern. On the other hand, we have seen that a canoe cannot be steered effectively from the bow, nor does the bow paddler have the advantage of being able to look along the length of the canoe to see the exact direction in which it is headed.

The exception to this rule is that in shallow water the bow paddler will be the one able to see underwater snags, rocks, or other obstructions, so it is his responsibility to be on the lookout for them and take any necessary action. The stern follows the bow's strokes or commands for evasive action. Developing teamwork in such situations is necessary but can be difficult. Faultfinding in cases of bad coordination is definitely a poor idea, particularly between people with a close personal relationship. If you feel an absolute compulsion to point out a mistake made by your partner, chew on your tongue for a while instead.

Teams that paddle together frequently often do quite well without using verbal commands very much. The stern paddler sees the bow draw hard to the right and automatically pries on the left to bring the stern over behind the bow. Fortunately, there are not many occasions in lake paddling that require rapid and close coordination, since welding two paddlers into an effective team is time consuming and the alchemy is subtle. Lakes provide a good place to begin the process of forming teams that may later want to test their partnership in the more demanding situations found on rivers.

TRIMMING A CANOE

The trim of a canoe refers to the angle that its lengthwise axis makes with the surface of the water in a normal floating position on a calm lake. The trim is affected by the distribution of any equipment being carried and by the positions and relative weights of paddlers. Thus, if a pair of canoeists tie their camping equipment directly amidships, when they launch the canoe it will have "level trim." But if when they take their positions the stern paddler sits on the stern seat, whereas the bow paddler kneels just forward of the duffel, the stern will sink somewhat and the bow rise. The canoe might then be said to be trimmed high at the bow, low at the stern, light in the bow, or the like.

The way a canoe is trimmed will radically affect the way it handles in the water. Careful attention to the trim of the boat can greatly ease the paddlers' tasks in many difficult situations. If the canoe is paddled into the wind, for example, trimming it high at the stern will result in its remaining correctly oriented without effort from the paddlers, so that they can devote all their effort to fighting the wind. On the other hand, if the bow is trimmed high, they may be unable to hold their course at all, and they will certainly waste a great deal of effort in the attempt.

Most canoes handle best in normal paddling when they are trimmed level or very slightly high in the bow. Particularly if there is a keel or a V-shaped hull, a level trim will probably give better tracking,

When wind and water conditions are normal, it is best to trim the canoe level, with the load balanced between the bow and stern. Thus, the solo canoeist will place a small load in the bow and paddle from just behind the center.

whereas a slightly high bow may make the canoe a little more maneuverable. An excessively high bow will tend to make the canoe slow and the handling poor, because the length of the canoe below waterline will be much shorter and the shape of the part of the hull that is under water will be quite different from the intended one.

Trimming a canoe high at the stern usually makes it quite difficult to steer and often results in a sluggish boat as well. Remember that a canoe is most easily steered when it pivots from the stern. A bow trimmed low will tend to hold the water, causing the stern to slip around the bow (as it does when one attempts to steer from the bow) without tracking well in its new course. At the same time, when one tries to make course corrections from the stern, the rear of the boat has less hold on the water because it is too high, though the bow seems anchored like the Rock of Gibraltar because it is so deep. The stern paddler fights to try to turn the bow around his position, but with poor results. The canoe should normally be trimmed high at the stern only for specific purposes, as when it is being paddled into the wind, for example.

Most canoes are trimmed well for normal paddling when baggage is loaded at the balance point and the paddlers are at the stern and bow seats. It is worth experimenting with your canoe, however. Variations in the weight of the paddlers will make a difference, as will a change from kneeling to sitting positions. Some canoes are very sensitive to changes in trim, and it is sometimes worthwhile to move seats or thwarts slightly to adjust the normal trim. If you are carrying duffel, moving it forward or back will change the trim and allow you to make adjustments.

When you are out on a lake, however, and it becomes desirable to change the trim of a canoe, it is usually best to have one or both paddlers shift to a different position. To trim the canoe higher at the bow, the bow person moves back; to trim it higher at the stern, the stern paddler moves forward.

Trimming for the Wind

As every canoeist soon finds, wind will catch the ends and sides of a canoe, exerting a good deal of force. Much of the art of lake canoeing consists of finding ways to use the force of the wind to assist paddlers as much as possible, and proper trim is one of the most important ways to achieve this.

When a canoe is trimmed level, the wind has the same effect on both ends of the boat and on both paddlers, so there is not a great tendency for the craft to be turned by the wind. This is somewhat of a simplification, of course, since if there are waves the canoe's ends will not be equally affected as they rise and fall. The effect of the wind on a canoe with level trim tends to be on the entire side of the boat. Thus, if you are paddling at a forty-five-degree angle into the wind, the side of the canoe on which the wind is blowing will be pushed by it. The net effect of the forward paddling and the push of the wind will be that the canoe will move in a course that combines the two forces, in a direction somewhere between the paddling course (straight ahead) and the course of the wind.

One of the simplest ways to use the wind to advantage, if it is not too strong, is to use it to eliminate the correcting element in the forward stroke of the stern or solo paddler. If you are traveling with the wind off the port side of the bow, for example, the bow can be trimmed a little high and the stern or solo canoeist can paddle on the starboard side. (The port side of any boat is to the left when facing forward; starboard is to the right.) The straight paddle stroke tends to turn the canoe to port, whereas the wind turns it to starboard and the two forces balance out. The work of paddling against the wind is then abated by eliminating the need for steering strokes.

If you are paddling straight into a breeze, you can trim the bow a little high and turn it a few degrees away from the wind on the paddling side, again balancing the force of the wind against the turning force of the forward paddle strokes.

With a stronger wind, this tactic becomes difficult to use. The bow is caught by the wind and pushed around if it angles out too far, and if it is brought in too close it may be thrown over to the opposite tack by the force of a stroke. The bow is pushed around by a strong wind because it is riding higher than the stern, thus presenting more wind resistance. The solution is to trim the stern high so that it will present the greater resistance. The higher stern will be blown away from the wind, lining the bow right into the wind, the desired direction. The paddlers can then paddle forward as hard as they like without worrying about steering at all, for the wind will hold the boat on course.

The same tactic can be used in reverse when paddling straight away from the wind. The bow should be trimmed high so that it will be pushed out like a weathervane, and the paddlers can again ignore steering problems.

When working at a significant angle to the wind, it is necessary only to trim the canoe level and then allow for the amount the canoe will be blown to the side in setting the course. That is, the bow of the boat must be turned somewhat more into the wind (toward the direction from which it is blowing) than a straight-line course would call for. The amount of correction necessary will depend on the strength of the

Paddling into a headwind. The paddler has moved ahead of the center of the canoe so that the bow sinks a little and the stern rises. The wind puts more pressure on the stern and keeps it pointed downwind, so the paddler does not have to steer at all and can put all his energy into moving the canoe.

wind, the paddling speed, and the design of the canoe. (For example, a canoe with a deep keel or V-hull will sideslip less and need less correction.) Some time is needed to learn to judge the correction necessary, but in strong winds most canoeists tend to underestimate the speed at which they are sideslipping.

If shore is visible from the canoe, it is easy to check the actual course resulting from both the wind and paddling by lining up two objects in the direction desired: a rock and a mountain, the edge of an island and a tree on the far shore, or a similar pair. As long as one remains in line with the other, the canoe is on course; if they appear to separate, you can correct the orientation of the boat immediately. Such a visual check is important when dealing with drift due to wind and waves. A compass reading will tell only the direction in which the canoe is being paddled, not the final direction resulting from both drift and paddling. Sighting on only one object on shore will indicate eventually if you are being blown off course, but it will take much longer to notice, and corrections will be less accurate.

WAVES

In the preceding discussion the effects of wind alone on a canoe were considered. However, if the wind blows for any length of time, particularly on large lakes, waves will be created, introducing additional complications. Waves result from the wind blowing from the same general direction for a period of time over a lake or other body of water. Bigger waves result from stronger winds and longer distances in which they can build up over sufficiently deep and unobstructed water. There are many variables in the formation of waves, but it is important to realize that on a large lake they can get quite big and can build up in a very short time. Some lakes only a few miles long, whose positions funnel winds from summer squalls over them, are known for rapidly forming large waves.

Beginners should exercise caution on lakes of any size to avoid getting caught in big waves, since even experienced paddlers sometimes have difficulty in handling them. When the wind starts to come up or there are signs of a storm, seek shelter immediately, before the waves have time to become too large. Once you are close to shelter, you can practice paddling in the waves, provided the situation is safe. Until you have had time to develop a feeling for the problems presented by a strong wind, be wary of getting too far from shore on big lakes.

Waves are gradually built up over some distance; they do not suddenly come into being at some point on a lake. A traveling wave being pushed along by the wind is an oscillation of the surface of the water. Individual water particles rise and fall as the waves pass, but most of the water stays in its place rather than moving forward. As a wave is pushed along by the wind it gradually becomes larger. This has important implications for a canoeist on a lake, because the natural inclination of the paddler caught out on a lake by rising waves is to paddle with the wind toward the lee shore. This may be the right decision, but it is important to realize that the closer to that shore one gets, the larger the waves will be. The waves will also be breaking on that shore, perhaps by crashing into rocks as six-foot breakers. On the other hand, the windward shore will have no surf at all.

The length of the waves, their height, and their steepness are all important to the canoeist. Waves built up by a wind blowing in the same direction are generally fairly long and gentle even if they are quite large. This kind of wave is the easiest type to ride because the faces of the waves are not steep, so a canoe rides over them rather than diving in and they are long enough to allow it to ride.

A wind getting much harder but still blowing in the same direction as the waves may tend to blow the tops over, forming whitecaps, which are somewhat steeper and will more readily break over the bow or stern of the canoe. As the waves get still higher and steeper, the canoe dives down into each trough, burying the bow or stern in the face of the next wave.

A changing wind complicates wave motions, with new waves forming and going in the new direction. Two or more wave systems sometimes add together, sometimes cancel each other. When the wind blows opposite to the direction of the waves, it eventually flattens them out, but in the interim they become very short and choppy. If they are very large, this can create difficult canoeing.

The methods described for paddling in windy conditions generally apply after waves come up also. Paddling straight into the waves is not difficult unless they become quite large or choppy. The ease with which the bow rides over each wave depends on the canoe design and the way it is loaded. All the weight should be as close to the center of the canoe as possible so that the bow and stern can rise easily over the crests of the waves. It is often worthwhile for both the bow and stern paddlers to move nearer the center of the canoe to lighten the ends.

To move the canoe sideways in strong wind or waves it is necessary only to bring the bow into the wind and then tack over to whichever direction you want to go. Paddling then holds the boat steady against being moved backward by the elements, and their pressure against the side of the canoe moves the craft in the desired direction.

If the waves become so high and steep that the bow is swamping badly when the canoe is run straight into the waves, particularly in short, choppy waves, it may be necessary to quarter into the waves; that is, to turn the canoe at an angle to them so that the bow can ride up easily and so that there is less of a tendency for the canoe first to climb steeply and then to dive into the next trough. It is more difficult to hold a canoe on course when quartering, and the paddlers may need to brace on their paddles (see Chapter 7) to maintain balance. There will, however, be far less chance of shipping water than when the canoe is run straight into the waves, as long as the paddlers can maintain balance and control of the boat.

When running with the waves there is again little problem unless the waves become unusually large or choppy. Keeping up a regular rhythm of paddling makes steering easier and curbs the tendency of the stern to bury itself in the front of an oncoming wave as the hull slides down the back of the preceding one. As long as the canoeists keep paddling, the craft will not slide back and the stern will rise easily as the wave overtakes it.

One can also run before the waves by using a sea anchor, either as an emergency measure or to save the effort of paddling. If an anchor might be needed, it should be made up in advance. Once the boat is pitching and taking on water, you will be too busy paddling and bailing to be able to take time out to rig anything.

A sea anchor is a brake dragging in the water against the direction of the canoe's movement. A cooking pot with a sturdy bail handle tied to a thirty-foot line serves well for a sea anchor. It should be attached to the stem of the canoe below the waterline. In the absence of a tie point on the canoe, you can attach a bridle by tying a loop in the end of the anchor line large enough to fit generously over the end of the canoe. Slide it over so that the line going to the anchor is directly under the keel, and either tie it to the rear thwart or seat or secure it by slipping the end of the loop under the seat and passing a paddle through the end.

When a sea anchor tied to the stern is thrown into the water, it drags the stern back, slowing the rate at which the canoe is driven forward by the wind and waves. The boat automatically stays oriented into the waves. With a sea anchor in place, the load kept near the center, and the stern trimmed a little high so that it will ride more easily above overtaking waves, a canoe will ride out some fairly heavy storms. Taking his bailer with him, the single boater or stern person can move just forward of the duffel to achieve the proper trim. Sitting in the bottom of the canoe increases stability. One advantage to running with a sea anchor in severe situations is that you can devote full time to bailing. Remember that running with a sea anchor eventually brings you to the downwind shore, where the waves may be breaking dangerously.

An island is often the best shelter from waves, since you can run with the waves past the island and then duck behind the lee side, where a safe landing can be made. Be a little wary of very small islands or rocks in heavy waves, however, since waves often bend around behind the island and add together to form one area of very high waves.

Fortunately, the canoe is a very seaworthy craft, and waves big enough to cause real problems are not common on lakes. With some practice the canoeist can learn to relish paddling through big swells. Most problems occur when inexperienced paddlers allow the canoe to be turned parallel with the waves, then panic and unbalance the canoe. Even after a capsize, however, if the occupants are prepared for the air and water temperature and stay with the canoe, an upset in a lake should not prove disastrous. The most important caution is to be aware of the possibility of wind and waves; don't risk going far from shore in a big lake without a wet suit and some experience of paddling in heavy seas.

NAVIGATION

Route finding in lake country is sometimes easy and sometimes requires great skill. One of the first things the novice should learn is how to recognize potential navigation difficulties.

The vantage point from a canoe is quite low, even if one stands up for a better view. From the boat one can gain very little perspective on the curves of the shoreline. It is often impossible to tell whether a stretch of land a mile off is the side of an island or the end of a peninsula, whether an opening in the shore is a continuous passage leading through to the next lake or simply a winding bay that dead-ends after a couple of miles. The canoeist cannot see around spits of land or twists in a channel, and despite the fine detail of a well-made map, out on the water one often cannot see enough to be sure of a position. For example, in a marshy area with a complicated series of channels about all one can positively say at times is, "We're in the cattails."

USING A MAP AND COMPASS

Gaining familiarity with map and compass work is the first technique to be cultivated if one wants to become skilled at route finding in lake country. One has only to read the journals of a few of the explorers of the vast North American wilderness to comprehend the magnitude of the difference between canoeing in unknown regions and paddling on lakes with accurate, complete maps. Because maps are now made by aerial photography, they are almost always accurate even in the few regions not adequately explored on the ground. Maps represent the accumulation of many years of knowledge, and until recently each map worthy of the name represented tens or hundreds of thousands of hours spent by explorers and surveyors in the field. Older partial knowledge, like the canoe trails of the Indians, might represent the work of a thousand generations. The modern paddler has centuries of recorded information on his map, but he has to know how to read it.

The best maps for canoeing in the United States are usually those produced by the U.S. Geological Survey, which can be found in various reference libraries or purchased from the Distribution Office, U.S. Geological Survey, at either Washington, D.C. 20025 for eastern

Simple navigational tools: a compass, a map measurer (which has a small wheel that can be run along a winding course to transfer the distance reading to a dial), a map showing a large river course, and a quick-sealing plastic bag to keep the map dry.

maps or the Federal Center, Denver, Co. 80225 for areas west of the Mississippi. Index sheets showing the maps available for each state are free and the maps, depending on the scale and inflation, are approximately one dollar each. Comparable Canadian maps can be obtained from the Department of Mines and Technical Surveys, Ottawa, Ontario.

A good overall view of an area can be had from the 1 : 250,000 series of maps, although with a ratio of about four miles on the water or ground to one inch on the map, details are limited. The 15-minute series of maps, 1 : 62,500 (approximately one inch to the mile) is available for much of the U.S. and is a useful size for detailed planning of trips. In other regions only the newer 7½-minute series is available. The scale on these is 1 : 24,000, which is sometimes a little more detailed than desirable, since a long trip may require an excessively large bundle of maps. Often special sheets covering a river or a national park are available, and these can be ideal for the canoeist. (Alaska and Canada are mapped in different series from those listed, but they are comparable.) Special canoe route maps may be available for some trips from other government agencies like the Forest Service or from private groups. However, Geological Survey maps set the standards and usually provide the raw data from which others are made.

Geological Survey maps normally include several types of information. At the bottom are a number of important ones. The date on the lower right-hand corner indicates the date of the survey on which the map is based. When two dates are listed, the second shows the year minor revisions were made, usually updating man-made features. These dates are quite important in deciding how much credence to give the information on the map. Maps dating back to the early part of the century should be regarded much less trustingly than more recent ones, as the makers did not have aerial photographs against which to check their interpretation of the terrain. Such maps are monuments to the dedication of the surveyors, but they sometimes contain errors. More important, things may have changed since the survey. A 1952 map will not show a dam completed in 1963 nor the fifty-mile reservoir that has since backed up behind it. More recent nontopographic maps are often needed to supplement information on man-made features.

The scale is shown at the bottom of the map, too, as is the magnetic declination in the center of the area covered by the map. Declination is shown numerically in degrees and graphically by two arrows, one pointing to true north, the other in the direction a compass needle will point. (A third arrow may show a grid direction that does not concern us here.) It is important to allow for declination whenever using a compass in conjunction with the map because the compass needle will orient itself with the earth's magnetic field, which is often quite divergent from geographical north–south lines. A declination of thirty degrees is not uncommon in much of the best North American canoeing country, and in northern Canada and Alaska the figure may be even higher. Even in an area with a modest declination of ten degrees, traveling ten miles on a course ignoring magnetic declination and assuming that the compass needle points directly north would land you on the opposite shore one and three-quarter miles from your destination, a fairly serious error by any standard.

Correcting for declination is simple enough if it is done methodically, although different people prefer different methods. One time-consuming but foolproof method is to use a pencil and ruler before leaving home and lay out on your maps a series of parallel lines which run along magnetic lines. You need only then lay a compass on such a map and line up the pencil grid and the needle to orient the map correctly. Other wilderness travelers use various memory aids to determine the relationship of compass readings to directions on a map. I prefer to work out the problem each time. The important point is that anyone planning much paddling off the beaten path needs to practice navigation with the map and compass and develop a system that works for him.

Suppose, for example, you are paddling on a large lake and have lost track of your position. You take a bearing on the tip of an island ahead and to the left and one on a point along the shore out to the right. That is, you sight with your compass to find out the direction of each of the landmarks. In order to compare these bearings with the map to see which island and point might correspond, you will have to convert the magnetic bearings to true ones. Some compasses have a means built in to set off declination so that the compass can be adjusted to read out in true bearings. In other cases the correction has to be made afterward, unless you have marked out a magnetic grid on the map. If you are somewhere in the western part of North America, the declination of the compass needle will be to the east of true north. In our example, let us suppose that the declination diagram at the bottom of the map shows magnetic north to be 16 degrees east of true north. Sighting with the compass, you find that bearing on the tip of the island is at 342 degrees according to the compass; that is, 18 degrees counterclockwise from the direction shown by the north end of the compass needle. A bearing on the point along the shore gives a reading of 121 degrees. Since the needle is pointing east of true north, however, these readings are magnetic bearings. To use them to find your position on the map, you will have to convert them to true bearings. If the compass were turned in the proper direction to line up with true north, it would have to be turned counterclockwise 16 degrees from the magnetic position, which would make the readings 16 degrees higher. The true bearings are 358 degrees, almost true north, for the tip of the island, and 137 degrees for the point. If the compass you are using has a mechanism for setting off declination, you would be able to read the bearings directly.

Having obtained these bearings, you can check the map for possible corresponding ones. A quick look does for a start; checking those islands on the map in the general vicinity into which you might have paddled, you can first see which ones are close enough in shape to the one ahead. From the water south of each of these islands, would there be a point visible along the shore to the southeast? Once you have found the possible combinations, you can check each exactly to see whether there is a location from which those precise readings could be obtained. This can be done exactly with a protractor and a straightedge or less accurately using the compass to measure the angles. If more than one place on the map satisfies the requirements, you must find an additional landmark or paddle on with the remaining possibilities in mind, waiting for another feature to come into view that will settle the problem.

It is important to remember when taking sightings like this that you will not always be able to tell whether you are looking at an island or a point or whether an arm of water is a river mouth, a bay, a channel, or whatever. You may have to paddle around the island or into the bay to the end.

Once you have identified one or more landmarks, both on the map and by sight, they can be used to establish your position or to set a course. Suppose, for example, that you are on a large lake and spot a recognizable island ahead. To establish your position, take a bearing with the compass on some well-defined point on the island, perhaps one end. If the end of the island is at a compass reading of 23° and the declination shown on the map is 17° west, then the true bearing for the end of the island is 40° (23° + 17°). Looking at the map, you will see that in order to obtain this reading you must be located along a straight line extending from the end of the island back into the lake in the opposite direction from the 40° bearing; that is, 180° around from it. It follows that if you draw a line on the map at an angle of 220° (40° + 180°) from the tip of the island, your location is somewhere along that line. This is the line along which you are sighting to get the 23° magnetic bearing.

If a second landmark can be found, perhaps the top of a mountain or the tip of a peninsula, another position line can be established by the same process, and your exact location must be at the point where the two lines meet. This method of establishing a position is most accurate if the two lines form right angles to each other and least accurate when they form a very narrow angle, because a small error in the bearing or in drawing the position line on the map makes a much greater difference when the angle between the lines is small.

Once a position has been established, you may be able to identify additional landmarks by drawing lines to them on the map, measuring the angles at which they lie, and then sighting with your compass along those angles. Such identification can help confirm your position or enable you to find a good landmark on which to set your course. Ideally, you should try to find one or two landmarks along the bearing that you want to follow to reach your destination.

Try to choose landmarks with well-defined points to take bearings so that they are as accurate as possible. A mountain with a sharp peak is better than one with a long, ill-defined summit. The long mountain may extend over several degrees, introducing that much error into your bearings. Similarly, a small island may be a better landmark than a large one because the sighting error is reduced.

A good compass and a lot of practice are all you need to become an effective navigator. Recognizing landmarks and making accurate sightings are skills that can be learned well with a bit of application. Get into practice on local trips when you know where you are going so that the skills will be available later on. For lengthy navigation on big lakes, it is useful to carry a cheap protractor and a ruler in the map case to simplify the chore of transferring angles from the map to compass readings and vice versa. Before leaving home, many canoeists like to draw on their maps a series of parallel lines that follow magnetic north–south lines. This gives a magnetic reference system on the map so that declination calculations don't have to be made. With practice, however, you will find that adjusting for declination becomes automatic.

Distinguishing landmarks on a map is also largely a matter of practice at going back and forth between a three-dimensional world, seen from a low point on the surface, and a two-dimensional view from the sky. Variations in elevation are normally shown on topographic maps by brown contour lines that show intervals of constant elevation. If a person were to walk along the path shown by a contour line he would not go up or down. The edge of a lake is thus a real contour line, and the imaginary ones around it on the map show where the edge of the water would be if the lake rose certain fixed distances. The contour interval, the elevation change between adjacent lines, is shown at the bottom of the map. In rolling country the interval between lines may be fewer than ten feet, whereas in a rugged canyon it may be two hundred feet. The usefulness of the contour lines will also vary with the country. Where enough distinct features rise above the general level of the surrounding land, a good map reader can easily locate them on the map because the contour lines show the shapes on the map as well. On the other hand, contour lines are likely to be of little value when the variations in terrain are small compared with the height of the forest cover, a situation not uncommon in some canoe country. In between these extremes is the rolling terrain in which contours may sometimes help the navigator, but only by confirming conclusions reached by other means.

STAYING FOUND

By far the most effective method of navigation in difficult lake country is to keep constant track of where you are on the map. Since this is also the best way to learn to use a map and compass, a novice should practice it from the beginning. Keep the map in some sort of transparent waterproof case so that you can consult it at frequent intervals. If you have to make much effort to look at it, natural laziness and a disinclination to break the rhythm of paddling will guarantee that visual checks on progress on the map will become less and less frequent. The same arguments dictate that you keep the compass in a convenient spot.

The most obvious technique for keeping track of your location is to watch the shoreline or islands being passed, relating the surroundings to their representation on the map. This should be the basis of most canoe navigation, with other methods used to supplement it. This technique will not work when you are crossing some distance from shore, however, and some shorelines are so confusing that it does not work in any case. In such situations it is important to recognize difficulties and uncertainties; clearly it is worse to "know" your position and be wrong than to recognize frankly that you are lost.

When compass navigation is necessary, it is best to take a bearing on a distinctive feature and then use the landmark for guidance than to try to keep the canoe on a particular compass course. In crossing a lake, for example, if you determine from the map that you want to hit the opposite shore after paddling on a bearing of 110 degrees, it is better to take a reading on an odd-shaped boulder or snag and then paddle toward it than to set the compass in front of you and try to keep the canoe pointed at the correct angle. This eliminates errors in aiming the canoe, takes into account sideways drift caused by wind, and allows canoeists to paddle at the most effective angle considering waves and wind, keeping an eye at the same time on the point they are paddling toward. When a direct bearing of this sort is impossible, other devices can be used. You can paddle to an intermediate point such as an island, then take a new bearing. You can use a back bearing, marking a distinctive point on the shore you are leaving and occasionally bringing the canoe into line with a compass reading back to that point until a landmark ahead can be found.

In fixing locations, a shoreline is as good a line of position as a compass bearing. A bearing on a single landmark fixes your position along a shoreline as it does on a road or a river, provided none of these bend back on themselves.

If you are aiming for a particular point along the shore, you should not paddle directly toward it unless it can be seen. It is better to aim deliberately wide to one side or the other so that when you reach the shoreline you know which way to turn. Otherwise, unless you are lucky enough to make a direct hit, you will be forced to search back and forth, never knowing quite how far to go before going back and trying the opposite direction. By deliberately aiming somewhat to the right or left of the hidden channel, the beginning of the portage trail, or camp, you can be sure immediately of which way to turn on reaching shore.

PORTAGING

We have already mentioned the basic methods of carrying a canoe. Portaging is simply carrying the canoe and equipment on land between two lakes, past rapids in a river, or around some other obstacle to navigation. The relative ease with which the canoe can be carried over forest portage trails is one of the features that makes it a superb wilderness craft.

Some of the types of yokes available to soften the task of portaging, particularly over long distances, have already been discussed. A yoke that is molded or carved to the shape of the shoulders is ideal, but other solutions please different people. Tying the paddles to the thwarts to form a yoke of sorts is one of the simplest, time-honored expedients. Lash the paddle blades to the center thwart and the shafts to the front thwart or seat so that the blades will rest comfortably on the shoulders when the canoe is carried. A bit of experimenting will determine the correct positioning. Cords or elastic fasteners can be left on the thwart and seat in the proper positions. My preference is to use cord tied in fixed loops on the middle thwart and loops of shock cord attached to the bow seat. With an arrangement of this sort the paddles can be slipped in quickly whenever they are wanted for a portage, with no adjustment necessary, as long as the same person is carrying the canoe.

Clothing, a single large knee pad not glued into the canoe, or various other devices can be used for padding when portaging the canoe any distance. It is not a good idea to use life preservers with kapok-filled, sealed plastic bags for flotation because the bags can be popped, which will allow the flotation to become easily waterlogged.

If a frame pack or a pack with an internal frame is being used on a camping trip, the canoe can often be comfortably portaged along with the pack by resting the center thwart on top of the shoulder straps. The load of the canoe can then be distributed between the shoulders and hips just as the weight of the pack is. This sort of heavy load is quite manageable for many canoeists, but discretion should be used, since in case of a slip it is harder to free oneself from the canoe, both because of the extra weight and because the thwart is between the high points of the head and the vertical tubes of the frame.

A useful aid in portaging is a tumpline, which allows some of the weight of the canoe to be transferred to the neck muscles. A strap two or three inches wide and perhaps a foot long is attached with cords or adjustable straps to the center thwart. When properly fitted to the individual, the tumpline can be slipped over the forehead so that the weight of the canoe can be shared between the shoulders and head, being shifted back and forth simply by raising or lowering the shoulders and sliding the tumpline headband backward or forward slightly. A great deal of weight can be carried for long distances with a tumpline by one who has practiced a lot, but this requires developed neck muscles. For most people the tumpline is useful mainly for temporary relief of the shoulders.

Finding a portage trail is often the most difficult aspect of the whole enterprise. Various markers are sometimes used to show the beginning of a trail, but it may require all the party's route-finding skills and a great deal of luck besides to find some portages. Along modern canoe trails there may be signs. Traditional markers are blazes on tree trunks or a tree with a cutoff top. In any case, the effort of finding a trail is well worth the trouble in densely forested or marshy regions. Bushwhacking with a canoe is ten times worse than with just a pack.

Use moderation in deciding on portage methods. One bad slip with a fifty-pound pack and a seventy-five-pound canoe can have unpleasant consequences for both you and the boat. If the trail is steep and slippery or covered with loose rocks, carry the canoe with another person, at least until you have reached more reasonable terrain. If you are alone, don't carry the duffel on the same load if the footing is bad. If you have a companion and the canoe is too heavy for you to toss onto your shoulders, don't attempt it; have your partner help, or work your way under from one end. Canoeing is supposed to be fun!

CHAPTER 6

CANOE CAMPING

The canoe is one of the most versatile means of transportation in wilderness areas that are traversed by navigable streams or rivers or that have large numbers of lakes. Such regions are quite common in North America, and thus the canoe was the preferred vehicle for many native Americans and the European explorers, traders, trappers, and adventurers. It remains one of the best ways to camp in many back-country sections today.

A canoe of a size that is easy to portage will carry a family of four, their camping equipment, and enough food for a trip of several weeks with no trouble. The same canoe will be adequate for two people on an expeditionary venture lasting for months. The canoe is unsurpassed in its adaptability. It can be used for camping trips into pristine areas by families with children still too young to walk, projects that are much more ambitious for backpackers. It can also provide a means for the adventurous to visit the gorges of remote white-water rivers.

There are a number of approaches to canoe camping, and no attempt will be made here to try to discuss every sort of shelter or method of cooking that can be used. The purposes of this chapter are to provide essential information and recommendations to those who have had little camping experience and want to begin to take canoe trips lasting longer than a day and to mention some of the differences between camping from a canoe and other lightweight camping, such as backpacking or bicycle touring, for the benefit of those who are new to canoeing but not to other sorts of wilderness trekking.

BASICS

To anyone who is just getting used to living outdoors or who learned to camp using great piles of heavy equipment hauled to the campground in a station wagon or pickup camper, canoe camping will be lightweight camping. On the other hand, those used to two-week backpacking trips where everything is pared to the bone to save weight will find traveling by canoe luxurious by comparison, since weight and bulk constraints are usually much less stringent. In general, it is best to keep weight and bulk as low as possible when camping by canoe, but unless the trip is very long, the portages difficult, or the canoe carrying a near-capacity load of passengers, one can indulge in a few luxuries.

The newcomer to lightweight travel will probably find that there are a number of costly items that will eventually need to be purchased. A good way to keep expenses down when just starting out and to learn a great deal about equipment at the same time is to rent gear. Shops catering to lightweight campers rent many items of equipment, thus enabling the beginner to gain experience with a far wider range of equipment than many very experienced lightweight campers have. This experience will allow him to find out what weight sleeping bag he needs, whether there is adequate space in a particular tent, and so on. Since there is also an active market in secondhand equipment, retired rental gear, discontinued models, and the like, renting for a while and forestalling a purchase may even save money by allowing you to wait for a bargain to come along.

The lists included at the end of this chapter provide a detailed compilation of equipment that may be needed on a particular trip and should be used for making up a checklist of equipment that will be taken. The beginner first needs to consider several major categories of gear. The backcountry traveler needs adequate clothing, shelter from the elements, equipment for cooking food, and suitable containers in which to pack everything.

CLOTHING

Proper clothing is important to the canoe camper for both comfort and safety, particularly if conditions may be cold. Basic clothing for canoe camping should be durable and loose enough not to bind when paddling or leaning over to push in a tent stake. If a little dirt bothers you, then choose colors and patterns that do not show it. In general it is possible to obtain good outdoor clothes at a reasonable price from surplus stores and similar sources.

For hot weather, choose lightweight clothing, but be sure to have long pants and long-sleeved shirts for protection from the sun, unless you are unusually well tanned. Many beginners far underestimate the burning capability of sun and water through long days, and the mistake can be very painful. A lightweight, wide-brimmed hat keeps the head cool and direct sun out of the eyes. Good sunglasses are essential. A bathing suit doubles well for hot-weather wear when skin protection is not needed.

Even during midsummer, nights tend to be cool in most canoe country. Bad weather, wind, and rain on a large lake can turn a hot day into a cold one rather quickly. It is important to have warm clothes that will retain some insulating value when wet, since all the most dangerous chilling situations the paddler may encounter involve being soaked to the skin. Cotton is virtually worthless as an insulator when wet, and it dries slowly, so the canoeist should not rely on blue jeans and cotton flannel shirts for warm clothing.

The outdoorsman's standby for wet, cold weather is wool, one of the best choices for basic outdoor clothing, although some modern substitutes are available as well. One advantage to wool clothing is that there is a great deal available at very reasonable prices in surplus and secondhand clothing stores. The military periodically rids itself of huge quantities of excellent quality woolen clothing that is perfectly designed for camping use. As a taxpayer you have already paid large sums for the manufacture of these items, so you may as well reap the rewards as a camper. With a little shopping care, you should be able to outfit yourself with heavy wool clothing for ten dollars or less for items that could easily cost seventy-five dollars in a specialty shop.

Clothing insulated with polyester batting (such as Dupont's Fiberfill II or Celanese Polarguard) is also excellent for wet, cold conditions. Such materials retain their thickness and much of their insulation when wet, and they dry very easily. They have better insulating qualities for a given weight than wool and are usually covered with smooth nylon, less irritating to the skin than wool. They also cost considerably more.

For warmth a wool cap is standard. Unlike the other extremities, the head does not suffer reduced circulation when the body becomes chilled, so it loses tremendous amounts of heat if left uncovered in cold weather. The experienced paddler will remove his hat when he becomes overheated in cool weather and put it on when he begins to feel chilled.

Long wool underwear is very helpful in cold weather, but you shouldn't bother to carry it at other times. Net underwear is cool when the weather is warm and warm when the clothes over it are closed, but it is generally made of cotton, which is not very good in cold weather. Wool net undershirts are excellent all year, provided they have a large weave, but they are hard to find.

Warm clothing is best worn in a number of layers rather than in one or two large, bulky items. Several light sweaters are warmer than one heavy jacket, because warm air is trapped between the layers. The layers also allow you to adjust the amount of insulation worn and will dry out far more quickly when wet.

A windbreaker of some kind is very useful. It should be roomy enough to be worn comfortably over the layers of warm clothing to keep a cold breeze from blowing through and destroying their insulating capacity. It can also be worn over the skin or underwear when one is working hard in cool weather. Some prefer an uncoated nylon shell, which is very light and breaks the wind well but won't shed water. Others like a jacket or pullover made of two layers of cotton or a mixture of cotton and nylon or polyester. Such fabrics are wind resistant, tough, and water repellent. Rain gear is essential on canoe trips and must serve for both camping and paddling. The standard material of which rain gear is made is a coated lightweight nylon that repels rain quite well but also condenses moisture from the body rather badly on the inside. Plastic rainwear is also commonly used, although it is less durable than coated nylon and shares the same condensation problem. Ponchos, which have good ventilation, solve the condensation problem, but they are not very good for canoeing, giving poor protection for the arms and being easily blown about in the wind and dangerous in whitewater. A rain suit is probably best, despite the condensation drawback. Some rain suits are now made of a coated nylon material with a thin insulating layer bonded to the inside to prevent warm, moist air near the skin from coming in direct contact with the cold, slick coating. This type of rainwear is more expensive and bulkier than the more common models but is worthwhile for those who expect very much cold and rainy weather.

Any rain gear that may be worn during white-water paddling must be snug enough so that it will not interfere with swimming. Voluminous garments bind the legs, catch the force of the current, and may snag on branches or rocks.

Wet suits may be necessary for paddling on long trips even more than on short ones, since there will be no warm car waiting at the end of the day's run. Any serious white-water paddling in cold water requires a wet suit, and prudence may demand one on other cold-water trips. A canoeist dumped into a cold lake has only a very few minutes to empty the canoe, right it, get in, and change clothes before becoming completely incapacitated, and one can hardly be sure of doing so in any conditions that might have caused a capsize. Wet suit recommendations are given in Chapter 2, but on trips not involving whitewater a compromise adopted by many is to take a short, ⅛-inch-thick suit to put on in situations where the extra margin of safety seems advisable.

Old, holey sneakers make excellent paddling shoes. For cold weather an oversize pair with wet-suit socks worn inside is good. Such shoes are excellent for protecting the feet from rocks, broken glass, and other dangers when it is necessary to wade, as it frequently is in canoeing. They are also admirably suited for muddy portages. Take along a second pair of shoes to wear around camp, for hiking side trips and long portages on dry trails, and for similar purposes. I prefer a sturdy pair of hiking boots for long portages over dry land, but others have different preferences.

SHELTER

The canoe itself can provide excellent shelter, and many experienced canoe campers prefer it to a tent. Most standard canoes can be turned over and will rest so that one side is well off the ground, enabling the canoeist to slip under it for protection against the rain, while having an open lean-to side. There is far more room to move about if the thwarts are removed, so canoes that are used much in this way should have thwarts that are easy to take out. In windy weather the canoe should be braced to prevent its moving around.

The canoe alone provides a roomy enough sleeping arrangement for one or two people, depending on its length. A fifteen- to seventeen-foot canoe will be adequate, by itself, for one person or, with a tarp, for two people. Since one side rests on the ground, it can usually be oriented to give good protection against even wind-driven rain, unless the wind is shifting constantly. It is not generally too satisfactory for long rainy periods in camp, however, since it is difficult to arrange enough room to sit up, much less stand. As an intermediate shelter that affords additional room and flexibility many people use a tarpaulin that can be stretched over the open side of the overturned canoe to provide an awning in front of it. More people can sleep this way, there is less need to remove thwarts, more protection is afforded against driv-

The canoe can provide a simple and comfortable shelter for one person, as shown here. The center thwart has been removed to give the sleeper more space. A camp stove can easily be used under the canoe, but a fire would have to be built in front of it, taking care to avoid overheating a fiberglass or ABS vessel. For two people it is best to carry a tarpaulin as well, which can be pitched over the canoe to extend the sleeping space.

ing rain, and sitting out a long period of rain in camp will be considerably more comfortable. A tarp can also be pitched alone when it is not convenient to haul the canoe to the sleeping spot.

A tarpaulin can be pitched by itself in a number of different ways, depending on the circumstances. Sizes between nine-by-twelve feet and twelve-by-twelve feet are the most common. Tarps are usually equipped with a number of grommets and tie tapes to make pitching in various ways convenient. The tarp made of coated nylon fabric is light, waterproof, and durable. A nylon tarp will commonly weigh between two and four pounds, depending on its dimensions and fabric thickness. Expendable plastic tarps are also available. Get one four to six millimeters thick and it will last through several trips. The tarp can be used to protect equipment during the day and even as an improvised sail.

Despite the advantages of light weight, economy, and simplicity when the canoe or a tarpaulin is used for shelter, many people prefer to carry tents for canoe camping shelters. Since it is specifically designed as a shelter, a well-chosen tent will be tailored to fit the needs of the camper exactly. The advantages of a tent are that it is quick to pitch and does not require you to portage the canoe up to the campsite, completely unpack it, and remove the thwarts. The tent may be roomier than a canoe and tarp and provide better protection against severe weather without elaborate improvisation. On a rainy day you can completely pack the canoe, except for the tent itself, before the shelter has to be taken down, and you can pitch the tent upon arriving in camp before all the other gear is unpacked. You can even set it up at lunchtime on a wet day to provide some relief from rain.

Although the canoeist can manage more weight and bulk than the backpacker, it is still best to keep the tent as lightweight and compact as possible. Tents designed for backpacking and mountaineering are used by many, both because the better ones are very well made and because many canoeists are also backpackers and mountaineers. There is no reason to have a half-dozen tents for different activities, but conditions do tend to be somewhat different. Backpacking tents will serve very well for canoe camping, but they are not necessarily ideal.

The standard two-man mountaineering tent is not particularly roomy, and it is not an easy place to dry wet gear. Some older styles of tents that can be pitched with an open front when winds are light can be more comfortable for canoe camping, particularly in areas where a fire can be built in front. Because they must be very light and tight against severe winds, mountaineering tents generally do not have any open sides or steep walls that might catch the wind badly. For many canoeing areas, severe wind is far less of a problem than prolonged rain, so that designs like the old Baker tent made in modern materials are quite comfortable to camp with. It is much easier to keep up your spirits after two weeks of rain in the north woods if you can stand up under the shelter of an open-front tent warming yourself before a cheery fire than if you have to crawl into a sopping, cramped, little A-frame tent. As with most camping equipment, a tent is a compromise designed to meet certain requirements, and when you pick one you should be sure that it best meets yours, rather than someone else's.

It is usually best to avoid large, heavy canvas tents designed for infrequent car camping. Besides being too heavy and bulky, such tents are usually not very well made. Nylon or one of the other synthetics is preferable as a material because of its strength, light weight, and resistance to rot. Nylon material may be coated or uncoated. The coated material is fairly waterproof, whereas the uncoated is very hard to make water-resistant. Small tents are best made with a roof of uncoated material that will allow water vapor to pass through, causing less condensation, with a separate rain fly made of coated material that can be pitched above it to shed rain. Small tents made of single layers of coated material are likely to be more economical, but the occupants will have a great deal of trouble with water condensing on the inside of the tent. In double-walled tents the waterproof fly is usually a separate unit, but in some designs the two walls of the upper part of the tent are incorporated into one structure.

High tents with steep walls designed for camping in relatively sheltered areas do not always require this double roof or wall, particularly if they are open on one side, since condensation is not much of a problem. If the tent is open, moist air will not be trapped inside and the occupants are less likely to come in contact with the walls and any condensed moisture. Thus, such a tent can be effectively made of a single layer of coated nylon fabric.

Whatever type of shelter is used for sleeping, when traveling in rainy areas it is worthwhile to carry an extra tarp to pitch over the cooking area, especially if campfires are being used for cooking instead of stoves. This tarp can be made of either plastic or nylon. The separate tarp prevents the regular sleeping shelter from getting too smoky. The extra shelter can also provide a relief from tent fatigue, simplify fire building, and assist in drying gear in wet weather.

SLEEPING BAGS

A good sleeping bag is one of the most important items of equipment for the canoe camper. In warm weather it may not be necessary, and one may well get by with a blanket roll or a cheap car-camping bag, but after a wet, chilly day, crawling into a warm sleeping bag can provide you with an understanding of the real joys of life, whereas an inadequate one will acquaint you with one of its genuine miseries.

A heavy, bulky bag designed for car camping can be used on short canoe trips, but it is best to have a lightweight, compact bag if possible. Backpackers and others who do lightweight camping will probably already own such a bag and have no need to buy a special one for canoeing.

Insulation in garments and sleeping bags is provided by the small air cells trapped in the insulating material. The amount of insulation provided is a function of the thickness of the layer of trapped air cells; the more thickness, the more insulation. Down has been the traditional material used for lightweight bags because it will expand to provide more thickness for a given weight of insulator and can be compressed into a smaller package than anything else. This is still true and down is still hard to beat for some conditions, such as very cold weather. However, down does have a big disadvantage. You have to take considerable care to keep down dry. Once it has gotten wet, a down bag will take days of bright sunshine to dry, and hot sun is not always a commodity available to the canoe camper.

A cheaper alternative to down as an insulating material for sleeping bags is one of the types of polyester batting such as Dupont's Fiberfill II or Celanese Polarguard. Polyester insulation has improved a good deal during the past few years, and manufacturers have begun to make properly designed lightweight sleeping bags using polyester filling. Although a polyester bag will not have as much loft (thickness) or fit into quite as small a stuff sack as a really good down bag of the same weight, it will have several other advantages. It will retain most of its loft even if it gets wet, and will thus retain some of its insulating capacity. It will dry out quickly. Finally, it will be a good deal less expensive. Comparisons are somewhat difficult to make, but a polyester-insulated bag is likely to weigh about one-third more and cost about one-third less than an equivalent down bag.

Regardless of insulation material, there are a number of design features that affect the warmth of a sleeping bag. The closer the bag fits the body, the less extra space there is inside for the body to heat as well as less extra weight and less surface area on the outside of the bag to lose heat to the cold air. Large rectangular bags are inefficient. Tight-fitting mummy bags are the most efficient shape, but somewhat roomier, compromise shapes are most popular, since most campers prefer a little extra space for moving around inside the bag. Most bags sold as mummy bags are actually roomier compromises.

Bags with seams sewn through to hold insulation in place are suitable only for relatively warm weather or for people who are both knowledgeable campers and warm sleepers. (Some people tend to "sleep warm," whereas others "sleep cold." There are wide variations in the amount of insulation that different people need to allow them to sleep comfortably. If you shiver in your coat while others are happy in shirt-sleeves, get a warmer-than-average bag.) Some sort of baffle system should be used to avoid sewn-through seams in bags designed for colder weather. A few are shown in the drawing.

Good quality in sleeping bags is important but difficult to judge. In the last few years, as backpacking and other outdoor sports have become increasingly popular, they have attracted a good many junk manufacturers as well as many more very good ones. There are ways to save money on outdoor equipment (some of which are discussed later in this chapter), but avoid discount operations for this kind of purchase, unless you have good reason to believe in their products and integrity. Good sleeping bags, tents, and other outdoor gear will last a long time, more than making up for their initial cost. Poorly made equipment is uneconomical because it falls apart quickly, often just when you really need it.

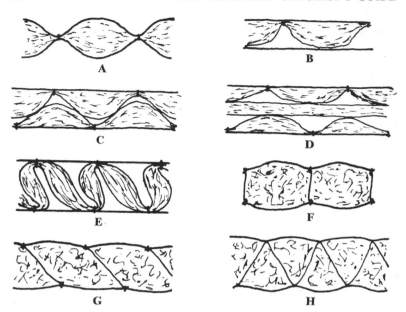

Some of the methods used to prevent insulation from shifting in sleeping bags. In **A** the inside and outside of the bag are simply sewn together to form channels or quilting. This method is inexpensive, but it can only be used in warm-weather bags, because the seams form cold spots. In **B,** used with continuous fiber batting like Polarguard, the batting is sewn only to one shell. The seams are protected slightly by the shell stretching smooth on the other side. This construction is still suitable only for warm-weather bags. In **C** two layers of batting are sewn to opposite shells, using offset seams, so that none of the thin spots coincide. Even more effective is the use of three layers of batting, as in **D**, with the outside layers sewn to the shells with offset seams and a central batt anchored only at the edges of the bag. **E** shows a construction method in which a single batt much longer than usual is looped back and forth between the two shells to avoid cold seams.

    F–H are construction methods using a lightweight baffling material to form compartments for loose-fill insulation, such as down or loose polyester fibers. **F,** known as *box* or *I-beam* construction, consists of baffles running perpendicularly between the shells. **G,** *parallelogram* construction, is similar except that the baffles slant between the shells. **H** is the most expensive and is generally more effective in bags made for very cold weather, which are not usually necessary for canoe camping.

It is difficult to tell whether a sleeping bag is well made unless you have had a great deal of experience because much of the material is hidden inside; you will probably have to rely partly on the reputation of the manufacturer and dealer. One thing to look for is the detail work in the sewing. Sewing that looks imperfect may still be strong if you have done it yourself, but in a manufactured bag it generally indicates poor quality throughout, except in bags sold as seconds because of imperfections. (The same applies to other camping equipment.) Check the quality and smoothness of operation of the zipper. See how many stitches per inch are used in the seams; fewer than eight, particularly in seams subject to much stress or wear, will result in premature deterioration. Too few stitches per inch also probably indicates that other corners have been cut inside the bag, where the buyer cannot see. Once the bag has been fluffed, thin spots in the insulation should not be present. Discuss the merits of various bags with friends and with the salespeople in several shops before buying one.

GROUND BEDS

It is far more comfortable for most people to have some sort of padding to go under the sleeping bag than to sleep directly on the ground. It is also more efficient in chilly weather to provide some insulation from the cold ground, since down-insulated sleeping bags are compressed under the body's weight to almost nothing and polyester ones are greatly reduced. A ground bed provides insulation underneath the body and much extra comfort when the sleeping spot is less than ideal. It also helps the sleeper keep dry.

The most common ground bed for backpackers is the urethane foam pad covered with fabric to protect it from abrasion and from absorbing ground moisture. Such pads have open cells like a sponge and can thus soak up water. They can be used satisfactorily for canoe camping, but some effort has to be made to keep them dry. Air mattresses and closed-cell foam pads are thus probably slightly better solutions for the

Three types of ground beds. RIGHT. An air mattress, which is excellent for canoe camping since it is not affected by moisture, is compact, and can even be used for flotation. This one is full length, which is not necessary, and is made of tough rubberized fabric (vinyl air mattresses are much too flimsy). CENTER. A closed-cell foam pad, which is watertight and needs no cover or protection from water. It gives less padding than the other two beds but is the warmest and lightest of the three. LEFT. An open-cell foam pad covered with waterproof material. It makes a comfortable bed but should not be immersed, lest the foam get wet.

canoeist, although open-cell pads will do for those who already have them or prefer them for comfort.

Closed-cell foam is filled with gas bubbles that are completely sealed by the foam material so they cannot absorb water. The closed-cell foam pad needs no cover, provides superior insulation, and is lightweight. It is more compact than the open-cell pad but less so than the air mattress. It provides less protection from the hard ground than either. A thickness of one-quarter inch is enough for insulation for most canoe camping, but greater thickness may be preferred for padding. Ensolite, Thermobar, and Volarafoam are some of the commonly available closed-cell foams.

Air mattresses are probably the most suitable ground beds for canoeists. They are quite compact when deflated, and most campers find them quite comfortable, though some would disagree. An air mattress is not quite as warm as a foam pad, because air circulating inside causes heat loss by convection, but this is a problem primarily in really cold temperatures that canoe campers do not generally encounter. The compactness of the deflated and folded air mattress, its comfort, and the fact that it cannot become soaked with water make it a good choice. An air mattress also holds the sleeper well off the ground, which can be a real blessing in wet conditions. Only durable, good quality mattresses are suitable. The cheap, unreinforced vinyl ones inevitably are punctured after only a short period of use. Choose only the heavy rubberized fabric type or the special lightweight rubberized nylon or polyester ones designed for backpackers.

Whether they use air mattresses or foam pads, most lightweight campers choose a short ground bed three and a half or four feet long. This is big enough to accommodate the torso with room to spare. A stuff sack filled with extra clothing provides a pillow, and an assortment of items provide padding and insulation for the lower legs and feet, which are more tolerant of lumps than the upper body. A vocal minority prefer to carry full-length pads or mattresses for the extra comfort they are said to provide.

If a tent with a floor is not being used, the camper should have a waterproof ground cloth of plastic or coated nylon or a sleeping bag cover with a coated bottom.

COOKING GEAR

A lightweight portable stove should normally be carried on canoe camping trips. It is convenient, particularly when you want a quick meal and dry wood is scarce. Even more important, however, is the fact that cooking fires and campfires are ecologically unacceptable in many places. Along heavily used lakeshores and rivers where party after party uses the same campsites there are often insufficient supplies of

Typical lightweight cooking gear for canoe camping: a couple of nesting lightweight pots with a cover that will do for a frying pan (unless one is planning on a great deal of fried fish), a small stove with a stand and windscreen, a pot gripper, and a fuel can.

A lightweight pressure cooker. This is very useful when stoves are used on long trips or to make possible cooking inexpensive dried staples like beans and brown rice.

dead wood. Live trees should never be used, nor should standing dead trees in heavily traveled regions. Even in large wilderness areas camping is concentrated in a few fragile spots that are easily damaged and made unattractive. Along dammed rivers the problem is exacerbated because natural flooding and cleansing of the banks no longer occur. By carrying a stove, you will ensure that you have a way to cook your food without making a mess. If you don't carry a stove, be prepared to back up your judgment by eating your food cold if suitable conditions for building a fire aren't found.

Stoves are also convenient. Many campers use them as a substitute for fire-building ability during wet weather, although making fires is a skill that should be cultivated, particularly for long wilderness trips, since fires provide the only practical way to dry out clothing, equipment, and morale during extended periods of wet weather. Nonetheless, it is sometimes convenient when one is pushing hard simply to collapse in the tent, prepare a quick meal, and get to sleep, rather than to go through the trouble of building a fire in pouring rain. Also, in many regions, particularly along desert rivers, the only wood that should ever be used for fires is washed-up driftwood. After an extended period of rain, such wood will be completely soaked, and it will be impossible to start a fire with it unless a dry batch can be found under a rock overhang or in a similarly sheltered spot. In these circumstances a stove is vital.

Stoves may be of the small backpacking variety or the more efficient pumped type. Relatively lightweight pumped stoves are available. The models burning kerosene or those that operate on white gas or naphtha fuel are the least expensive to run, but many campers prefer the convenience of butane or propane fuel. For canoe camping either is suitable.

If you are going to rely on fires in heavily wooded country, you should carry an ax. The only way to be sure of getting dry wood after long periods of rain is to split open standing dead wood. Wood that has been lying about on the ground will be soaked through, and breaking branches off live trees is both inefficient and inexcusable. A full-length ax with a handle of at least twenty-seven inches and a head of two and a half pounds or so is the most efficient tool for splitting logs, assuming it is sharp and you have practiced using it. A hatchet makes a poor substitute. Saws are helpful, though not essential, for cutting, but a saw will not take the place of an ax because it cannot be used for splitting. A lightweight folding saw is a good substitute for an ax in areas where you expect to rely on driftwood, but in such circumstances do not count on getting dry wood after a week of rain.

A nesting set of three or four aluminum pots, equipped with bails for easy carrying, is normally used for cooking. The largest should hold at least six quarts, more if you plan to cook for more than four people. It is best if the bails lock in the vertical position, so the pots cannot tip when they are being carried or when hung on a green stick over a campfire. Expensive sets lined with Teflon or made of stainless steel reduce burning of food and make cleaning much easier. To save money, you can collect a set of tin cans of appropriate sizes, using bailing wire for bails. These usually last a season before rusting out.

Pans used over stoves stay relatively clean on the outside, but the soot that builds up from cooking over a campfire is a nuisance. If you carry a fabric bag for each pot, they can still be nested without needing to be thoroughly washed on the outsides. At washtime, just wash the insides and wipe off excess soot from the outside of each pan and put each one in its storage sack, leaving most of the carbon on. Such blackened pans absorb heat more efficiently than shiny ones.

Many conveniences are preferred by different camp chefs. Some pots have removable handles. Small, clamping potholders will grip most pans and are indispensable for many cooks, but others maintain that a glove or a shirt cuff serve as well. Ladles are favored by some, adjustable pot hangers to dangle stew over the fire by others, and a grate to go over the cooking fire by still others. Pick your own little cooking luxuries, but don't take everything.

A few specialized pieces of cooking gear are worth mentioning. If you plan to fry much fresh fish, take a decent frying pan. An aluminum pot cover will do for occasional jobs, but it will tend to burn and cook unevenly. A good frying pan is well worth the weight if you use it. One of spun steel or a somewhat heavier aluminum model will do, and a Teflon lining may be worthwhile. Be sure to take a spatula. Lightweight pressure cookers designed for mountaineers are available, and for those who take very many long trips they may be worth considering, as they make it possible to use many economical and palatable dry foods that take too long to cook to be practical otherwise. Normal dried beans, brown rice, lentils, split peas, and the like can be cooked without difficulty. Reflector ovens permit the preparation of various baked luxuries when one has a fire and is willing to take the time to bother, but using a reflector oven well requires some practice. A dutch oven is simpler to use, but even the aluminum ones are rather heavy and bulky. Improvised dutch ovens can be managed with a couple of pans and an aluminum pie plate that fits inside them.

Personal utensils should be kept simple. Some campers carry just a cup and a spoon, but others prefer somewhat more elaborate arrays. Aluminum cups are an abomination; they let the food or beverage contents cool off too quickly and burn your fingers and lips when it is hot. Steel cups are easier on the hands and lips than aluminum, are durable, and will not melt if left close to the fire or even deliberately heated. Plastic is the most popular material for cups because it doesn't burn the lips and keeps drinks hot longer, but plastic is harder to clean and will melt if accidentally left too near the fire. The same comments on materials apply to bowls and plates if they are carried.

Biodegradable soap is normally carried for washing dishes and pots. Use it sparingly and well away from the lake or stream. Use warm or hot water if you use soap, to avoid leaving an unpleasant film of mixed soap and grease on utensils. A pot scrubber is very useful, preferably one that does not rust and doesn't contain soap. The green ones made by 3M are particularly good.

Any fire you build should be left cold. If you can't shove your hand down into the bottom of the bed, you haven't finished. If there are already charred rocks for a fireplace, leave them so that the next party won't get any sootier. If there aren't any, cover your fireplace with sand or mineral soil before you use it so that you won't leave fresh scars, and scatter the cold ashes when you are done.

SAVING MONEY ON CAMPING GEAR

There are a number of ways to save money on expensive equipment such as clothing, tents, and sleeping bags. You can purchase very good outdoor clothing in surplus stores and secondhand clothing outlets. Roomy wool clothes may look unfashionable, but they are ideal for canoeing. With a little shopping, you can purchase most clothing items at a considerably lower price than the cheapest and flimsiest street clothes.

Many outdoor suppliers that cater to backpackers and others who travel light are now big, corporate businesses. (In fact, quite a few have been taken over by huge conglomerates whose main business may be making electronics gear or floor wax.) They bring out catalogues twice a year, and when design changes are made the leftovers from the last year are often sold at a reasonable price. Rental gear is also generally sold off at the end of a season rather than being kept around until the following year. Find out when the stores in your area have such sales and make arrangements to get there early.

As outdoor activities have become popular among those with more money than tenacity, the secondhand market has become a good source of equipment for bargain-hunting campers. Bulletin board notices, garage sales, and classified ads are often good places to find bargains. Check out prices in catalogues beforehand to be sure you are getting a good price on used equipment. In this area, it is usually best to stick with name brands and inspect the item carefully to see that it has not been damaged by misuse. With sleeping bags, check to be sure that interior baffles have not been torn out by incorrect washing and that the down is not matted together.

CARRYING YOUR GEAR

Containers for stowing equipment are one of the canoe camper's greatest problems, since items borrowed from other styles of lightweight camping, particularly backpacking, are less suitable. Packing equipment in a canoe improperly is probably the most common beginner's mistake.

Many solutions to the packing problem have been tried, with varying degrees of success in different situations. The first prerequisite of camping gear containers is that they be large enough to carry all the necessary items in a few portable loads. They should be easy to load and secure into the canoe, keeping the center of gravity of the boat low. It is a great advantage if they are waterproof, which for canoeing means *absolutely* waterproof. For any trip with significant portages they must also be easy to carry.

Avoid scattering large numbers of small packages and items around the canoe because they get in the way and will probably not be secured adequately or protected against moisture. It is time consuming to load and unload them and they are easily lost, either in an upset or while you are trying to get out of camp early. All equipment and food that is not actually in use during the day should be packed in one or two large containers.

My own preference is for either modern backpacking frames or large, undivided, soft backpacks. Both of these are easily tied into the canoe (and they must always be tied in securely) and are ready to portage or carry up to a campsite above a river or lake with no special preparation. One such pack should carry one person's share of gear for any but very long trips, and on those an extra pack can be taken in each canoe. The gear itself is packed in heavy waterproof bags that can be stowed inside the soft packs or tied to the pack frames.

Most equipment should be in or on the packs, except for river gear, lunch, extra clothing, and camera equipment. Lunch, extra clothes, and items like sunglasses and insect repellent are often carried in a small waterproof day bag tied to the seat. When not in use, cameras may be carried in special waterproof bags or in an army surplus ammunition box carefully secured to the canoe. The latter provides the best protection for photographic equipment so long as the seal is checked beforehand for waterproofness. To do this, fill the dry box with rocks or weights and sink it under a foot or two of water for an hour; then open it and find out whether there was any seepage. Ammunition boxes should be tightly secured in the canoe so they cannot slap about in case of an upset, because their corners are sharp.

All these precautions against gear getting wet or lost may be somewhat excessive for moderate trips on calm lakes, though they are clearly essential on white-water tours. There is a lot to be said for consistent practice in protecting equipment, however. Most experienced paddlers have had an unexpected upset at one time or another, perhaps most frequently when conditions were so easy that they became careless. On camping trips the availability of warm clothes and sleeping bags often makes the difference between a pleasant trip and a miserable one, and on some occasions they can be a life-and-death matter. Sloppy packing habits guarantee that problems will occur sooner or later.

Making packs watertight is perhaps the biggest packing headache. Packs made of coated fabric normally do not even approach the state of being waterproof. Some people have success with multiple plastic bags sealed with twists, overlaps, and rubber bands. However, most canoeists find that the plastic bags develop leaks in short order, and sloshing bilge, splashing waves, rain, or a capsize will manage to get water through even pinhole leaks. Some outfitters sell good waterproof bags that can be put inside packs. Those made from thin, unreinforced vinyl are not very durable, but some of the ones made from heavy coated fabrics are quite good. Several surplus products work well. There are some good surplus rubberized duffel bags about eighteen-by-fifteen-by-six inches, big enough for a sleeping bag and a few clothes. The old standby that holds a great deal of gear is the delousing bag, a flat, rubberized black bag five feet long and two and a half feet wide when it is laid out flat. The top lip comes together and is rolled over and tied. These are fully waterproof, although I prefer the extra safety of a large, heavy plastic liner or individual heavy plastic bags for critical gear. Delousing bags are fairly durable except for the cotton ties, which have to be replaced after a few trips, and they are the cheapest large-volume alternative, short of making your own bags, for thorough waterproofing. Delousing bags and rubberized duffel bags are still available at some surplus stores, though the supply finally seems to be getting low.

If plastic bags are used for waterproofing the inside of packs that are not waterproof, the bags should be fairly heavy and should be double-sealed. At least for important items, two independently sealed bags, one inside the other, should be used. Be sure to handle with care plastic bags meant for waterproofing, mend any pinhole leaks with tape, and carry extra bags. Squeeze extra air from such bags while you are packing, lest they be popped when squeezed. Packs should be thoroughly cleaned before use, to remove grit and debris that might cause leaks.

Another good solution to the packing problem is a rigid, watertight box built so that it can be carried like a pack. One such pack is available commercially. Packs of this type could be made from fiberglass to fit the shape of the canoe.

LOADING A CANOE

All duffel should be stored in the center of the canoe as low as possible. If a large load is being carried, heavier items should be nearer the center and lower. Heavy items packed below the roll center of the canoe will actually stabilize it, whereas weight above it will try to stabilize the boat upside down. Heavy items mistakenly placed near the ends of the canoe will make the craft difficult to turn and will also cause it to plunge deeply into waves, rather than ride over them.

With all gear and paddlers aboard the overall trim of the canoe should normally be even. The techniques of trimming to the bow or stern may be useful in special circumstances, but even then avoid exaggerating, because a canoe much heavier in either the bow or stern will not handle well. Remember that when paddling into a headwind for long distances it is useful to trim the bow slightly low so that the stern rises, catches the wind, and orients the canoe like a weathervane, leaving the paddlers free of the need to make steering corrections. Duffel should not be far off-center, however, since if the wind starts to raise large waves, the bow will begin to bury itself. It is often most convenient for the stern paddler simply to move forward a few feet to change the trim or for the solo paddler to work from in front of his load rather than behind it. Then the paddler can quickly change the trim by moving back to a normal position again. Packs that are well lashed to the canoe cannot be moved very easily when it is riding six-foot waves.

It cannot be overemphasized that all packs and equipment should be securely tied down. Besides the danger of loss in a capsize, items that shift around the canoe when it is bucking in waves are a definite liability, since they are likely to throw the paddlers off-balance just when they can least afford it.

Items that are kept apart from the main duffel for ready use need to be tied in also. In rough water, however, long lines can be a hazard to people if there is an upset. Thus, to attach a water bottle to a seat or thwart, tie a small loop to the bottle and a spring clip to the seat or thwart. The bottle can then be easily released for use or removal, but there is no four- or five-foot length of parachute cord that might tie your fate too closely to that of the canoe. The bailer can be tied to the seat with light cotton cord that would break in an emergency.

CHOOSING A CAMPSITE

When possible, it is a good idea to pick a campsite before necessity presses too hard, since a good one rarely seems to be available as twilight approaches. If you are pushing on late, it is particularly im-

A river runners' camp in the lower canyons of the Rio Grande. The campers have chosen to carry their gear an extra distance and camp on a rock shelf, rather than on the comfortable sand of the dry wash, to avoid the danger of being caught by a flash flood. In wilderness like this, care must also be taken to prevent canoes from being blown or washed away.

portant to map your progress to avoid having darkness catch you either along a lake shore that is nothing but marsh or entering a twelve-mile-long canyon with sheer walls going up for hundreds of feet. A night spent midstream on a boulder is educational but not very restful.

Most of the attributes of a good campsite are fairly obvious, even to the novice: a dry, flat spot with good drainage to pitch the tent; a fresh water supply; an easy landing and safe place to put the canoes overnight; dead firewood and a suitable fire site, if a fire is to be built; and a pleasant view. On some really well equipped rivers you may demand a hot spring to soak away the efforts of the day. Other factors may not be obvious to the beginner, however. Where insects are a problem, as in many of the best canoeing areas, an open, breezy knoll will be a better campsite than a more sheltered low spot. Mosquitoes, in particular, tend to be quelled when the evening wind comes up. In canyon country it is often a good idea to consider where the morning sun will rise. In cold weather it is hard to get off before the warmth comes up over the rim, so it is well to pick a spot that will catch the sun as early as possible. In hot weather you might prefer the opposite side of the canyon, where the cool morning shadows are retained longer.

In deserts, dry washes can make quite risky camps, since a flash flood can come down one as the result of a storm many miles away. Camps and canoes are both more safely situated well above the bottom of a wash. Narrow washes with steep sides are particularly hazardous; even if you hear water before it actually comes down, it may be impossible to escape.

In regions inhabited by bears and moose, prevent unwanted midnight encounters with them by not parking on game trails. This mistake is easy to make, because along the shores of densely forested lakes and rivers clear spots are often the ends of game trails. This precaution is particularly important in grizzly country. Find a spot to camp where you will not be in the way of a disgruntled bruin in the middle of the night.

When choosing a campsite on a riverbank, remember that rivers can rise overnight, particularly when the flow is controlled by upstream dams. Observe the bank and know enough about the nature of the watershed upstream to tell you what to expect; keep in mind that a six-inch rise in the water level can often flood a large area.

ORGANIZATION IN CAMP

Arranging camp chores is largely a matter of personal preference and circumstances, but the work will be made easier if you consider it when you do the packing. Make sure you know just where all the items are that may be needed when you first get into camp. A tent, tarp, or rain fly should be readily accessible, not buried underneath everything else, so that on rainy afternoons you can set up a shelter right away without tossing all the other gear out into the wet to find the tent. It is usually simplest to separate the next evening's meal when packing in the morning, too, so that it can be pulled out easily. This is especially helpful after getting into camp late.

A definite routine to take care of a few obvious but easily neglected details is important. When pulling into a prospective campsite to check it, beach the canoe well and tie it to something sturdy or leave someone to hold the painters. It is embarrassing at the least and possibly life threatening to look back over your shoulder from your proposed tent site to see the canoe and all your gear, unattended, heading through the next rapid. This mistake is easier to make than you might think, as demonstrated by the number of experienced paddlers who have had it happen (though most of them would prefer to forget the incident). The same difficulty can occur on lakes if the wind comes up; it is impossible to swim as fast as the wind can drive a canoe. Once the canoe is unloaded, whether or not it is being used for shelter, it must be brought up beyond reach of possible waves or a rising river and thoroughly anchored if there is any possibility of wind. A playful gust coming down a side canyon can easily pick up a canoe and blow it thirty feet down the beach into the river. If there are no trees to which the painters can be tied, you can load rocks in a pack for an anchor or bury a stick in the sand with a line tied around the middle.

Wood gathering, fire building, cooking, and pitching a tent can be apportioned according to any scheme that works, provided no one gets stuck with always doing unpleasant jobs. If there are men in the group who seem to think that kitchen chores are women's work, they should be disabused of this quaint notion at an early stage in the trip. In wet weather the cooking fly should be pitched immediately by one or two members of the party while the others are carrying up gear and securing the canoes. Then the job of fire building or heating up a pot of soup on the stove can be started immediately.

WATER

By definition, finding water will not be a problem on a canoe trip, but obtaining suitable drinking water may be. It is best to be conservative when deciding whether water is fit to drink without treatment, particularly on long trips on which a seriously ill person might cause the party real problems, besides spoiling a vacation. Some rivers are perfectly clean, though they are getting hard to find. Side streams may be safe but should not be assumed so. In general, any water downstream from human habitation should not be trusted. It is also important to be wary in regions where livestock are grazed. In many remote desert regions, for example, even small herds of cattle in a large area make the water generally unsafe because they concentrate along watercourses.

Except where industrial wastes have polluted the water with exotic poisons, water can be made safe by boiling it vigorously for twenty minutes. Chemical purification is generally safe to use for drinking water, although it is not quite as reliable as boiling. Tablets that release either chlorine (Halazone) or iodine (Globaline) as they dissolve are available. Perhaps the most convenient (certainly the cheapest) means of chemical purification is, however, a plastic dropper bottle filled with household chlorine bleach. Add ten drops per gallon of water, shake with the cap loose so that chlorinated water

A large collapsible container like this is useful for carrying water up to camp and for purifying it in areas where it is unsafe to drink untreated water.

reaches the neck of the bottle, and allow to stand ten minutes. Double the bleach and the time if the water is cloudy or smelly.

EQUIPMENT CHECKLIST FOR CANOE TRIPS

Take what you need to; leave the rest at home with the kitchen sink.

canoe
paddles
extra paddles
pole
knee pads
bailer and sponge
life preserver
waterproof storage containers

pocket knife
cigarette lighter (kept on body in
    cold weather)
water bottle
water disinfectant solution
food
extra food
first-aid kit

pack or frame
warm clothing, including hat
sun hat
rain gear
wool long johns
wet suit
windbreaker or paddling jacket
extra warm, dry clothes in waterproof container
boating shoes
wool socks
swim suit
sun cream
sunglasses
extra pair of prescription glasses
retainer strap for glasses

flashlight
maps (include walk-out maps on remote rivers)
compass
guidebook
insect repellent
head net
extra matches in waterproof container
candle or chemical fire starter
repair kit
toilet paper and trowel
camera and film
fishing tackle
money
extra rope for shuttle

FOR WHITE-WATER

spray cover
flotation
helmet

rescue line
long ropes for lining boats in rapids

FOR CLOSED BOATS

spray skirt

float bags

FOR OVERNIGHT TRIPS

shoes for hiking and camp
cook kit
stove
fuel

tent or other shelter and necessary line and stakes
sleeping bag
ground cloth

collapsible water storage jug
frying pan and spatula
cup
bowl
spoon
pot grippers
soap
pot scrubber

pad or air mattress
mosquito netting
towel
toilet articles
carbide lamp and carbide
ax
saw

Chapter 7

RIVER CANOEING

There is a special charm in gliding through the water lilies of an exquisite pond in the evening light, a unique pleasure in the rhythm developed by two well-coordinated canoeists stroking down a long bay, and a challenge in the waves that can develop on a big lake. Still, for many paddlers the essence of canoeing is the anticipatory thrill of coming around a bend in a river. The ears strain for the sound of rapids that may lie ahead; eyes try to reach around the spit for a glimpse of the water downstream and for possible landings in case they are needed. Paddles stroke to bring the moment of revelation sooner or are held at ready in case of the need to act quickly.

One of the most obvious attractions of river canoeing for adventurous paddlers is the challenge of white-water. The fast ride, the puzzle that must be unraveled to interpret the movement of water dropping through a maze of boulders and to pick out a passage through it, and the mastery of the canoe that is necessary to actually make the run— all combine to make white-water paddling the ultimate test of the canoeist's skill and of a paddling team's coordination.

Not all river running is white-water paddling, however. Much fine river canoeing is through easy water with at most a few riffles (easy rapids with small waves requiring maneuvering only to keep in the main channel) or perhaps a couple of portages around difficult sections. River canoeing even on easy water has a special quality because of the continuity of a river run, the sense of passing down a living ar-

156

The extra challenge presented by the current flowing around the hull of the canoe and the ever-present mystery of what one will find around the next bend lend a special attraction to river canoeing. Aluminum canoes such as this have proved excellent river craft, although other materials have some advantages.

tery of the continent, and the feeling of immersion for a day, week, or month in its rhythms.

There are a number of basics that any river runner has to understand to be able to paddle even flat-water sections of a river safely, which will be considered before the special problems of white-water are brought up.

THE ANATOMY OF A RIVER

Rivers vary so in their basic characteristics that any detailed study would require several volumes; all we can attempt here is to take note of some features that are of particular importance to the canoeist. The paddler must quickly develop a recognition that there are vast differences between one river and another. Having successfully run a few rivers or a few dozen often breeds overconfidence and a lack of appreciation for the problems that may arise elsewhere. At Saint Louis, the Mississippi River is already huge and still has over a thousand miles to run before reaching the sea, but in that distance it drops only a little over 400 feet in elevation. The Colorado, another of America's great rivers, drops that distance in the Grand Canyon every fifty miles. Other, smaller rivers drop the same distance much faster without developing the tremendous turbulence of the Colorado. The differences are enormous, and one should develop an appreciation for them before deciding to run a particular river in a canoe.

Rivers in general rise in a network of small streams so that one river drains a large basin, extending perhaps even for hundreds or thousands of miles. In regions that receive a great deal of precipitation, relatively small drainage basins may still produce large rivers. Where annual precipitation is low, even a huge watershed may be drained by a small stream. The big southwestern rivers are fed by vast areas: the Colorado drains virtually all of Arizona and large parts of Mexico, New Mexico, California, Nevada, Utah, Colorado, and Wyoming. In such large watersheds, even small rivers can become raging torrents as a result of storms hundreds of miles away. Although any river floods at times, this type is far more subject to flash flooding and is more likely to take boaters by surprise (because the precipitation is taking place far away) than those draining smaller areas.

Rivers may drain low regions or high ones, and the vertical drop of the river is obviously one of its most important characteristics. (The drop is simply the number of feet of elevation that the water runs down over a particular section. It may be expressed in feet per mile or in total numbers.) A river cascading down many hundreds of feet for each mile traveled is not canoeable. On the other hand, a river like the Yukon, with an average drop of only a little over a foot per mile for the last two thousand miles of its course, can have only a very few rapids or falls and will generally be quite sluggish. The greater the vertical drop for each mile the river flows, the more turbulent and powerful the currents will be and the faster the movement.

The drop per mile, or gradient, does not tell the whole story, however. The volume of water being carried by a river is just as important. A river of fair size when it is carrying three thousand cubic feet per second of water may have moderate white-water in a mile with a drop of thirty feet, but when spring melting swells the runoff to twelve thousand cubic feet per second, the same section will turn into a turbulent maelstrom of surging currents. At the first level the rapids may be perfectly suitable for running in open canoes by moderately experienced paddlers, whereas at the second it would probably be foolhardy except in specially prepared boats.

Other factors are important. Any river or stream carrying much more than its usual amount of water will be far more serious than a waterway of the same general characteristics running at its normal level because a great deal of debris will be picked up and will jam here and there and because obstacles will be found in main channels that would be washed out if the river ran at the same level most of the time.

Average gradients, useful to the canoeist, can be gained from bridge elevations and topographic maps, but they tell only the average story. A twenty-foot-per-mile gradient can mean that the river drops at a fairly regular rate for that mile or that it drops fifteen feet over a waterfall and then takes the rest of the distance to slide five feet. Because of resistant layers of rock or dams of boulders washed out from side canyons, many rivers lose most of their elevation in isolated places of this type, thus forming rapids considerably more serious than their average gradient might indicate. Such waterways are known as pool-and-drop rivers.

A river's flow is influenced by the channel in which it runs, which in turn is cut and shaped by the river. Gravity drags on the water and pulls it downhill, but friction against the bottom slows its flow. Increased friction reduces the flow, whereas a greater slope increases it. If the river is deeper, the higher water flows not on the actual bed but on the water below, which is itself moving. Friction does not begin to drag on the higher layer of water until it is moving faster than the lower one, so water higher in the river flows faster. At the surface there is a slight drag against the air, so the fastest-moving water in any clear channel is normally just below the surface. The air drag is quite minor, however, so for practical purposes one can consider the top layer of water as the part of the river with the highest velocity downstream. Similarly, friction against the banks slows the water at the sides of the river and the fastest flow in a straight, clear channel will be in midstream.

Of course, as the riverbed drags on the water the water is also dragging on the sand, dirt, rocks, gravel, and silt on which it is flowing. When the drag is sufficient, particles are pulled downstream and may be lifted up into the flow of the water itself. The faster the current, the greater the frictional drag and the greater the number and size of pieces of sediment that are carried along with the flow of the water. Smaller particles are more easily moved, so a slow-flowing stream with a bed of finely ground material may carry much of it along, though an otherwise identical one with a bed of heavy rocks and gravel will move very little detritus. A river carrying sediment will not be able to carry as much when it slows down, so anywhere that the speed of the current is reduced, one can expect to find deposits of material carried down from above. Such bars will be larger and more frequent in a river heavy with sediment.

GRADIENT AND VELOCITY

The rate at which a river flows depends on its gradient or drop per mile, the width of the channel, and the amount of water being carried. Obstructions, the amount of frictional drag on the bed, and the winding of the river's course also affect the velocity of the current, but for simplicity, consider a straight, smooth channel. If the channel retains the same shape but gets steeper, the water will naturally accelerate and begin to move faster. If the same width is maintained, the water will also become shallower, since the same total volume of water per minute must still be moving past each point. In general, on any given river between major tributaries, a section that is both wider and deeper than elsewhere indicates a slower current, and a speeding up of the water without a narrowing of the banks indicates a shallower channel. An even faster current is usually created when the course both steepens

Rapids like these provide the ultimate challenge to the river canoeist, particularly when they are found in remote wilderness canyons where serious mistakes can be costly. They should never be attempted until one is sure the run would be safe.

and narrows, because the higher layers of water then still have a deep lower layer to reduce friction. Similarly, an increase in the volume of water running down a river usually produces a higher current velocity because the extra water can flow over the top of the lower layers, with consequent reduced friction.

Although the overall width and depth (or both) must increase when the river slows, there are likely to be some shallows formed by deposited sediment, because the slower current can carry less.

BENDS

Consider a bend in the path of the river, perhaps where it has to detour around a strong rock formation. The swiftly moving surface water in the center of the channel keeps flowing in a straight line while the water hitting the outside of the bend is deflected and slowed. Water from the center of the river slides over the outside water and piles up against the bank, perhaps rolling or smashing against it, depending on the power of the river. This piling up forms a slope on the river surface as a whole so that some of the water coming around the bend and sliding up the surface of the hill of water does not flow all the way to the outside of the curve but moves on around it without hitting the bank. The water left to meander around the inside of the bend, which lacks the momentum to carry up the slight slope now formed by the water flowing around the curve, is the slowest-moving part of the river. The water slowed on the inside of the bend will drop any sediment it is carrying, forming a bar of silt, sand, gravel, or small rocks. The outside of the bend, receiving the full force of the current, is cut away so that the channel may be worn deeper there and the bank may be undercut. The bank may then fall into the river or overhang it, depending on the strength of the material and the rate of erosion.

Several characteristic features, governed by the force of the water, its height, the sharpness of the bend, and the nature of the banks, can be expected at a river bend. The current nearly always is fastest and the channel deepest at the outside of the bend. It is slower and shallower on the inside and there is likely to be a bar there. Good landing and camping spots are often found on the inside bank of such bends. Undercuts are common on the outside. If there are trees along the banks, they are frequently found falling into the river along the outside edges of bends, since the river cuts away the ground in which they are rooted. Rivers sometimes undercut rock walls also, so that the river deflecting against an outside cliff may run underneath an overhanging rock ledge. Water thrown against an outside wall in a powerful river may dive down as it comes against the bank or be thrown up in a breaking wave. In either case, a vertical corkscrew motion is created.

EDDIES

Another characteristic feature of river bends is the eddy that often forms on the downstream side of the inner corner. As we have seen, fast water tends to flow toward the outside of the bend, pile up on the far bank, and travel rapidly around the channel there. The water level thus becomes higher along the outside of the curve, particularly in a fast-moving river. As gravity tries to equalize the level of the water surface, some of the water that has traveled around the curve is drawn back into the lower pool around the inside of the bend. At the top of the pool, where the main flow is shooting past, some of the water is dragged out by the friction of the current rushing by. This combination actually creates an upstream flow near the inside bank below the curve, with water entering at the bottom, pulled in by gravity, and water pulled off by the primary current at the top. This upstream current, called an eddy, is one of the most important of all river features, particularly for the paddler.

Eddies form not only around curves but also on the downstream sides of boulders, below projections from banks, and almost anywhere else where the flow of the current is deflected by an obstruction. For the canoeist the eddy is a resting spot in the middle of chaos, to be used for inspecting what is below, for making upstream progress, for setting up the canoe to make the next maneuver, and for a host of variations on these techniques. Proper use of eddies is the key to successful white-water paddling, so the canoeist running rapids needs to study them constantly. Even on relatively placid rivers eddies are generally the best landing spots.

A boulder standing in the middle of a river not completely covered

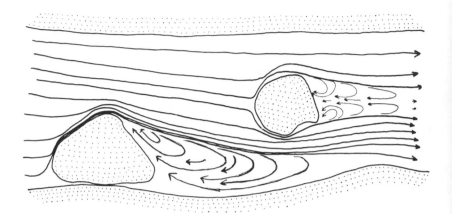

Eddies. Water flowing rapidly past obstructions results in an upstream current below the obstacle. This reverse current, or eddy, is formed because the main flow of water is deflected by the obstacle and shoots past, leaving a low spot downstream of the island or boulder. Some water flows back into the low spot to fill it up, causing the eddy current, and this water is in turn dragged off at the edge of the eddy by the force of the main current. The eddy line is the fairly sharp and turbulent meeting line between the two currents. The drawing shows two eddies, one formed by a midstream boulder, with an eddy line on each side, and one behind a rock at the side of the river, with one eddy line.

by flowing water splits the current. The water rushing past the boulder on both sides then continues downstream, leaving a space downstream of the rock. As with the bend, there is then a low spot on the surface and gravity will drag some of the water back up to fill it, creating the characteristic upstream current of the eddy. Also, as with the eddy around the bend, the current rushing past drags water from the eddy along with it. The circulation that is formed has water entering the eddy from the sides well downstream from the rock and flowing upstream toward the boulder and then off to the sides, to be sheared off by the main current.

There is a fairly sharp boundary between water moving upstream in the eddy and the main current rushing by. This juncture, with water rushing in opposite directions on either side, is called an eddy line. The eddy line may be quite turbulent in large or fast rivers, but it often looks deceptively calm. It is a useful feature for the capable paddler, enabling him to spin the canoe rapidly into or out of the eddy in a fast, almost effortless turn. For the beginner, crossing a strong eddy line is a real and often unexpected challenge that will ensure a few swims for experience.

Eddies come in many varieties and sizes. An eddy formed by a boulder may be considerably shorter than the length of the canoe, forming a haven for only the very alert and skillful paddler, or it may extend for some distance. On a large and powerful river an eddy from a big boulder may extend a quarter of a mile downstream and the eddy line can be wide and elusive, slithering into whirlpools at the touch of a paddle.

CHUTES AND STANDING WAVES

A sudden narrowing of a river's channel backs water up behind it, creating a rapid drop below, even where there is no drop in the bed. The current pours swiftly through the narrow section, creating a chute of water. Such chutes tend to be accentuated because obstructions that narrow the riverbed are often accompanied by drops in the underlying strata and because the rushing water pounds and erodes the bed immediately below, thus increasing the drop.

Typically, where the river narrows into a chute and then widens again, the water undergoes rapid acceleration as it pours through, and it must then slow down again as it strikes the more gradual bed and water surface below. In slowing down, the water loses energy by bouncing off the ground or the other water below. In a vertical waterfall this results in spray and gushing water. (The actual energy dissipation results mainly in heat, but this is not noticeable to the canoeist.) At

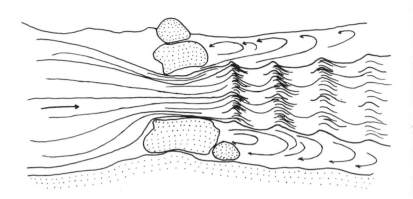

A chute. When a fast-moving river is forced to go through a narrow channel, for example by the boulders that have fallen into the bed in this drawing, the water backs up behind the narrow spot and then accelerates rapidly through it. When the water slows down again on the other side, the kinetic energy picked up in the drop is dissipated in a series of standing waves below. At the edges of the river below many chutes, such as this one, are eddies behind the boulders that formed the restricted channel.

Haystacks, or standing waves. A side view of the standing waves that form below most chutes and drops where the water is deep enough to flow on continuously. The water that has speeded up in the drop hits the less-inclined bottom below and bounces up to form a wave. It then drops again and bounces again, so that a series of progressively smaller waves is formed. When these are large and breaking at the top, as the first one here is, they are often called haystacks.

the bottom of a chute, however, the fast water pouring down striking the calmer water below generates a series of waves called standing waves, because they stay in the same place while the water moves by. These waves can range in size from little riffles a few inches high to great, rolling monsters of ten feet or more. Those that break at the top are known as haystacks, from their appearance.

BOULDERS AND ROCKS

It is interesting and enlightening to study the effect of the same rock on fast water at different levels of runoff. If a boulder projects well out of the water, an eddy will form behind it. A canoe can certainly crash into the rock, but the current deflecting off it has a certain amount of cushioning effect and helps the paddlers draw the canoe over to one side or the other. As the water rises to just cover the rock, so that a little of the current is flowing over it, the eddy below remains much the same but the rock is harder to see and the deflection of the canoe hull is less—it is easier to run directly into the rock.

As the water comes higher still, with the rock several inches below the surface, a sufficiently strong current will create a "hole" below the rock, a vertical eddy in which much of the water dives well below the surface and rises again downstream, while some of the breaking aerated water rolls back down the upstream side of the standing waves that are formed. Such holes (known as suck holes, souse holes, and various other names) can be quite small or large indeed. Whether or not a hole is formed, a rock just under the surface often becomes a "sleeper," close enough to the surface for the canoe to crash into but creating so little disturbance when viewed from upstream that it is hard to detect.

At even higher water levels, the hole will often wash out and the presence of the rock below will be marked only by a series of standing waves well downstream. The standing waves tell the canoeist that the boulder is covered with more than enough water to clear the hull of the canoe.

RAPIDS

The exact pattern of turbulence that is formed by a rock depends on its shape, the way the current strikes it, and a host of other factors. Real rapids are complex, which is why they are interesting. Chutes, eddies, standing waves, and holes of various sizes are linked in dynamic patterns called rapids as the water winds its way through a series of obstructions. Such rapids, formed where a large group of stones and boulders obstruct the path of the river, do not occur randomly but are generally in narrow sections of canyons, since otherwise the river would simply find its way around the barrier. They may be formed by a number of particular actions, the most common being falling stones from the side of the canyon and outwashes from tributaries. Thus, the experienced river runner looks intently for possible rapids just downstream from side canyons entering the main watershed or where a talus slope is visible ahead dropping down from one wall of the canyon. (Talus is an accumulation of large blocks of stone that have fallen from a cliff above, usually forming a steep slope rising from the river.)

ROLLERS AND KEEPERS

Holes, as mentioned, are formed when water plunging over a short drop dives under the surface and some of the turbulent mixture of air and water forms a roller, a wave breaking back upstream. An open canoe is easily swamped as it dives into a hole, but this is equally true when it encounters a large standing wave. Rollers and holes have a special nature because a buoyant object like a canoe or a swimmer wearing a life preserver will not be carried under with the main current but will instead float in the trough. It may not be carried on over the roller wave beyond the hole because the surface current is running back down the wave surface. Except in quite powerful water the situation is not often really dangerous, although a canoe may easily be swamped, as the hole will rarely hold an object for long.

There is an important exception to this generality. A roller formed below a regular drop that extends all the way across a river or stream is often a "keeper" or "stopper," a wave that may hold a floating object for long periods. Such keepers are all the more hazardous because they are often quite small and innocuous looking. Unlike most holes, there is no exit to the side, which is why they do not eject floating objects. A swimmer or canoe remains trapped in a normal hole only as long as he or it remains in the center, and it is usually not long before a leg or a bow is caught by a side current and dragged out. In a keeper extending the width of the river, there is no exit to the side.

Keepers of this type are nearly always formed by man-made dams; even a small dam can form an effective one. A canoe that gets across the current in such a spot can roll over and over there for days. A person may repeatedly be washed underwater, float up into the roller, and then float back down again, to be shoved under by the falling water from above. Such spots are extremely dangerous and should be treated with great respect.

Although a very few boulder-formed holes are true keepers, these generally occur only in large rivers. The only natural feature that forms a stopper similar to a man-made dam is a rock ledge that extends across a river and is broken off in a sharp line to form a uniform drop from one bank to the other, a relatively rare structure. When formations of this type are found there are usually some irregularities that produce flaws in the roller wave so that objects trapped behind will eventually wash out.

RUNOFF PATTERNS

The annual cycles that rivers follow are important in understanding them, as is knowledge of the artificial variations introduced by man. Rivers that are fed mainly by the melting snows of mountains will normally crest sometime during the spring or early summer, then gradually drop to lower and lower levels in late summer and fall. Exact patterns vary a great deal, though, as do annual deviations from the average. Some rivers carry high water for only a short period, perhaps a few weeks, whereas others have a long, steady runoff that holds the water level high for months. Still others are more likely to reach high levels from heavy thunderstorm activity rather than snowmelt, so that high water levels are more variable and hard to predict.

Besides the complications of natural runoff cycles, most rivers are dammed so that runoff is more or less controlled on at least some sections of the river. Large, free-running rivers are now a rarity in most parts of North America. The pattern of flow in a dammed river is likely to change radically from one part of it to another: the river may run free for a number of miles, then go through a flood-control dam, which might allow relatively natural levels of water to pass except during periods of high runoff, when the level is reduced until the quantity flowing into the dam decreases, at which time the discharge will be increased. Farther down there may be a hydroelectric storage facility diverting nearly all the flow of the river from the channel for a number of miles. The flow below this whole facility will depend on power needs. If the power plant is used for peaking power, for example, nearly all the discharge will probably take place during evening hours. A host of other kinds of dams may be found, including water diversion projects that pump the whole river off to another state, drying up the river below or reducing it to a minimum flow.

Investigating the patterns for a particular section of river is important to the canoeist because the water level is important to him. If a particular run is canoeable, it will usually be so only at particular water levels. When the river is too low it may be impassable, require an excessive number of portages, or simply be unattractive. Whitewater runs are normally suitable for canoeing, particularly with open boats, only at certain water levels. Any river is dangerous in flood stage, hence the paddler must know in advance whether a river is rising rapidly in the spring, whether flash flooding might suddenly raise the water level, or whether a release from a dam upstream might bring the water level up several feet in a few minutes.

BASIC RIVER PADDLING

The first differences the beginner will encounter when moving from lakes to rivers are the techniques for launching and beaching a canoe. Where possible, you should exercise the same care as on a lake shore, but put-in and take-out points on a river are often even poorer than those encountered along lake shores. Ideally, you will find a quiet eddy with a gradual beach accessible by a good trail. Often, however, the best spot available is at the bottom of a steep bank among sharp rocks. This is where the advantages of canoes made of rugged materials become apparent, since a certain amount of scraping is sometimes unavoidable. It may be necessary at times for the second person to enter the canoe while it is still partially aground, to avoid having the

Practice launching and landing the canoe in moving water before heading downstream. A sandbar such as this one is the ideal spot, but it may not always be available. If it is not held in carefully, the upstream end of the canoe can easily be spun off by the current.

craft carried off by the current as he is still trying to board. Such tactics are to be avoided when possible, if only as a point of pride; learning to jump in and out of the boat quickly will be useful, but elegance in launching and landing is not always possible.

Your first attempts at river paddling should be made in moderate current with no white-water downstream. Scout the river for a suitable landing spot to be sure you can get out safely. Until you have had some experience with paddling in moving water, it is foolhardy to expect you will be able to land before the river goes around a bend into unknown territory. The best way to learn river canoeing is to go out with an old hand, which allows for a much less conservative approach without sacrificing safety. Unless the river is without real rapids and the water is warm and everyone is a strong swimmer, life preservers should be worn. If the water is really cold, wet suits are essential.

A canoe floating freely downriver will travel a little faster than the current. Like the water, it is powered by gravity and slides on a surface that is already moving. The motion is practically frictionless until the canoe is going faster than the water; then drag against the hull develops.

There is an old myth that one cannot maneuver unless one is going significantly faster than the water, which is true if rudder-type strokes are being used to steer. A novice should already be aware, however, that such strokes are far less effective than strokes such as the draw, pry, and sweep, and in river canoeing timid strokes are nearly always abandoned for decisive, powerful ones. One can maneuver equally well in most circumstances whether one is going faster than the current, at the same speed, or slower. Different methods can be used, but the assertion that one must have "way" to steer is nonsense.

In river running it is not necessary to paddle all the time to get where one is going, as it is on lakes. One may sometimes paddle to move faster, but river paddling is often done mainly to keep the boat oriented with the current or to set it in the proper channel rather than to move intentionally faster downstream than the current.

When a canoe is allowed to drift, it will not maintain any particular orientation to the current but will swing first one way and then the other. In deep water with no obstructions, the angle of the boat does not matter, but as a general rule it is best to keep a canoe oriented with the flow of the water. If one should accidentally strike a rock just under the surface, the worst way to strike it is broadside. Since a canoe running sideways down a river presents a far larger profile than one lined up with the river, such a one will also be far more likely to strike a rock.

The basic strokes used in river canoeing are the same as those of the lake canoeist, but, as mentioned, the river runner tends to prefer the more powerful strokes because of the nature of the paddling. In a river one often needs strokes that will move the canoe over powerfully and quickly at a moment's notice. The lake canoeist may prefer subtle strokes that will make minor directional changes or hold a course against the wind with a minimum of effort and without interfering with normal paddling rhythms. The river canoeist sees a rock ahead and has to move over fast; economy of effort is not a consideration. The river runner relies heavily on the draw, pry, and scull strokes and has also adapted similar strokes known as braces (discussed later in this chapter) to meet the special demands of white-water paddling. For the beginner, however, real mastery of the normal forward strokes, back paddling, the pry, the draw, the cross-draw, and sweeps is essential. One should be able to do these strokes equally well on either side of the canoe.

FERRYING

The most basic river maneuver is ferrying, a technique of moving across the current without being carried downstream. It consists of angling the canoe over in the current and then paddling upstream while maintaining that angle so that the boat is carried across the river while its downstream motion is slowed or stopped. If the stern is angled against the current and the canoeists back paddle, the crossing is a back ferry. If the bow is pointed upstream and angled against the current and the canoeists use a forward stroke, it is a forward ferry.

The ferry is basic to handling many river situations. Suppose, for instance, that one is paddling down a flat but fairly wide and swift river with steep banks, looking for a lunch spot or a place to spend the night. A little beach, which was concealed from view upstream by a large cottonwood, suddenly appears just off to the left on the other side of the river. If the occupants of the canoe simply point the bow over to the left and start paddling for shore, the current will carry them far downstream before they reach shore. They will then have to try to labor back upstream and probably have to give up if the current is very strong.

The correct technique is to ferry over to shore. As soon as the canoeists see the spot, the stern person draws or pries the stern over to the left at an angle to the current and both paddlers back paddle. Most of the effort of the back paddling works to counteract the downstream force of gravity and of the current, holding the canoe level with the landing spot. The angular component carries the canoe over to shore.

Ferrying is also usually the best way to put a canoe into the proper channel to run a particular section of river and is often suitable for avoiding obstructions. It is one of the most frequently used techniques in river paddling, whether by novices on mild streams or experts paddling difficult white-water. The back ferry is used when it can be, because it is convenient. The canoe has only to be angled over a little to be in back ferry position, and it is as easily reoriented when the ferry is completed.

As the current becomes stronger, forward ferries often become necessary, particularly if it is important that the canoe not be carried downstream at all. Since back paddling is always less powerful than propelling the canoe directly forward, the forward ferry will work against much stronger currents. The difficulty with the forward ferry is that it is performed with the stern headed downstream, not the position in which the boat is normally paddled. This presents no difficulty if one is ferrying all the way across the river, perhaps to move from one shore to the other to examine a blind section of river below, because in

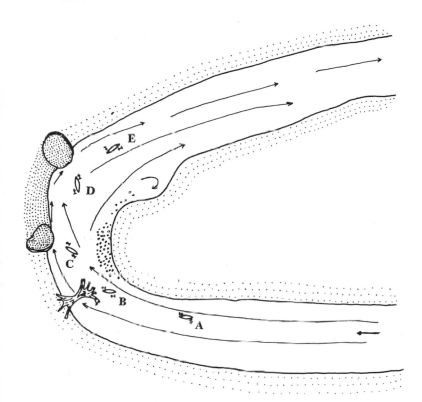

Back ferrying around a river bend. This is a typical river canoeing situation where the river goes around a sharp bend. The main current would carry the canoe first into the sweeper, or fallen tree at the left, where the paddlers would probably capsize and might be trapped underwater. Aiming the canoe toward the inside of the bend might work, but it would accelerate the canoe's velocity downriver. The paddlers take the better solution of a back ferry. At **A,** the bow paddler is still paddling forward, but the stern pries his end of the canoe over to set the ferry angle. Both canoeists then back paddle and the current sweeps the boat over to the right side of the channel to miss the tree. The back paddling also slows progress and allows inspection of what is to come while ensuring that if any obstacles are struck, the force of the blow will be reduced. After passing the sweeper **(B),** the paddlers reduce the force of their back paddling to allow the boat to be carried out into the main channel and avoid the characteristic gravel bar at the inside of the bend **(C).** They then continue to back ferry to keep away from the outside bank **(D).** After rounding the curve, the bow resumes forward paddling while the stern draws his end of the boat back to a position parallel with the current **(E).**

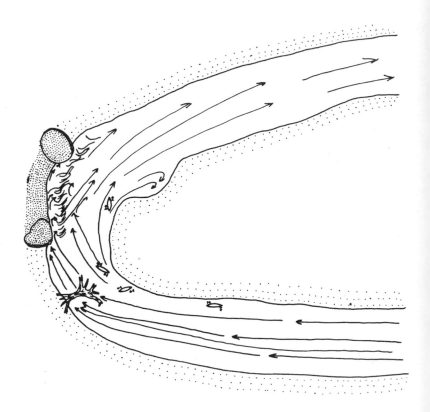

Back ferrying around a bend in high water. The same bend is shown here at a higher level of runoff. The current is much more powerful and dangerous now. The gravel bar at the inside of the bend is well underwater, and a huge curling wave has formed on the outside of the bend where the force of the current strikes the bank and is deflected. The canoeists decide to back ferry again, but this time they paddle hard to hug the inside of the bend, where the current is weaker. A mistake here that allowed the canoe to be taken into the sweeper or the outside of the bend could result in calamity. After rounding the bend, the paddlers can either continue to back ferry, which would bring them into the eddy, or resume forward paddling down the river.

this situation the canoe does not have to be turned in midstream. As we shall see, it is also quite easy to use a forward ferry when moving between eddies. But in other circumstances it is a matter of judgment whether the time lost in turning the canoe is compensated for by the extra power of the forward ferry.

The forward ferry is the favorite of the solo paddler most of the time because back paddling is even less efficient when paddling alone. Back ferrying in moderate currents is excellent practice for the single paddler, however. It will greatly improve both power and control in the back stroke. Try both the regular back stroke and the cross–back stroke, using a twisted body with a forward stroke on the opposite side of the canoe. The latter is a particular favorite of those who paddle decked white-water canoes, but it can also be used in an open boat. (A decked white-water canoe is one that is closed on the top except for one or more cockpits for the paddlers, to permit running very difficult white-water. A decked canoe is usually narrower than a conventional open canoe.) The single paddler doing a back ferry will often alternate between the regular and cross–back strokes, as one corrects the directional bias of the other.

You can calculate the ideal angle for a ferry by using elementary trigonometry, but as a practical matter you must learn it by experience. As long as the current speed is slower than the speed that the canoe can be paddled (forward or back, depending on which type of ferry is being used), the canoe is angled over as far as possible without losing ground. This angle becomes less and less as the current gets stronger. However, when the current becomes faster than top paddling speed, a canoe can travel farther across the river for each foot it is carried downstream by angling farther over again. It is rarely desirable to angle over more than forty-five degrees, however, even though theoretically you would get farthest in very fast water by paddling almost straight across. Problems with waves, entry into the current, and the danger of heading downstream broadside generally make this a poor alternative.

BOW AND STERN RESPONSIBILITIES

In lake paddling, most of the responsibility for setting a course and thus for calling out any necessary corrections falls on the stern paddler. This is the natural mode of operation simply because most steering is done from the stern. The bow paddler may call for a stroke to avoid an obstacle that can only be seen at the last minute, but otherwise he only sets the paddling rate.

In river canoeing the bow paddler, with a much better view of the river ahead, necessarily takes a far more active role. Steering generally consists of keeping the boat oriented with the current or in a ferry position, but rapid maneuvering may often be necessary to avoid striking rocks or other obstacles. The bow paddler will normally see such hazards first, so he leads or commands the response. This may vary sometimes with the situation and the experience of the two paddlers. Two people paddling a canoe must form a team, however, and when one yells a command, the other should respond by carrying it out immediately, asking questions later.

The simplest set of commands is based on a call for the desired result: "forward," "back," "right," or "left" are indications that the other paddler should move his or her end of the boat that way, with whatever stroke is called for by the circumstances. To ferry left, the bow paddler might start back paddling while calling "Left!" to the stern to get the angle set, and then "Back!" If the stern paddler was paddling on the starboard side, he would use a pry or reverse quarter sweep; if on the port, a draw. A team that paddles together regularly and becomes well-coordinated often needs only occasional commands. The stern keeps his end behind the bow most of the time, and in other maneuvers he is likely to know what his partner intends.

RIVER SAFETY

Before discussing paddling techniques for handling specific river problems, it may be well to discuss a few generalities, the most important of which have to do with safety precautions. The need for life preservers and adequate clothing, including wet suits for cold water, has been discussed but cannot be overemphasized. Circumstances differ, but when in doubt, wear the appropriate safety equipment. A good swimmer may not need a life preserver on a calm, warm river, but if the river is not known, white-water may lurk around the next bend. You may not plan to run it, but in case of an accidental upset you may swim through it quite unwillingly. In heavy rapids only a life preserver can assure one of enough time at the surface to be able to get sufficient air. Don't plan on grabbing a life preserver laid nearby in the canoe; if there is a chance that you may need it, wear it. In any upset you will have enough to do without trying to grab a vest and put it on.

Appreciation for the debilitating effects of cold water is also vital. If the water is cold enough so that you cannot wade around in it comfortably, the consequences of a spill must be weighed. One cannot last long in cold water without a wet suit.

Paddling in groups is usually the most sensible way to travel. On moderate rivers it may be safe enough for experienced people to paddle with a pair or even a single person in a canoe, but even the most expert will rarely canoe in white-water alone. Beginners must have others around for assistance. This is generally more practical in river canoeing anyhow, because shuttles are far less expensive, time consuming, and tedious when there are a number of people and canoes in the party. Since river canoeists normally put in at one place on a river and take out at another, a shuttle is inevitable on most trips. Although numbers do not guarantee safety if other precautions are not followed, the lack of numbers does ensure that the margin of safety will be slim, particularly for novices.

Proper advance knowledge of the river to be paddled is the most absolute of all safety rules. An expert may paddle down a river without knowing what is below because he knows what to watch for and never goes beyond a point where he can pull out of the current to inspect the river below. Novices, however, cannot know enough of their own abilities or the possible hazards on the river to use this method. Get detailed, *advance* knowledge of the section to be run,

The cardinal river safety rule is to portage all rapids unless you are *sure* they can be run safely. These canoeists are finishing a carry around a set of rapids in an extremely remote river canyon, where an injury or a lost canoe could be serious.

preferably by walking or driving along the shore and inspecting the water. Detailed descriptions from experienced people who appreciate the river's difficulties and the abilities of you and your group may be a reasonable substitute, but don't give much credence to information from a local nonboater or an ace kayaker who doesn't remember what it is like to be a beginner and has never even paddled a canoe, or to casual suggestions from a daredevil friend.

The fact that your informant has run the river section that you are interested in and knows your level of skill does not mean that his information is adequate for you. You may be told, for example, that another person of limited paddling experience went down and had little trouble. However, the fact that the paddler is inexperienced also means that he might not have recognized possible hazards that could change. The runoff level at which the other person went down the river and its level when *you* paddle it are vital. It will not be the same river when carrying twelve thousand cubic feet of water per second as it was when running at twelve hundred. Many rivers have gauges located at particular points that can be used as reference points for discussion, but it is also vital to be sure that the gauge has not been changed.

On dam-controlled rivers, release amounts and schedules are important for both safety and enjoyment, since the amount of water being released from the dam will determine the water level of the river. Large releases may make the river dangerous, or they may be the only thing to make it runnable. Calling the agency that controls the dam should often be standard procedure before driving to the river. On long trips you should also try to find out what the delay period is before a release reaches a particular section of the river.

Normally, it is only safe for a beginner to trust conversations with really experienced canoeists who also take an interest in novices and understand what their true capabilities are. The neophyte at river running must remember that runs that are trivial even for intermediate boaters may be far beyond his capacity. Progress both in paddling and in river reading skill is often rapid, so the difference in capability between a beginner and a canoeist with a year of river experience can be great.

A great deal of information can be obtained from maps, bridge elevations, and river descriptions in guidebooks, but most of it will be usable only after the paddler has had at least a moderate amount of experience. Even then, secondhand data should be viewed with a skeptical eye. Methods of judgment differ, and some guidebooks are notoriously inaccurate. Even those that are generally good are bound to have flaws, perhaps a portage around a fifteen-foot waterfall that was somehow dropped from a page proof. Ultimately, the canoeist is responsible for his own safety, which means scouting whenever the river ahead cannot be seen and retreat would be difficult. For the beginner, this often means scouting in advance a whole run from the shore.

One should be particularly wary of partially scouting a river from a road or trail, noting that 95 percent is straightforward, and assuming that the little section one cannot see is the same. The remaining 5 percent is the most likely location for a nasty rapid, waterfall, or dangerous bend. A sheer canyon or a rapid drop is just the place in a river where a road or trail is most likely to wander away to easier terrain. Scouting a river badly is often worse than not scouting it at all, since it can lead to a false sense of confidence.

When actually running a river, follow the same rules of scouting ahead whenever a passage cannot be seen and stopping before the point of no return is passed. You can often hear rapids, but not always, and there are other possible hazards as well. Rapids are often indicated when the river disappears ahead, with only the top edge of the drop visible. The bow paddler can stand to try to see what is ahead, but it is often impossible to tell from the water whether the river drops one foot or twenty. Landing and walking ahead to check is the only safe solution. Exercise care in rounding blind turns, and if the water is swift it is often necessary to scout such bends from above.

Unless one already knows the river or it is very slow, it is generally safest to travel around bends as far inside as depth permits. The slowest water is there, and if problems occur ahead one is close to the eddy that usually forms around the inside corner. Various kinds of dangerous waves, swift water, and fallen trees are all likely on the outside of the turn, which may make the best sporting run—but only if one is sure of its safety. In low water the outside will be the most likely place to avoid running aground.

The greatest danger in river running is posed by sweepers, fallen trees or logs that have washed down the river and extend across the channel. If the canoe's path is blocked by a midstream boulder, the current will normally be diverted around it and will tend to carry the canoe around too. If a crash and a capsize do occur, normally the worst consequence is to have the canoe broach (be caught broadside) on the rock while the canoeists are thrown into the water. A tree hanging across the water with its branches dipping into the current does not divert it, however, nor does a log jammed across a chute between two boulders. The canoe may be caught and turned over, or the paddlers may simply be swept out unceremoniously while the boat slides under. The real danger, however, is that a swimmer dumped from a canoe may be caught by branches or snags protruding into the water and be unable to free himself. Many deaths have resulted from this kind of trap, even among experienced and well-equipped boaters. Avoid sweepers at all costs and keep a good lookout for them. When traveling under overhanging vegetation in milder circumstances, the bow paddler should not grab branches to slow or stop the canoe because the current will swing the stern around. In general, holding canes or branches is not a good idea at all, but if it is done the person in the stern should do it.

The beginner should try to learn to gauge current speed as soon as he starts to paddle on rivers. It is not too important to be able to estimate the speed in miles or kilometers per hour, though this is useful, but you should have a good feeling for the relative speed of the water compared with paddling speed. Then it is possible to judge whether or not you could land on a spit if trouble appeared around a bend or if scouting is essential because the current is too strong to fight. The speed at which canoeists can paddle depends on skill, strength, boat design, and other factors, but some rough figures may be useful to indicate the order of magnitude. Hard back paddling will probably result in a speed of approximately one or two miles per hour, with forward paddling being two or three times that. To give some idea of limits, a winning speed for a two-man racing canoe in international flat-water competition over a course of a little over six miles is somewhat over eight miles per hour. This is much faster than even a championship team could possibly paddle a normal canoe. Ten miles per hour is a fast speed for a river current, and speeds faster than fifteen miles per hour are quite rare. In steep drops, turbulence begins to limit the speed at which water can travel.

When a river divides into two sections, it is generally best to keep to the larger branch, particularly if there is a drop visible, because the larger channel is less likely to be obstructed. One cannot avoid a drop by taking a smaller channel (except by portaging), since the water level will be the same when the two converge again.

Easy drops on a river often begin with rather shallow riffles over beds of small stones. The river becomes shallower where the water accelerates. (Remember that since the same quantity of water goes by every point along the shore between tributaries or diversions, the width or depth must be reduced if the water goes faster.) In such cases an inverted **V** of smooth water often points out the main channel. Such a **V** is also often the best channel marker in chutes of serious whitewater, but cautions must be observed there. In riffles, the paddler's main concern is staying in the main channel and away from the shallows. Bars form at the insides of bends, downstream of obstacles in the water, and anywhere else that the water is slowed. They will often form for various reasons diagonally across the river and the current will turn to run over these perpendicularly over the bar. Noting the current's shift will warn the canoeist about the bar and should also alert him to reorient the canoe to keep it parallel with the current. This is particularly desirable at shallow spots where the canoe's bottom might hit something, because the boat is far more likely to capsize if broadside to the current.

The novice must learn as soon as possible to recognize the signs of obstructions in the water. These are likely to be harder to see in slow-moving water than in more difficult fast-moving currents, because water slipping easily by a rock or stump does not roil around nearly as much as water ripping by quickly. Nasty rapids may be more difficult to read than the signs made by a few underwater boulders in slow water, but they are easier to see.

The most obvious sign of an obstruction, other than the top of a rock that clearly has underlying support, is a V with the point upstream. Such a V is always the result of something in the water's path, either breaking the surface or just under it. Another sign of a bottom scraper is a smooth hump, or pillow, in the water, formed by water sliding over the top of a smooth boulder. The shape of a pillow is quite different from that of standing waves, which occur in regular series of decreasing size and are crested, whereas pillows are rounded. Standing waves occur in deep water and mark a good course for the canoeist if they are so big as to present a danger of swamping the boat.

In clear water you will often be able to see subsurface rocks, but it may be difficult to judge their depth and to tell whether the canoe will clear them or you will have to dodge. If the current is fast enough to form a pillow over the rock, the shape of the pillow and its position with respect to the rock indicate the depth of the water. If the water forms riffles over the rock, it is barely covered. An obstruction submerged a bit more deeply will have a pillow directly over it. A more deeply buried rock will have a pillow formed somewhat downstream.

In rough water a calm spot is not formed by chance but is the protected area downstream of a slightly submerged object. If you are trying to reach the calm spot, do it from downstream. Running directly for it from above will almost certainly run your canoe's bottom over a rock.

To avoid obstructions in river canoeing it is important for the beginner to break the habit of steering around them, as is most often done when paddling on lakes. Remember that the canoe has a good deal of forward momentum when it is traveling in a swift current and that gravity and the force of the surrounding water are both working to carry the canoe along downriver right into any obstacle in its path. There is an additional danger as well: if the paddlers try to steer the canoe around a boulder, for example, using sweep strokes, they add to the downstream speed of the canoe while turning it sideways, so in the likely event that they cannot avoid the rock, the canoe will not only hit it but will hit broadside. This will frequently cause the canoe to broach on the rock, with its center caught on the boulder and the current pushing on both ends, pinning the canoe. The situation is exacerbated by the current pushing on the bottom of the canoe, tending to roll it upstream and capsize it. Then the pouring water rushes into the canoe, exerting incredible force that not only holds it on the boulder but may bend or break it.

In river canoeing it is usually best to avoid obstructions by using strokes that move the whole canoe directly to the side or by back ferrying. In the first case, one paddler pries while the other draws or equivalent sculling strokes are used. The solo paddler pries or draws, as necessary. All the power of the strokes is concentrated on moving the canoe in the proper direction. The canoe is kept aligned with the current so that it presents a smaller target as it sweeps past rocks and will be more easily carried around by the cushion of water in a near miss. If a hit does occur, the boat will be far less likely to broach on either the boulder struck or the next one downstream.

Back ferrying also has advantages for evasive maneuvering. Although the canoe is angled somewhat against the current, the angle is not too great and is kept under control. Much of the force of the paddling is against the current, so the forward progress of the canoe toward the obstruction is slowed, the paddlers are given more time to react, the cushioning current around a boulder also has more time to act on the canoe, and the potential force of a collision, if it does occur, is reduced.

One of the first things the canoeist must learn before paddling on faster rivers is how to get in and out of eddies. The eddy is the refuge for the paddler in swift current, a resting or landing spot to examine

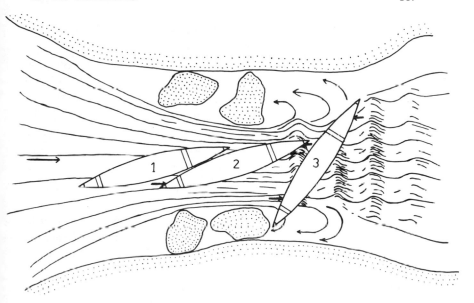

Broaching in a chute. It is important in many situations on a river to keep the canoe aligned with the current. Here a canoe is shown entering a chute just a little askew (1). The canoe accelerates with the water as it goes down the drop, and it is still accelerating when the bow hits the slowing water in the standing waves below (2). Since the boat is at an angle, the slower water hits one side of the bow, pushing it back, and it is also decelerated because it is starting to climb the wave. This pushing of the water on one side starts to rotate the canoe, and as the canoe begins to slow, the fast water behind pushes on the other side of the stern, increasing the force acting to turn the canoe. As a result, the canoe is spun into a position across the current (3), in which unskillful paddlers are likely to lose their balance and where the canoe is much more vulnerable to damage if it should hit a rock.

the river below, relax muscles and nerves for a few minutes, or beach the canoe and get out. In quick water it is impossible for a paddler to master the situation without some ability to enter and leave eddies with grace and control. Otherwise a river run may be exciting, but it is likely to be expensive, since few can afford to lose very many canoes. It may also be disastrous, if the river turns out to be at all dangerous.

The art of river canoeing is to run through swift water in control, not in daredevil escapades.

At first glance, entering an eddy might seem easy enough. The canoeists might simply point their bow at it and paddle forward. In a mild current this tactic might work, although some awkward and unexpected turns and shifts of balance are likely even then. If the current and thus the eddy are moderately strong, however, what happens to the team simply trying to paddle directly into the eddy is instructive. As the bow crosses the eddy line it is caught by the upstream eddy current and begins to move that direction. Most of the hull, still in the grip of the main current, continues to be swept downstream. As a result, the canoe quickly turns 180 degrees and the bow is rotated back out of the eddy. Assuming that the paddlers are not thrown far enough off-balance to be dumped into the river, they are left floating along backward, looking upstream at the receding eddy.

On the next attempt, our determined canoeists may try driving into the eddy really hard, so as to break through the eddy line before they are carried on downstream by the main current. This is in fact the best method of all, but only after some important refinements in technique have been learned, to avoid the fate about to befall our persevering friends. As they drive through the eddy line, the bow is again swung upstream (though not as far) so that the canoe is broadside as it enters the eddy. The bodies of the paddlers and the canoe itself have built up a good deal of downstream momentum, but the bottom of the hull is now caught in the upstream current of the eddy. The result is a simple application of the laws of motion: the paddlers, paddles, and upper part of the canoe continue traveling downriver, whereas the lower part of the hull begins moving upriver, with the effect of a rapid capsize downstream. If our friends are lucky they and the canoe end up floating around in the eddy, where it is at least easier to put things back together. If not, the capsize may occur with only half the canoe in the eddy, so that all are washed out again and proceed downstream in disorder.

The ferry provides the simplest way into an eddy. The canoeists bring the canoe along parallel to and very close to the eddy line, back paddling as they approach, to avoid overshooting. As the eddy is approached, the bow continues back paddling while the stern draws or pries his end into the eddy as high as possible. Good timing is important here, as it always is in eddy maneuvers, but this will come with practice. A couple of fast, powerful strokes may be necessary to force the stern through the eddy line and set the angle of the canoe, but once it is set, both paddlers should back paddle hard. The main current now works for them. Instead of sweeping the upstream end of the boat by, it works on the downstream end and pushes it into the eddy after the stern, leaving the canoe settled nicely in the eddy and pointing downstream. The main errors likely to be made are in performing the actions too slowly or indecisively, but the result will be normally just to miss the eddy, with the canoe still heading downstream and the paddlers in balance. The canoeists are then ready for another attempt or for evasive action in case of downstream problems, rather than being left out of balance with the canoe spinning out of control.

Paddlers of closed white-water canoes playing in a chute. The canoeists are ferrying back and forth between two eddies on opposite sides of a big drop. Only experts would even consider running an open boat through this section.

The forward ferry can also be used to enter an eddy, and because the strokes are more powerful it is more effective. This technique should be practiced by beginners to enter eddies in large sections of otherwise unobstructed water, since it requires that the bow be facing upstream, and if the eddy is missed the canoe is left running down stern first. More important, in turning the canoe upstream or back down after an abortive attempt, the boat is left in a bad position for broaching, a likely situation for novices in an area with many rocks.

The solo canoeist can ferry in and out of eddies, too, but because of reduced power and control of the angle of the canoe, it will require more dextrous handling of the boat. The single paddler will thus often prefer the forward ferry or the leaning strokes for entering eddies that follow.

The easiest way to get out of an eddy is usually to paddle out the weaker downstream end, where the eddy line is far less powerful. In faster rivers eddies may be found that are too strong to permit this sort of exit, but by the time he is paddling in this sort of current, the canoeist should have learned the braces and eddy turns. Ferrying into the eddy (also termed *setting in*) and paddling out the lower end are sufficient for beginning river runs.

The Braces

The paddle brace. This stroke, the key to modern white-water canoeing, is the technique of leaning hard on the extended paddle, using the resistance of the water to support most of the weight of the body. Strong braces enable canoeists to balance reliably even in turbulent water, because the brace is like a portable outrigger that the paddler can extend or withdraw at will.

Braces have many subtle applications in difficult water, but mastering them is well worthwhile for any paddler, whether or not he ever expects to canoe in white-water or large waves. Learning the braces develops a great deal of confidence, and strokes such as the draw become far more powerful as the canoeist gains faith in his ability to lean out on his paddle. Once the braces have been learned, one begins to appreciate the incredible versatility of the canoe.

The high brace. There are two distinct braces used in canoeing, each with many variations. The high brace is similar to a draw stroke, with the paddle held high, both forearms pointed upward, and the shaft above the chest, often above or even above and behind the head. In the high brace the power face of the paddle pushes down on the water. The blade may lie almost flat on the water or tilt as high as the perpendicular, and the side-to-side angle may vary as well, depending on the purpose of the brace. Most commonly, however, the paddle is fairly flat in a brace and closer to vertical in a draw. The two strokes tend to blend together in white-water canoeing, for in many rough-water situations a combination is needed.

The low brace. In the low brace the paddle is held as though one were just starting a recovery from a forward stroke, with the blade parallel to the surface of the water as though it had just been feathered; it is angled out to the rear. The forearm holding the lower part of the shaft is pointed straight down and presses the nonpower face of the blade down against the water.

You should obtain some initial practice with the braces on flat water before trying them in the river, in order to develop a little confidence in the technique of leaning on the paddle. To be effective a brace must have a great deal of the paddler's weight on it; a timid brace may be worse than none at all. The low brace is the easier to learn for most people; in fact, novices often instinctively use a pale version of it for steering corrections at the end of a forward stroke when paddling at the stern or the center of the canoe.

Sit in the canoe and stick the paddle out at an angle of sixty degrees or so, rock over to the paddle side, and lean on the water. Keep this up until you are putting much weight on the paddle and tipping the canoe some distance. If you are paddling with someone else, have him lay his paddle down and try to tip the canoe over toward your paddle side while you hold it up with a low brace. Keep this up until you have developed some confidence in the power of the brace and can lean out on it *hard*. Be prepared to tip over a few times while practicing braces—if you don't, you're not really trying.

Once you can lean over and recover with the low brace, try starting

Practicing the low brace on flat water. The paddler has brought the canoe up to speed and is leaning over on the paddle in a low brace position. The canoe is slowing and pivoting around the paddle. The nonpower face of the paddle— the side that faced forward during the regular paddling—is down against the water.

The low brace in fast water. The canoeist is across the current, riding over a standing wave, and leaning downstream as one must to avoid capsizing or taking on water. The low brace is being used to lean on, so the paddler needs to rely less on balance. The drag of the paddle in the water will also help pull the canoe over the wave. Note that the paddling-side hand pushes down on the paddle shaft, whereas the off-side hand pulls up on the grip.

with the paddle all the way back at the stern, with the outside edge raised an inch or two. Lean over onto the paddle and sweep it slowly forward. This sweep should result in an even more powerful bracing action and will also turn the canoe in the opposite direction from the sweep. Practice this also until you are confident of it. Then paddle the canoe forward at a good rate until you have reached top speed and lean over onto a low brace, first without the sweep, then with it. Note the turning effect of the brace when the canoe is moving. The brace has the same rotational effect if the canoe is stationary and the water is moving. Try a number of braces after paddling the canoe up to speed. You should be leaning strongly into the turn if you are bracing hard.

Once you are confident of the low brace try the high one, and be even better prepared for a few dunkings. It is important to learn how far you can lean out on the high brace before falling into the water. Start the high brace like a draw, reaching out as far as you dare, then a little farther. Lay the paddle a bit flatter on the water than you would

Practicing a high brace on flat water. The canoeist has paddled the boat to speed and is now leaning over on a high brace. The paddle supports his weight, and the canoe turns around the paddle. Note that the power face is down and the hand holding the grip is high. The face of the blade is angled slightly up.

in a draw so that you can reach farther. For this long reach the paddle shaft should pass over your head. Learn the high brace from the kneeling position so you have good control of the canoe through your legs. Practice tipping the boat and righting it with the brace, and if you are paddling double, have your partner try to tip the canoe against your brace. Try sculling on the brace, which will enable you to lean on it continuously. As with the low brace, paddle the canoe up to speed a number of times and then lean out on a high brace, experimenting with placing it a little forward and a little back, noting the effects. Use some draw strokes in the same way as the brace.

Develop both the low and the high braces on both sides of the canoe in flat water; then you are ready to try them on the river.

Eddy Turns

Braces give the canoeist another tool to deal with the problems of entering and leaving eddies. Although ferrying can be a useful method in many situations, it is a bit too slow and weak for others. It is often possible to enter an eddy only by driving directly into it at the highest possible point. To do this, one must have some way of counteracting the tendency of the canoe to flip over to the outside of the turn. The method used is the same a bicyclist uses to prevent tipping over as he goes around a tight corner: leaning into the turn. By using a brace, the canoeist can also lean to the inside of the turn without needing to worry about the exact angle needed. With the brace to push on, a strong lean can be used and the canoe can simply be pushed back upright at the end of the turn.

However, in many situations the brace can do something more than just allow the paddlers to lean into the turn. It can provide the same anchor against slipping that the tires of the cyclist do. Consider a canoe being paddled tandem with the bow paddling on the right and the stern on the left. A tricky section is coming up and there is a large boulder in the center of the river just ahead, which they will pass just to the left. The eddy formed by this boulder will be just the place to stop and get a good look at the passage below. As they approach the boulder, the bow paddler makes a couple of diagonal draw strokes to point the canoe at an angle toward the very top of the eddy, knowing that the higher the canoe hits the eddy line, the easier and surer the entrance will be. Both paddlers drive hard as the canoe passes the boulder, and the bow of the canoe hits the top of the eddy at an angle of about thirty degrees. As the bow enters the eddy, the stern paddler continues to power the boat forward, so as to be sure that it punches on through the eddy line. But as soon as the nose of the boat has pushed into the reverse current, the bow paddler leans far out to the right and forward and plants a high brace deep in the eddy. The effect is dramatic. Not only does the lean and grab of the paddle prevent the bottom of the boat from being swept out from under the canoeists, but it also acts as an anchor that prevents the canoe from slipping toward the outside of the turn and provides a pivot for the turn itself. The canoe whips around the paddle in a sharp turn and ends facing upstream near the top of the eddy. This, the classic eddy turn, is very ef-

The paddler of a closed boat using a high brace for an eddy turn into the main current, which travels from left to right in the photograph. The boat has just entered the current from the eddy at the lower right and is pivoting around the paddle. Note that the canoeist is leaning into the turn and downstream on the brace.

fective and is one of the most satisfying river maneuvers to perform. The solo canoeist paddling on the right side of the boat would make the turn in almost the identical way, though he would have to drive the bow of the canoe in a little farther before reaching out for the brace.

Several details are critical to the successful eddy turn. It is essential that the bracing paddle be in the eddy current. The brace is effective as a pivot because the blade is embedded in water going in the opposite direction from the downstream momentum of the canoe. If the brace is thrown too early, so that the paddle is in the main current or the eddy line, it will not serve its purpose. The canoe must enter the eddy at enough of an angle so that the bow drives into the slack water. Beginners tend to aim at too shallow an angle because they are afraid of hitting the boulder, which will result in a weak turn and often in missing the eddy altogether. The boat will turn into the eddy only if the bow is planted in it as well as the paddle. If only the paddle blade is in the upstream current, the canoe will still make the turn, but it will remain in the main current, floating down backward.

The ideal eddy turn is the one using the high brace, made into an eddy on the paddling side of the bow or the solo paddler. This turn is much more powerful and precise than the one to the stern's paddling side or the off side of the single paddler. The difference is great enough that some canoeists prefer to switch paddling sides to have the bow paddle or single paddle on the inside of the turn. Whether or not you prefer this method, it is important to practice the off-side turn as well, since situations arise when it must be used.

The same initial procedure is followed when a turn is being made into an eddy on the off side. The paddlers drive the bow of the canoe into the eddy as high as possible and at an angle sufficient to guarantee penetration. Hitting the top of the eddy is even more important, because there will be far more sideslipping in an off-side turn. As the nose of the canoe enters the eddy, the paddlers lean into the turn. The bow person continues to paddle forward hard until the bow is well into the eddy and then switches to a cross-draw or pry to spin the canoe around. The stern braces to the inside, normally using a low brace. This brace will keep the canoe from tipping, but it does not have the pivoting effect of the brace in the eddy, for the stern's brace will be out in the main current until the turn is completed. As soon as the turn is completed, the bow must go back into a forward stroke.

The solo paddler cannot rely on this weaker brace but must lean into the turn and keep paddling, relying on balance to stay up. A sweep on the outside is generally used to help bring the canoe around. It is important to note that leaning too far into the turn is rarely the problem, especially for beginners.

A canoe leaving an eddy across a strong line of differences in current runs perhaps an even greater risk of capsizing than one entering an eddy because the current it suddenly encounters is that of the powerful main channel. It is often desirable for several reasons to cross the eddy line at the top, its strongest section. If there are difficulties downstream, the maximum space possible should be allowed to maneuver into position to meet them. Furthermore, the powerful crosscurrents at the eddy line can be to the skilled canoeists' advantage. With proper bracing techniques, they can use the force of the water shooting by to turn the canoe effortlessly downstream again or propel it far across the channel.

As with the turn into the eddy, the first principle of reentry into the main current is to lean into the turn. More generally, lean the canoe downstream as it enters the main channel. *Do not lean upstream* (a lean upstream seems to be instinctive in beginning canoeists). The water rushing under the bottom of the canoe that is entering the current will grab it and rip it out from under the boaters, dumping them into the water upstream. Any lean in this direction will guarantee a capsize at bewildering speed. Leaning downstream counteracts this tendency of the river to pull the bottom of the boat out from under its occupants.

When entering the main current, use braces again when possible to stabilize the downstream lean, lending it additional stability. Bracing downstream is particularly powerful while the water is moving faster

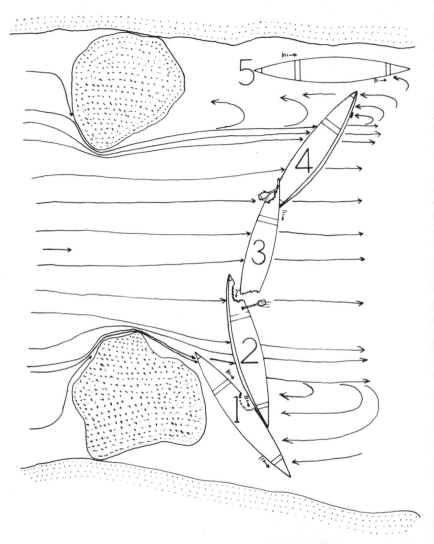

Eddy turns into and out of the current. This maneuver, often known as the **S**-turn, links two eddy turns to cross a chute of fast water, and it shows turns for both leaving and entering an eddy, with the paddles on both the most advantageous sides of the canoe and the less favorable sides.

In **(1)** the paddlers are just leaving the eddy, paddling hard into the eddy than the canoe because the water shooting under the paddle gives it additional lift, making it virtually impossible to capsize a canoe that is leaned well downstream against such a brace.

As with the turn into an eddy, maximum stability is obtained when the solo or bow paddler is on the brace side, the inside of the turn. This is far less important when leaving the eddy than when entering it, however, because a strong lean is safer on entering the main current. One does not have to return to an upright position as quickly because of the continued action of the current on the bottom of the boat. A single paddler simply leans hard downstream while continuing to paddle on the upstream side, if necessary, whereas the stern in a team boat uses either a high or low brace. The situation on leaving an eddy is also less critical, because the eddy itself provides the perfect spot to switch paddling sides if that is wanted, without risk of having an emergency occur during the change.

To turn downstream out of an eddy, simply drive the canoe into the eddy line at an angle of about forty-five degrees. As the bow enters the main current it will tend to be swept downstream. If the bow person is

line, with the canoe angled upstream. They hit the current as high as possible to make maximum use of its power to carry them across. As the bow enters the current, it leans hard downstream onto a high brace **(2),** which catches the current and spins the canoe to prevent it from being capsized upstream by the current tugging at the bottom of the hull. The stern continues to paddle forward hard. Once the canoe is turned and in the main current, the downstream lean can be reduced and the bow can resume hard forward paddling **(3)** to catch the eddy on the other side before the boat is carried too far downstream. As the bow enters the eddy on the opposite side, again at a good angle **(4)** and traveling fast, the stern paddler leans into the turn and holds the boat up with a low brace while the bow pries in the eddy current. (A cross-draw could also be used.) This is a less powerful turn than it would be if the paddles were on opposite sides so that the bow could use a high brace and the stern continue to paddle forward hard. As soon as most of the canoe is in the eddy and the danger of capsizing is over, the paddlers pull forward hard again to get high in the eddy **(5).** They are now in a position to cross back over if they wish, using either an S-turn in the reverse direction or a ferry.

paddling on the downstream side, he can simply brace well forward and the force of the water on the blade will complete the turn. The canoe makes a fast pirouette out into the current and is off downstream in one graceful movement. If the bow person is paddling on the other side, a bit of sweep accomplishes the same purpose. The single paddler uses the same methods as the bow of a tandem boat, reaching forward with a high brace for the turn, or, when it is needed, putting a little sweep in the forward stroke on the upstream side. With a fast enough current, depending on wave formations, the sweep may not even be necessary. A strong downstream lean is always essential, however.

The exit from an eddy can also be the beginning of a ferry across the channel, perhaps to reach another eddy, to make a landing on the shore, or to position the canoe to avoid obstructions below. The bow is driven through the eddy line as before, though as fast as possible and at the sharpest angle that will still get the nose of the boat through, perhaps thirty degrees. At this point, make an effort to maintain the angle of the canoe as it enters the main current, instead of allowing the boat to be whipped around by the force of the water. Drive the canoe as far out as possible before the brace is used, since the key to retaining the ferry angle is getting the whole hull into the main current so that the current is not pushing one way on the bow and the eddy the other way on the stern. If there is a stern paddler, he should continue to drive forward and maintain the canoe's entry angle. If the bow or single canoeist is paddling on the downstream side and uses the high brace, it is used a little farther back than in the eddy turn. The blade angle is set so that the current pushes the paddle as well as the canoe across the river.

Ferrying into a fast jet from an eddy is quite effective once the paddlers have acquired the knack. Forward momentum is attained with the help of the eddy current before the main channel is entered, so that when the canoe does break through the eddy line it is pushed rapidly across the river while the forward momentum is being lost. Skilled paddlers often ferry back and forth across a fast jet without even bracing, simply by using a downstream lean to avoid being tipped over and the strength of the current to carry them across. Beginners should make full use of both their braces and forward paddling power, however.

There are numerous combinations that can be worked out using eddy turns, backward eddy turns, forward and backward ferries, and similar maneuvers to move back and forth in particular sections of a river. White-water paddlers speak of playing a rapid, working out all the combinations that can be used in a given spot in the river. Moving back and forth between eddies using different techniques is, in fact, one of the best ways to learn to handle a canoe well in fast water and to ready oneself for more difficult rivers.

One common combination is a forward ferry across a fast chute between eddies on either side. After entering the water as described, the canoe is carried across into the opposite eddy and will enter it in the classic ferry position. All the paddlers need do is to lean and brace downstream as they are carried across, then push back up into balance as the far eddy is entered. The process can then be repeated going back the other way.

Another method of crossing between two eddies is the S-turn, a combination of two eddy turns. The canoe is driven out of the eddy on one side with an eddy turn, and as it turns partway downstream, the paddlers drive it across the channel, still leaning downstream. When the bow enters the eddy line on the other side the balance is shifted, a brace is thrown on the other side, and an eddy turn is made into the far eddy. The whole maneuver is graceful and exciting.

WHITE-WATER PADDLING

Once a canoeist has mastered eddy turns in moderate currents, he is ready to attempt easy white-water runs. There is, of course, no really clear distinction between one level of difficulty and the next, nor between two kinds of difficulty. Classification systems exist, but at best they give an imprecise approximation to allow comparison between one river and the next.

The term *white-water* implies a good deal of turbulence, froth, and foam whipped up by water cascading over stones and boulders, being thrown about as it races downstream, and in its turn beating against obstructions in its path and gradually wearing them away. Although it means different things to different paddlers, white-water always implies challenge and excitement. A successful run down a rapid will demand of the canoeist a careful assessment of the river and the path of the water, an analysis of the way in which the canoe can be maneuvered through, and then a precise execution of the whole sequence, perhaps including a number of last-minute changes in plan as a new view is gained from the water level.

The elements of judgment and planning, of memorizing a run and the actions that will be needed to come through it, cannot be overemphasized. It is the point most likely to be neglected by beginners but never by experts. Experienced canoeists may seem sometimes to approach and run a section of white-water while paying little or no attention to it, but this is because the serious paddler can often analyze a simple section at a glance. A seemingly heedless leap into the maelstrom is made not because the master is unconcerned with what is around the bend but rather because he has noted an eddy where the canoe can be pulled in for a look at what is below and because long experience has convinced him that there is no chance of missing that eddy.

Reading water, memorizing its course, and being able to recognize the same features equally well from shore and from the middle of the water are the most difficult white-water skills to acquire and the most important. A river runner who knows both the water and his own skills precisely and can match them up without major errors will be a far more competent canoeist on the water than one who has superior paddling skills but only a vague idea of what he can run and what may prove too dangerous.

Chutes

The most elementary white-water run is that of paddling straight down a chute. The most important thing to ascertain is whether there is enough clearance for the canoe to be able to run the chute without being caught in a bottleneck or running aground. In particular, one should watch for disturbances in the center that might indicate projections just under the surface. Most chutes are clear, though, both because their power rapidly sweeps obstructions away and because their concentration of a large flow in a small area ensures good depth.

At the bottom of a chute there is normally a pool with a series of standing waves indicating deeper, slower water where the energy of the current from the chute is dissipated. Such waves are a good sign whose absence should make one suspicious of a shallow spot or a sharp rock at the bottom of the chute. But even in the best of circumstances canoeists should expect to encounter several problems at the chute bottom. First, as the bow of the canoe runs into the slower water, it meets resistance when it plunges down and is pushed back by its own buoyancy and by the backward drag of the slower water. At the same time, the stern remains in the fast water of the chute and is pushed forward. In this situation there is a strong tendency for the canoe to broach (to be pushed perpendicular to the current), especially if the paddlers have allowed it to swing around to an angle with the line of flow of the water. Broaching at this stage is often serious because several other pitfalls may await the canoe that swings across the current here. The boat might be caught on a downstream boulder, the fast water of the chute may capsize the broached canoe, or the standing waves may cause problems for the paddlers. In case the wave below the chute is a keeper, a crossways position is the worst possible one for the canoe.

A beginner running a chute should normally concentrate on keeping the canoe straight and paddling hard at the bottom to keep it that way and to push on through the standing waves below. As those waves become larger, however, they may cause problems of their own for open canoes, since the bow or stern can plunge into the troughs between waves and take on a large amount of water. One such plunge is not serious if the paddlers can eddy out below and bail the boat, but taking on water in the middle of a rapid is a portent of more problems to come. The bilge (water) is a "live load"; it does not stay neatly tied under the center thwart like a duffel bag but slides around and throws the balance of the canoe off at the most inopportune times. Thus, a line of big haystacks at the bottom of a chute should warn beginners off unless there is ample safe water below and the relation between the paddlers' dress and the water temperature is such that they need not fear a dunking.

Standing Waves

For the paddler of a closed white-water canoe with a spray skirt (described in Chapter 9) sealing off the cockpit, standing waves generally mean a fun ride. The canoe may plunge through some waves so that they break in the paddler's face and bob up so high on other waves that he may have trouble reaching the water with the paddle; since there is no worry about swamping, the paddler can charge through with impunity. Alternatively, he may ride through sideways, either kneeling in balance or bracing on the downstream side. Conventional cruising canoes can be made watertight too, with the addition of a spray deck, a cover made of fabric, plywood, or fiberglass that covers the canoe, except in cases where the canoe has a cockpit with a rim for spray skirts. Spray decks give the paddlers of standard canoes many of the options of the owners of true white-water boats, although it is usually still impossible to develop a reliable Eskimo roll except in the specialized canoes. (Canoeists with suitable boats can learn to right a capsized canoe without leaving it, using their paddles for leverage against the water. The technique is called Eskimo rolling because it was first developed by Eskimo kayakers. See Chapter 9.)

Paddlers of open canoes need to exercise a good deal of care in ploughing through standing waves, lest the canoe be swamped. When paddling through difficult rapids it is not uncommon to ship a good deal of water, and you will often have to bail in the next calm stretch or pull over to shore or into an eddy at the end of the rapid. You have to calculate your prospects carefully before starting a run, however. Each gallon of water shipped guarantees a little more trouble with the next haystack, and if you reach the end of a run where a rock has to be dodged with half a boat full of water you will find out how hard it is to move all that weight around.

If standing waves are high enough to be threatening, the canoe can often be sneaked around to one side, where the waves are a little smaller and more manageable. The canoe will also plunge less if it is angled somewhat with respect to the waves. This maneuver, known as quartering into the waves, allows more of the hull to be lifted at the same time while reducing the amount of pitching so that less water is likely to be shipped. The canoe will roll more when quartering, however, so paddlers must be ready to brace to hold it steady.

Braces can be used in two ways to steady a canoe during a run through rough water. If you feel the canoe tipping too much to one side or the other, you can throw a quick brace to right it. This is a reactive or corrective brace, used on the side toward which the canoe is being tipped. It is less desirable than other techniques because it tends to be a last-minute maneuver leaving the canoeist always a little too close to capsizing for comfort and often resulting in a capsize if it is not strong enough to correct the situation. In the most common type of capsizing, where a fast current is sweeping the bottom of the canoe out from under the paddlers, the reactive brace will normally be upstream, which is a weak brace because the current tends to catch the paddle blade and sweep it under.

The better bracing technique is the anticipatory brace, like the one used in an eddy turn. The paddler notes ahead of time which way the current will act on the canoe, then leans and braces in the opposite direction, normally downstream. With a team of two paddlers, the appropriate member braces while both lean. A single paddler may have to lean without a brace, holding the paddle ready for a reactive brace on the other side if the lean does not go far enough. Normally, one should lean and brace downstream; it is quite unlikely that a canoe will capsize in this direction against a brace, and the push of the paddle against the water helps the downstream gunwale to float clear of waves. The lean keeps the upstream gunwale high. One advantage of anticipatory bracing is that if it fails, you can still use a reactive brace on the other side. Leaning out on a downstream brace is a good position from which to survey the water to come. The position lacks the desperate quality of the reactive brace.

It is possible for a canoeist to run standing waves sideways in an open canoe, leaning downstream, with a downstream brace with the paddle on that side, but this is not usually a good idea except in closed white-water boats. The canoe is extremely vulnerable to complete swamping when running this way, since a wave breaking over the gunwale will dump water in the length of the canoe, while a boat running straight or quartering will take in water only over the bows. A swamped canoe aligned across the channel will be difficult to reorient and will be in the worst position if it should be carried into a rock.

Rollers and Holes

These are often play spots for paddlers in special white-water boats, provided these spots are not too large and not keepers. Paddlers of closed white-water boats, which are sealed against shipping water, delight in running holes sideways, reaching far out with a deep downstream brace to pull out or dropping the bow or stern into the hole to pop out on the buoyancy bounce.

For the open canoe, though, even one with a spray deck, holes are good places to avoid. Tiny holes are generally downstream of rocks too close to the surface to provide clearance for the hull, and larger holes will swamp an open boat in a split second. Spray decks are not generally strong enough to stand the pressure they would receive if immersed in a large hole. In fact, even paddlers of white-water boats who do much playing in holes usually reinforce the decks of their boats with special beams or bulkheads to prevent the decks from collapsing under the pressure. A paddler playing in a hole with a white-water canoe can easily sink the bow six feet into the water before popping out, and the pressure on the deck at this depth will be about 2.5 pounds per square inch.

If a small dam with a roller below it is being run in an open canoe, it should be taken straight on, with the canoeists paddling hard as the bow enters the roller to push it on through and keep from broaching. Such dams may have quite small waves and may be run in open boats, but the danger of even a small wave should not be underestimated. Even a six-inch wave caused by a dam or shelf can be a dangerous keeper, and safety precautions must be observed. Do not overlook the possibility in shallow water that the dam itself will catch the canoe as it goes over; the bow then becomes buried in the roller.

Large dams should never be run in canoes by any but experts who understand the possible hazards. Little dams or ledges of a foot or two may not be too hazardous if enough care is exercised. Rescuers on the shore with safety lines are often good precautions in such circumstances. The situation should be evaluated by an experienced paddler. It is particularly foolhardy for inexperienced canoeists to try to shoot dams or weirs.

GROUP PROCEDURES

White-water paddling is a poor sport for solitary canoeists or even single canoes with tandem crews. To make the activity reasonably safe, it is normally necessary to have a minimum of three canoes, and more will be needed if some members of the party are inexperienced in water of the level of difficulty being attempted. Although good canoeists sometimes make white-water trips with only one boat, these are usually done in water much easier than they are used to paddling or with the understanding that risks are being taken beyond those normally considered acceptable by river runners. White-water paddling is quite a safe activity, but only when good safety precautions are observed. A beginner in rough water cannot possibly appreciate the risks that would be involved in running without companions, and novices should always run with groups at least until they have become knowledgeable.

It is best to learn to paddle white-water with a club or experienced friends. Progress is bound to be very slow if a number of beginners have to learn together without experienced companions. For safety they will have to be conservative in deciding what to undertake. They also will not have advice available to point out errors and methods for correcting them. If it is at all possible, then, learn how to paddle white-water from experts. The American Canoe Association (4260 E. Evans Ave., Denver, Co. 80222) may be able to supply information on canoeists in your area. If you must learn with other beginners, start with water close to the road, without dangerous spots, and ending in quiet water. Be doubly cautious about life preservers, wet suits, and stationing rescuers with throwing lines where they might be called for.

For group trips involving white-water, it is best to have one person designated as a leader with responsibility for the safety of the group and the authority that goes with it. This ensures that decisions will be made with some thought rather than just happen, provided the leader is competent. He decides whether a rapid is safe to run for those who wish, or whether all or part of the group should portage. In a group of more than a few canoes, the leader will generally designate one as lead and one as sweep, probably the two most experienced teams. The general rule of travel is that no canoe passes the lead canoe or drops behind the sweep. Thus, if the lead canoe pulls into shore to inspect the river ahead or to allow the party to catch up, each canoe as it comes down pulls into that spot or one nearby, which avoids the possibility of a less experienced team accidentally running into a rapid or getting too far ahead and into trouble. The second rule is that no canoe allows the one *behind* to get out of sight, or at least no farther than demanded by circumstances. Hence, at the end of a section of swift water coming around a bend, a canoe should pull into the first possible eddy to wait for the next boat to appear, so that if anyone capsizes or gets into trouble, a rescue team is always posted just downriver, normally within sight. Where the correct channel is not obvious, this rule also ensures that each team can normally see where the one before it went.

In large groups of widely varying ability, it is prudent to alternate more and less experienced teams. Often teams should be split, putting novices in boats with experienced paddlers. In one fashion or another, be sure that someone with a good understanding of emergency procedures is not too far away when needed.

In sections of swift water, canoes need to be wary of getting too close as well as too far apart. If a canoe gets in trouble and broaches on a rock, it is poor form for the next boat to be running so close behind that it piles into the first.

Emergency items for the whole party should be carried by the sweep rather than an earlier canoe, particularly on rivers where getting back upstream is difficult or impossible. It is bad planning to have the party's large first-aid kit a mile downriver when an accident occurs at the other end of a canyon with rock walls dropping right into the water.

DIFFICULTIES

Canoeists who exercise reasonable care should encounter few, if any, true emergencies. Having one paddler gash a knee after a capsize could be a life-threatening situation if the weather and water were cold and the person had no wet suit, if no materials were available for building a fire or giving first aid, if the other members of the party were ahead and did not realize a canoe was missing for an hour or two, or if other important precautions were ignored. On the other hand, for a properly prepared party, such an accident would be annoying and would entail some minor difficulties, but it would not be a true emergency in the sense that anyone was in serious danger.

Basic precautions are the party's first line of defense against difficulties. In white-water, good quality life preservers should be mandatory in most circumstances, though there are arguments for running keepers without them. For paddlers of white-water boats, helmets are likewise mandatory. When one is floating upside down in a rapid, setting up for an Eskimo roll, collisions between rocks and one's head tend to be detrimental to proper concentration. In serious white-water, many open boaters prefer to wear helmets too, because there are situations that arise swimming a turbulent rapid when one could receive a blow to the head. In going over a ledge feet first, for example, the last part of the body to go over is the head, which can easily strike the edge of the ledge. Even a few moments' unconsciousness in the water could be fatal.

Throwing lines are good pieces of safety equipment. A moderately heavy rope that has been stretched and worked enough so that the kinks are well worked out is best. Polypropylene floats but does not always handle as well as other materials. Three-eighths-inch diameter is thick enough to be easily grasped by someone in the water, although some people prefer a lighter line. Opinion varys on whether a throwing line should have some large grab ball on the end. Some use floats with monkeys' fists tied in the ends, some only floats, and some simply knots. Others argue that any of these is far too prone to catch between rocks and that the advantages of the floating end—that it is easy to hold and throw—are outweighed by this danger. Personally, I prefer a three-eighths-inch polypropylene rope that floats and has high visibility, with nothing on the end.

A throwing line must be coiled correctly and be readily available. Anyone carrying one should also practice throwing it in advance to make it worthwhile. People with these lines can be stationed on shore below a difficult drop when the channel is near enough to shore. Once the line is correctly thrown, the person on shore can sit, run the rope behind his or her back, and hold it with the hand on the opposite side of the body from that going to the swimmer. Throwing lines can also sometimes be tossed from a canoe to a person in the water, in which case the opposite end should be tied to the rescuing canoe with a quick-release knot in case the line catches somewhere. Do not have rescue lines (or any other lines) trailing around in a canoe; they must be neatly coiled and fastened where they can be reached quickly but will not loosen accidentally. A piece of shock cord mounted on the canoe is a good holder. Loose lines can wrap around both a point on the canoe and the leg of a swimmer with very unpleasant consequences.

When an open canoe capsizes in a rapid, the first and most important rule for the paddlers is to get to the upstream side of the boat. A canoe may hold a ton of water, moving down the river at the same rate as the current. If the boat then broaches a rock, first the inertia of the water inside, then the pressure of the surrounding water will press it solidly against the upstream side of the rock. The space between the canoe and the rock is thus not a good place to be, rather like the area between the bumper of a moving car and a brick wall into which it is crashing. Other considerations, such as hanging onto paddles, staying with the canoe, keeping it upside down to retain air and buoyancy, and attempting to guide the boat past rocks and into the nearest eddy are all important, but the primary rule is to stay upstream of the canoe.

Swimmers who are not in danger should immediately start for shore with the boat and paddles. A boat will often eddy out to one side anyway, and some assistance from swimmers may bring it in. Friends may be along to rescue you soon, but don't wait for them; start working for shore. The extra few feet gained can make the difference between getting to an eddy or washing on down into the next rapid. Remember that the farther your boat is carried, the greater the likelihood of its having an encounter with a hungry boulder.

The painters at the ends of canoes are useful during rescues. When swimming, it is often easier to tow a canoe with the painter than to hold the boat itself. It is nearly always easier to get out of the water onto a boulder while holding the painter rather than a deck or gunwale. If swimmers stay with the canoe, a rescue boat can toss a swimmer its stern painter and tow him with an upstream ferry while he holds onto his own canoe and continues swimming to aid in the rescue. If a boat has been lost or abandoned and a rescue boat is trying to salvage it, a painter is essential to give the rescuer something to hold. In this situation various methods are used for holding the painter while the boat is being towed. Some hold it in their teeth, others with one hand. It can be tied to a thwart with a quick-release knot but should never be tied so as to require more than an instant to undo, lest the boat being towed carry the rescuers into difficulty.

When a choice presents itself, people must be rescued first, boats second, and paddles last. Never assume that swimmers are all right until you have absolute assurance, not only from them but to your own satisfaction. Saving a boat is always secondary. Remember that inadequately clothed swimmers cannot last long in cold water, even though they may think they are all right.

This priority applies equally to swimmers dumped into the water. The normal caveat to stay with the canoe applies only as long as it is safe to do so. If the water is numbingly cold and shore is relatively close, drop the boat and head for land, especially if there is no prospect of getting the canoe into an eddy quickly. Similarly, if the boat is headed for a drop that seems dangerous, swim for safety if that is feasible. No one wants to lose a canoe, but neither is it worth risking your life to save one.

If a canoe is broaching on a rock, quick action by the paddlers may avoid compounding the difficulties. One person may be able to leap out onto the rock or into the water, depending on depth and other circumstances, and push the boat free. Care needs to be exercised in this tactic, of course, particularly to keep from being caught between the canoe and the rock. As the boat comes up against the rock, lean downstream, toward the rock. It seems to be instinctive to lean away from the rock to avoid the collision, but this is wrong. As soon as a canoe broaches, the water builds up against the upstream side and the water rushing under the hull also tends to tip the boat the same way, sweeping the bottom out from under and capsizing the canoe upstream. Leaning downstream gives the current time to swing the boat free and the paddlers time to act. If water once comes up over the upstream side, it begins to fill the canoe; in a few seconds the hull is filled with water and the whole force of the current is pushing the canoe against the rock, trying to break it in half.

Removing a broached canoe from a rock once it has filled with water and has the open end facing the current can be a major project. It cannot be done simply by lifting the canoe off but only by moving it in a direction so that the current will carry it on around the rock and release it. Advance practice and quick application are important because the water is constantly working on the canoe, doing more damage and settling it more and more against the boulder. With an aluminum canoe the rock makes a bigger dent, and with a fiberglass boat it breaks in more of the side. If the canoe is in a position where no one can safely reach it, then of course it must be abandoned, at least until it reaches low water. If it is possible to get out to the broached boat, however, it is often possible to rotate it off the rock so that the current is no longer pushing on the open side of the canoe, then pull it off with the current's help.

Tie any lines to the canoe at the sturdiest points you can find, but never try to pull off a canoe that is badly stuck by just hauling on a line tied directly to a thwart. You'll simply pull off the thwart. Tie a line first to one end of the canoe and then to a good anchor on shore, so that if the boat is freed and the rescuers lose their grip on it it won't be at the mercy of the rapids again. If only a little of the canoe is in the water, it can normally be lifted by several people and rotated out. If it is thoroughly stuck, tie a line to the lower end of a thwart near the rock and opposite the end toward which a release seems easiest, generally the end sticking out farthest from the rock. Bring the rope around the hull, over the top side of the canoe, and pull from upriver toward the other side. This distributes the force onto the hull as well as the thwart. It rotates the canoe on around the rock and off it, into the water, to release the grip of the current.

Getting rope under the canoe in the upstream direction and tying it to a thwart several feet underwater is often next to impossible. I first saw one way of accomplishing it, called the Steve Thomas Rope Trick, illustrated in a safety bulletin of the Coastal Canoeists. The rope is passed downstream under the canoe, brought back up over it, and tied into a loop around the boat with two half hitches. The whole loop is then pulled and rotated in the other direction so that the half hitches travel down around the bottom of the canoe and upstream under it. When the half hitches are pulled around back to the top they are undone, the end of the rope is tied to the top of the thwart, and the knot is slid down as far as one can reach. The rope and knot are then correctly positioned and the rescue attempt can be made.

If the strength of the thwart is questionable or initial hard pulling seems to be overstressing it, a second rope or the other end of the same one can be similarly attached to a seat or second thwart.

SWIMMING IN FAST WATER

In addition to those already mentioned, there are several points to remember when you capsize. In your first experience of swimming in rapids you will find that it is not swimming in the normal sense. The water will carry you every which way, particularly if you are separated from your canoe. Keeping your head out of water long enough to get air can often be a struggle, but if you breathe when your head comes out and keep your wits, you should be through the worst part fairly soon. Presumably, you will have had many opportunities to swim in white-water before you risk canoeing just above a really dangerous rapid or waterfall. If you are wearing a life jacket, you'll bob to the surface pretty frequently, even in a rough rapid, and in a mild one you'll be on top nearly all the time.

Get your bearings and take stock of the situation right away. Where is your canoe? This is an essential question: if it is nearby and the circumstances are favorable, you may be able to catch it and tow it to shore; if you are downstream of it, you have to be careful not to be caught between it and a rock.

You must also ascertain quickly any other serious dangers threatening you. The hazards of cold water have been mentioned several times, but they cannot be overemphasized. If you are becoming severely chilled, you must get out as quickly as possible. Check immediately downriver to try to see where you are being carried, and correlate this information with any you may have from previous scouting. The most serious danger is from sweepers, brush, or log jams—try to avoid these at all costs. If you are being unavoidably swept into sweepers, go in face first, which will make it likely that if you are caught you will be faceup in the water. Swimmers washed under logs back first frequently have their faces pushed under.

After sweepers, dams and other keepers are the main possible dangers other than falls, large dams, or man-made diversion tunnels, hazards that should have prevented your canoeing in the first place. If you are carried into a keeper and cannot swim over the roller, try to kick off from the bottom if you can reach it. Swimming over to one side will often bring you to an escape point. Finally, you can try diving as deep as possible to reach the lower current that shoots underneath.

As a general rule, swim down a rapid with the feet headed downstream. It is better to ward off rocks with them than with your head, particularly if you are not wearing a helmet. Always wear shoes when canoeing white-water because of the danger of cut feet. Keep working for shore or for a nearby rescuer or eddy, except when you need to position yourself to be washed down a chute at an advantageous point. The current will drop you in eddies quite frequently. Take advantage of the first chance to let it help you out. *Don't try to stand up in a fast current* unless it is very shallow. You might trap one of your feet in a cranny between the rocks.

SAFETY RULES FOR RIVER RUNNING

1. Carry a good life jacket for each person in the canoe and *wear it*.

2. Learn the limits of your skill both in paddling and in evaluating river runs, and keep your canoeing within those limits and the ones imposed by your equipment and your party. Be particularly conservative if you are the leader, and do not be sloppy in ascer-

taining the level of experience of your group. You are assuming responsibility for their lives.

3. Always work up to more difficult runs by making easy, safe ones first to check out your equipment, conditioning, and paddling skill. Do this whether you are a beginner or an expert. Don't expect to start the new canoeing season in the same form that you ended last season.

4. Don't canoe alone. The normal minimum for safety is three boats.

5. Always scout any sections where you cannot see the next sure spot to beach safely. When in doubt, portage.

6. Prepare for the water temperatures that will be encountered. White-water runs in spring frequently require wet suits for safety. Wool or similar synthetics that retain some warmth when wet are necessary on most canoeing trips. Boaters who have capsized often need active rewarming on shore to prevent hypothermia.

7. Avoid sections of a river that have serious hazards: dams and other keepers, log jams and sweepers, bends with curling waves or overhanging ledges on the outsides, waterfalls, and the like. Portage if necessary, and run such sections only if the party is truly experienced and strong enough to do so safely.

8. Learn the techniques of mouth-to-mouth resuscitation and basic first aid, with special attention to the problems of shock and hypothermia.

9. Secure all lines in the canoe so that they cannot accidentally entangle a boater in a capsize.

10. If you tip over in fast water, stay on the upriver side of the canoe and keep your feet downriver. Swim for shore or for eddies, and abandon the boat if necessary for your own safety. Don't try to stand up in fast water.

CHAPTER 8

POLING A CANOE

It is ironic that poling should sometimes be considered a subject separate from the general run of canoeing, since poling should be a basic skill for every canoeist, particularly the river runner. Poling is generally the best way to ascend rivers and streams and is often the best way down rapids, especially those that are shallow and intricate. A good canoe poler can travel in many places where the paddler cannot, and the art of poling can teach any canoeist a great deal of river lore. Poling is particularly valuable for wilderness travelers because it opens up many shallow stretches to travel and can save a lot of lining, tracking, and portaging.

Poling, like much of the rest of canoeing, goes back a long way into American history. Backcountry travelers who used the canoe for transportation knew the value of poling both for shallow water and for upstream travel in general. Paddling upstream is hard, unrewarding work, and it is often virtually impossible to make any progress at all. In shallow water the paddle scrapes bottom without being able to go deep enough to gain real purchase on the water. In these situations and others, poling is far superior.

Like paddling, poling has gone through a revolution as the result of new materials, and modern canoeists are still discovering new possibilities that have been opened up to them. The special advance for poling has been the development of the lightweight pole of tubular aluminum. Wooden poles with iron or steel shoes generally weighed in the neighborhood of seven pounds each. An aluminum pole of the same length (usually twelve feet) should weigh under three pounds. This difference in weight makes a tremendous difference for the poler because of the length of the pole. The heavy wooden pole cannot be swung around rapidly and easily because the heavy ends are each five feet away from the canoeist, so moving them requires considerable effort. With an aluminum pole, swinging the whole length is not difficult, and many techniques are possible that could not be used with heavier poles.

LEARNING TO POLE

The first step in learning to pole is to become used to standing comfortably in a canoe. Most standard cruising canoes can be used for poling. Decked white-water canoes, which have no openings on top except for narrow cockpits, cannot be used for poling because there is nowhere to stand. Short, open canoes with a length less than sixteen feet are far from ideal, but there are few other requirements. You should have footwear that will not slip too badly on the bottom of the canoe when both shoes are wet. If the canoe itself does not have a nonslip surface many shoes will work better if you put on the soles a couple of strips of adhesive tape of the kind used to put a gripping surface on stair edges.

It is easier to balance while standing in a canoe than most people think, and polers also gain a good deal of stability from their poles. To start off, probably the simplest way to get the knack is to go out on a local pond or lake on a warm day, prepared for a swim. Stand in various positions in the canoe and push yourself around with the pole, using it on both sides. Try standing with your feet planted on opposite sides of the bottom and rock the canoe back and forth enthusiastically. Find out how far you can tip it without capsizing or falling out. If you work at this exercise seriously you will get wet, but the experience will teach you a lot about what you can do. Try standing on one side of the bottom so that the canoe tilts over and pole from that position.

A few hours of such practice will allow you to progress much faster when you start to pole on moving water.

For your first try at poling on a river, pick a spot that is fairly shallow and has a moderate current so that you can concentrate on the basics without being too nervous about dumping and can learn the simplest maneuvers and the proper techniques for positioning yourself in the canoe in this situation before trying more difficult water. From this point your progress should be quite rapid, and you will have no trouble guiding it yourself.

Much of the technique of poling comes quite quickly as soon as it is tried. Basic control of the canoe is more instinctive than with paddling, because it is often accomplished simply by pushing against the pole in the appropriate direction and transferring the force to the canoe through the feet. Since the pole is in direct contact with the bottom of the river or lake much of the time, there is no problem in learning to push on a less substantial medium, as there is in paddling. Particularly in rivers, there is nearly always something solid to push on with the pole. There are subtle differences in the way a canoe acts, depending on foot placement and weight shift, but you will absorb many of these during the first few hours of poling.

POLING UPSTREAM IN MOVING WATER

On quiet water the poler may have difficulty finding a good bottom to push on and may either have to resort to the paddle or have a special attachment on the bottom of the pole to push on mud and muck. The bottoms of rivers and streams are generally quite solid, however, at least where the current is moving, because the sluicing water carries away any light, silty material. Even rivers with very muddy banks usually have solid bottoms a little way out. You may sometimes have to work back and forth to find the best compromise between having to work against the current and finding the best footing for the pole, but this is the craft of the poler, who takes the river by stealth rather than strength.

For poling, the downstream end of the canoe should be trimmed lower than the upstream end. Assuming that the bow is pointed upstream when you are poling up against the current, the stern should be lower in the water, which will cause the current to catch the stern and drag it downstream so that the bow will always tend to swing back upstream. The canoe then tends to be self-orienting or directionally stable. If the bow were loaded heavily, the canoe would tend to swing suddenly around whenever the bow made a slight angle with the current and the pole was removed from the bottom.

Similarly, when moving downstream, assuming the bow is pointing down, the bow should be trimmed a little heavily, again so that the current keeps the canoe aligned by pushing the downstream end of the canoe along with more force than the upstream end.

If you are not carrying much of a load and are poling alone, this means that you should normally stand a little back of center when poling upstream and a little ahead of it when poling down. If you are carrying a passenger or a load, you can adjust the weight so that you can stand where you like.

As with paddling, when you are poling alone you can achieve the best directional control from near the center of the canoe. For poling straight ahead, you may prefer to stand farther astern, but turns are more difficult from that position. The most common poling position for going upstream with an unloaded canoe is thus a little behind the center of the canoe, which will trim the stern a little down and still put you near the center of the boat. (You can equally well point the stern upstream and pole from a little toward the bow end, facing the stern, of course, if this is advantageous.)

The most common method of poling upstream is climbing the pole hand-over-hand. Stand with one foot on each side of the centerline of the boat, partially facing the poling side, so that the opposite foot is somewhat ahead of the other. Thus, if you are poling on the right side of the canoe, the left foot would be advanced, a little behind the center thwart, and the right foot would be a foot or two farther back. Face somewhat to the right. Ideally, the bow of the canoe should be a few degrees to the right of a line directly upstream. Shove the pole down to the bottom just behind you, then push off against it, leaning some weight on it, and climb up the pole hand-over-hand. When you reach the top of the pole, toss it up out of the water and put it down again a little ahead of you. Resume pushing as the forward momentum of the canoe carries the canoe past the pole. This efficient movement can be kept up for long periods, and you can easily adjust the speed. You can also stop and hold the canoe steady against the current with the pole on the bottom for a rest or a look at the situation ahead.

TURNS

When poling, turns are normally made by pushing the pole against the bottom in a suitable direction, preferably without interrupting the normal stroke. Turning in the direction of the side on which you are poling is usually quite easy. As the pole moves back toward the stern, simply push out on it with the lower hand while pulling with the upper. If the canoe is moving well, you can also place the pole out to the side somewhat and drag it on the bottom, putting as much weight on it as possible, but this method is undesirable unless you also want to slow down or stop.

It is harder to turn the canoe to the side opposite that on which you are poling. The normal method is to push the pole underneath the canoe as it is moved back behind the body during the normal stroke. With practice this turns the canoe quite effectively. If the boat is traveling forward slowly or is stopped, you can also place the end forward and out, away from the front of the canoe, and push the end directly around.

To make a major change in direction, it is best to turn toward the poling side. Thus, if you wanted to turn completely around and head in the opposite direction, making the turn to the left, it would be best to switch poling sides first if you were poling on the right. To turn hard, set the pole out close to the side of the canoe and somewhat to the rear, put some weight on it, and push out hard on the pole, using it as a pivot and transferring the rotational momentum to the canoe with the feet. Accomplished polers can turn a canoe a full 360 degrees in this way, beginning from either an upstream or downstream direction.

OTHER UPSTREAM TECHNIQUES

There are several methods for pushing upstream at a faster pace than that allowed by climbing the pole hand-over-hand. One is the hand-over-hand switch, in which your hands climb the pole rapidly in the conventional manner, but instead of pulling the pole up out of the water and moving it forward at the end of each stroke, you turn it end-for-end at the finish of the stroke and push the opposite end of the pole into the water on the other side of the canoe. This switching allows a more rapid and continuous push for a short distance, as in pushing up through a drop, for example. Climb the pole until your hands are two or three feet from the end, and then make the flip. You can make this motion with the pole staying on the same side of the canoe, too; doing it several times steers the canoe correctly, but it is most effective when alternated from side to side.

Another powerful stroke used in shallow rapids is the quick jab, but this technique requires a special attachment for the pole except in the shallowest water. The method is to hold the pole with hands spread fairly wide and high enough on the pole so that it hits bottom when extended back at a considerable angle. Shove back on the pole hard, pull it forward to grab the bottom again, and make another jab. Executed properly, this is a fast, jackhammerlike stroke that moves the canoe continuously. Because the pole is pulled forward through the water, there is a great deal of resistance to the forward movement if the water is more than a foot deep. The quick jab can be effective in water up to three feet deep if an extension is added to the end of the pole. Fitted with a socket and held on with a quick-release pin or other device, a three-foot-long extension rod is used to jab at the bottom and will drag far less as it is pulled forward through the water.

The windmill stroke, in which the pole is flipped over at each stroke, can be used for cruising in many situations. Instead of climbing up to the end of the pole, the canoeist using the windmill stroke makes a hand-over-hand motion in the middle of the pole, turning it over at the end of each thrust on the same side of the canoe. The stroke is effective only when the canoe is moving well, so the poler would normally switch into it only after starting with the normal hand-over-hand. Make the thrust with both hands in the windmill, and as it is completed, slide the forward hand up the pole and reach the backward hand under to flip the pole over so that the upper end drops forward into the water. As this end hits bottom, the lower hand lets go and reaches up to grab the pole above the other hand. Both hands should be on the pole again as the canoe passes it and another push can be made, at the end of which the pole is flipped again. The motion is not difficult to learn on flat water, but it takes a skilled poler to use it effectively in fast currents.

SNUBBING DOWN

In easy water, the canoeist can pole downstream using exactly the same methods as those that are standard in upstream travel. However, for descending more difficult stretches the poler usually wants to make slower, not faster, progress than the current and the method used in these situations is known as snubbing. For slowing the canoe's progress during regular poling, the canoeist drags the pole against the bottom, putting more weight on it to brake harder, but snubbing is far more effective in maneuvering the boat to the exact position where it is wanted, slipping it back and forth between eddies and channels and stopping to look over the next section. The poler can also switch quickly from snubbing to poling back upstream if he has chosen the wrong passage, because the pole is angled downstream when snubbing.

When snubbing, stand on the downstream side of the center thwart of the canoe so that the current will hold the more heavily weighted end oriented downriver. As with poling upstream, take a position in the canoe at about a forty-five-degree angle to the keel line so that you can brace against the pole. Unlike upstream poling, though, the hands do not usually move up and down the pole. Set the pole against the bottom to slow the canoe or stop it, lift the pole a little to allow the canoe to slide downstream a bit, and again place the pole's end on the bottom to halt progress.

With snubbing, progress is made by a continuous series of short little spurts. The canoeist snubbing in swift water keeps touching bottom, absorbing a little shock with the arms and body, then moving the pole down to the next spot where purchase can be gained. Until you have some practice, it is important to avoid letting the canoe start moving too fast, since the shock of the pole hitting bottom when the canoe is moving quickly can be heavy and can easily unbalance a beginner. Keeping the pole well forward reduces the chance of catching it between rocks and being swept overboard by it. In fast sections it is sometimes best to drop one hip onto the bow seat for stability, from which position it is easy to resume standing. If the canoe does start moving too fast, the best recovery is often to step back behind the center thwart and drag the pole, with as much weight as you can apply to it. Except in the fastest currents, you should be able to slow the canoe back to manageable speed this way. The main advantage to snubbing over dragging is that it is far easier to move the canoe where it is wanted.

PADDLING WITH A POLE

Although it is only an inch or a little more in diameter, because of its length the pole can exert considerable force as it is drawn through the water even when it does not touch bottom. The poler can use it as a double paddle, taking a stroke first on one side and then the other, from either the standing or sitting position. This is a particularly useful method when you are passing over a section of water so deep that the pole will not reach bottom. A few strokes with the pole quickly bring you to shallower water again. For a change of pace, you can paddle quite a distance with a pole while sitting, moving along very efficiently.

TRAVELING WITH A POLE

There are several major advantages to poling. One is that a great deal of canoeing can be done in stretches of river too shallow for enjoyable paddling. What is learned in poling these sections will serve the canoeist well when paddling big, deep rapids on other occasions. The poler need not worry about shuttles, or even scouting. He can start from any bridge and pole upstream, automatically scouting the downstream run back to the car, which may be made by poling hard, snubbing, or running with a paddle. Poling can be done safely alone in shallow water even in cold weather.

The competent poler on a downstream wilderness run may be able to avoid the necessity of portaging or lining some rapids after gaining confidence in the technique of snubbing. This is particularly true in shallow rapids that would require difficult maneuvering to descend with a paddle. Despite fast currents, a good poler can easily ferry a canoe completely across a river to gain a good passage on the far side, provided the water is not too deep. This ability complements one's paddling technique beautifully, since it is often in fast, shallow sections that the paddle is weakest, paddlers having to scratch desperately at the bottom while trying to fight the current in a ferry.

The poler moving upstream or down progresses from eddy to eddy, seeking out not the channel but the shallow sections closer to one bank or the other between eddies, then ferrying quickly across the channel to reach a better passage on the far side. Even for the most confirmed paddler, poling is a tremendous education, for he sees the pattern of the river's flow at leisure and from downstream, features that the downstream paddler can only glance at quickly over a shoulder. It is a pity that the pole has become so badly neglected as a means of propelling and controlling the canoe, since it is in many ways a more versatile tool than the paddle.

Poling is primarily a technique used by one person in each canoe, except by real experts. A canoe being poled by two accomplished people with a well-developed sense of teamwork is formidable indeed, but without considerable advance practice a team of two polers is much like a Keystone Cops routine, fun in warm water but not recommended on a cold wilderness river. The best way to combine the skills of two canoeists on a river who have not mastered double poling together is to have the upstream person kneel and use a paddle while the downstream end of the canoe is handled with a pole. This method can be mastered quickly by most tandem pairs. The paddler adds extra power and mainly needs to avoid throwing his standing partner off-balance.

Safety considerations for poling are much the same as for paddling. Going out on rough or cold water inadequately prepared is asking for trouble. Poling is inherently quite safe, but because it is more easily managed as a solo activity it is important to exercise good judgment. On easy streams solitary poling is an enjoyable and safe activity, but overconfidence is one of the main enemies of safe canoeing. A little periodic thought about the consequences of a small misjudgment or slip will act as a good deterrent for those getting a little too bold.

CHAPTER 9

THE WHITE-WATER CANOE

It has been pointed out in a number of connections that any canoe is bound to be a compromise in design, with sacrifices made for any advantage that is gained. There are many subtle differences among different open cruising canoes that make a canoe more suitable for one purpose than another. For paddling in white-water, those characteristics that contribute to maneuverability and seaworthiness are at a premium. The ultimate craft at this end of the spectrum is the decked, white-water slalom canoe. Because it was developed primarily for competition, this type of canoe is often called by its designation in racing classifications, the C-1 if it is a one-person boat or C-2 if paddled by two people.

C-1s are often mistaken for kayaks by the uninitiated, and inveterate open boaters sometimes claim that is all it is. However, the C-1 is paddled by a kneeling canoeist using a single-bladed paddle and all the techniques of the open boat canoeist. C-1s are readily distinguishable from kayaks even without looking inside to see the knee pads, foot braces, and seat or thwart to lean against rather than the low kayak seat. Even though it is usually the same length as a kayak, a C-1 has much more volume, so it is fatter and fuller throughout.

The standard decked canoe is built from fiberglass or a similar laminate, with the hull and deck forming a continuous curve. A C-1 will generally be thirteen feet two inches in length and a C-2 fifteen feet, the minimum lengths allowed in white-water slalom competition. It has a good deal of rocker and no keel. In the deck, openings with rims allow paddlers to get in and seal the boat completely against the entry of water with a spray skirt that fits tightly at the paddler's waist and has an elasticized edge that stretches over the coaming, the outward-curving rim of the cockpit. The paddler cannot shift around much to different positions in the cockpit, a factor considerably reducing comfort, but the bracing system in the white-water canoe is set up so that a paddler can lock himself into the boat, easily transmitting the forces exerted on the paddler to the hull. With the canoe sealed against the entry of water, the paddler in a decked canoe can blast through haystacks with impunity, lean the canoe over on its side in an eddy turn, or can even capsize and turn the boat back up by skimming the paddle along the surface of the water and pulling up on it. The skilled paddler of a white-water canoe can play in rapids that no sane canoeist would attempt in an open boat. Using this canoe does have a price, however. It is finicky to handle, it has poor flat-water performance, its load capacity is reduced, it is difficult to carry bulky or odd-shaped luggage in, it cannot usually carry passengers, and it is impossible to pole. Decked white-water canoes are specialized boats that are nearly ideal for their intended purpose, but they lose much of the versatility of the cruising canoe.

TYPES OF WHITE-WATER CANOES

Even within the specialized arena of the decked white-water boat there is a great deal of variety. The type of boat just described is designed for slalom competition or for pleasure paddling in rapids. There is also a downriver race through white-water that is a contest strictly for speed from one point on a river to another. Special decked canoes called downriver boats made for this race are extremely fast and seaworthy but are very unstable and hard to maneuver. They are not useful for any other purpose and are intended only for expert paddlers.

Slalom boats and recreational variations on them take a number of forms, too. Boats designed primarily for racing by top competitors and labeled as such by their makers often sacrifice durability for the lightest possible weight. Even experts reserve them for racing, and they will not last long in the hands of a novice. They may also have features that make them harder to control than standard white-water boats.

The best boats for general use are those heavy enough to be fairly durable. Unfortunately, weight alone gives little information on the quality of a boat. The best fiberglass canoes are made with laminations of a number of layers of woven cloth, which may be of glass, synthetics, or a combination, saturated with resin, but with all the excess carefully worked out. The most sophisticated constructions use epoxy resins with special cloths and a vacuum process for removing excess resin, but this technique is not currently used to make commercially marketed boats. If you are looking for a white-water boat, try to find a knowledgeable person to help you. Learn all you can about boat construction and take your time. White-water canoes are scarce enough so that you may need to spend some time looking. Both manufacturers and those wanting to sell new or secondhand boats are often around at major races. Consult the magazine *Canoe* or write the American Canoe Association (address on page 208) for schedules of these. The canoes made by the Seda Company and by Easy Rider are good ones to use as a basis for comparison.

There are variations in C-2s that may be worth considering. A third cockpit in the center may be included, which can be used to carry a passenger for cruising or be closed off with a cover when not in use. It enables a solo paddler to use the canoe as a somewhat sluggish C-1. Most frequently it is used as a handy hatch for loading and unloading the boat on long trips. It is difficult to appreciate the utility of this feature for canoe camping until one has worked through the end openings of a normal C-2 a few times. Another variation is to make a white-water touring canoe by having the deck extend across at both ends as far as the normal paddling positions and in somewhat at the sides, but with the rest of the area forming one large cockpit surrounded with a coaming so that a strong, removable spray deck with skirts for the paddlers can be installed. Such an arrangement cannot be designed to withstand major pressure as a regular C-2 can, but it gains many of the advantages of the open canoe while retaining much of the white-water performance characteristic of the C-2.

THE SINGLE-DECKED (C-1) WHITE-WATER CANOE

The single-decked canoe is definitely an individualist's boat. There is no assistance or companionship from a second paddler to help one power through waves and against the wind, nor is there anyone on the canoeist's off side to throw a welcome brace as the bow penetrates the eddy line. The C-1 paddler has all the joys and pains of self-reliance. The unknowing will comment on his "kayak," whereas kayakers will either shake their heads at the C-1 enthusiast's eccentricity or joke about it unmercifully. One not only has to be a rugged individualist to

A C-1 designed for slalom competition and recreational white-water paddling. The hull has a great deal of rocker and is very maneuverable but not very fast. Note that the paddler is wearing a life preserver and a helmet to protect his head from submerged rocks. If the water were at all cold, a wet suit would be essential also.

paddle a C-1; this type of personality is also necessary just to own one and carry it around on the car.

The dedicated canoeist trying out a single white-water boat gravitates naturally toward the single canoe rather than the kayak because the paddling strokes and position are the same he is familiar with. There are also some special advantages to the C-1 over the kayak. The single canoe paddler can put tremendous power into his or her strokes, being able to bring more of the trunk muscles into play than can the kayaker and having the advantages of a solid grip at the top of the shaft and plenty of reach with the blade. The canoeist has far more reach from the kneeling position than the kayaker, who sits almost in the bottom of the boat, and the canoeist's brace is much stronger than the kayaker's. The volume of the C-1 floats it higher in turbulent water, bobbing over waves into which kayaks dive. The C-1 paddler stays drier and has much better visibility in his kneeling position than does the low-slung occupant of the kayak.

In fairness, we must also note the disadvantages of the C-1 compared with the kayak. The kayaker has less power in the forward stroke and the brace than the canoeist, but he has the potential for a fast tempo of strokes that need no steering component (which would waste time and energy) because of the double-bladed paddle that is dipped in first on one side and then the other. He has a brace or an Eskimo roll (the technique of righting a capsized kayak) available on the side where it is needed, without having to switch the paddle over. The C-1 paddler generally has more problems when fighting an upriver wind because he sits higher, the boat floats higher, and he must make constant steering corrections. The C-1 turns more easily than the kayak, but reverse maneuvers in it are more difficult in every respect except for visibility.

Matters of comfort are arguable. The advantages to riding higher have been mentioned. In a kayak the lower back tends to ache after a few hours and the legs may fall asleep. In a C-1 many will find that their legs feel cramped from the constant kneeling position. Individual adjustment of the seat or thwart and the bracing system will often take care of this. Wet suits bunch at the back of the knees when one is kneeling in a canoe, but this problem is easily solved by cutting patches out of the suit at that spot and either leaving the areas behind the knees open or covering them with thin nylon material.

Because of its extra width, the C-1 begins as a more stable boat than the white-water kayak. The canoeist negates the advantage, however, by kneeling and thus raising his center of gravity and by sacrificing the kayaker's ambidexterity in bracing. The C-1 paddler with his kneeling position can extend the blade of the paddle much farther out, gaining leverage and the ability to catch helpful currents that the kayaker cannot reach. The canoeist's brace is so good that one can sometimes see a C-1 paddler bracing in a large hole hanging below his boat for some time, but he is constantly faced with situations where he must switch paddling sides, maneuver desperately to come into a difficult spot with the correct side in position, or sacrifice the advantages of a downstream brace because his paddle is on the upstream side.

Paddling the C-1

Learning to paddle a C-1 seems to be largely a matter of perseverance and commitment. Most strokes are the same as those used in solo paddling of a normal cruising canoe, but the boat is far less forgiving of errors in technique. Ambidexterity is desirable, but paddlers differ in their feelings about the desirability of switching sides in the middle of a run. It seems best to learn all the strokes well on both sides and then decide whether the brief period without a blade in the water is worth the advantages gained by switching.

Reverse strokes and the inverted sweep used to turn the canoe toward the paddling side are the most difficult maneuvers to learn well in the C-1. Only practice will make them efficient and reliable. The C-1 paddler must also learn to lean strongly to one side while paddling on the other in order to compensate for the pull of the current on the hull when crossing eddy lines with the paddle on the less advantageous side of the boat.

Once a canoeist has gotten used to the directional instability of his new craft and can control it reasonably well in moderate water, the technique of the Eskimo roll, described in detail below, should be learned. The roll is a critical part of the white-water canoeist's technique. A reliable roll not only provides the means for a recovery after an upset, without leaving the boat, but also develops the confidence that the paddler needs to really lean out on the paddle for braces and eddy turns. In fact, the paddler will almost certainly find that his paddling ability in a cruising canoe will improve after he masters the roll, simply because he will become much more confident in his braces and draw strokes.

In the C-1, however, maximum use can be made of these strokes because there is no need to worry about taking in water over the gunwales in an overly enthusiastic draw. Bracing can be used to maximum advantage for the same reason. The most stable position for riding through big waves is often to allow the boat to turn across the current and to brace downstream. Provided the water is deep and there is

Paddling a C-1 backward through a slalom gate. The spray skirt fits tightly around the canoeist's waist and the coaming of the canoe cockpit, keeping water out even if the boat capsizes. The loop at the front of the skirt allows him to release the skirt quickly if necessary.

little danger of hitting submerged rocks, this is a very easy, enjoyable way to ride haystacks. However, with an open boat the method is usually inadvisable because it is too easy to have a wave break over the side, dumping water in the entire length of the canoe. There is no such worry in a C-1, and the paddler can lean the boat over on its side to ride through big waves if he wishes. Similarly, there is no danger of taking on water around the bows if one rams straight into a big haystack. Even if the paddler is completely covered with foam and spray, the canoe remains watertight, so the paddler is free to concentrate on matters other than the danger of taking in water.

The C-1 paddler who has mastered the basic techniques of whitewater can play in many rapids that would be virtually unrunnable in an open canoe, even one with a spray deck. Holes that are not too dangerous can be run sideways, with the paddle planted in a high brace downstream; or the bow or stern can be planted in the hole so that the end of the boat first dives in and then is popped out by the water pressure, either flipping the boat end-over-end or popping it out into the air. Quite a strong deck is needed for such maneuvers because of the tremendous pressures that develop under a few feet of water. Boaters who make a practice of playing in holes generally use foam beams running vertically inside each end of the boat to keep the decks from collapsing.

As with open boats, safety should be a paramount consideration for the C-1 paddler, especially since he is more likely to venture out in potentially dangerous water. Solo paddling is extremely hazardous, and for a novice to paddle alone in white-water is idiotic. Safety precautions such as having experienced people to lead all trips, scouting rapids before running them, and portaging when in doubt are no different from open canoeing. C-1 paddlers need life jackets in virtually any water they are likely to paddle, and they will require wet suits more often than not. Although open boaters may choose to paddle without helmets even in challenging white-water, it is essential that the paddler of a closed boat wear a helmet, because in case of a roll the head is the lowest part of the body during the time the canoe is upside down, and even a minor glance against a rock could be fatal to the canoeist if it stuns him. Helmets should be worn at all times for white-water C-1 paddling. A spare paddle is often carried on the front deck, secured with clamps, shock cord, or Velcro tape. Grab loops on the ends of the boat are essential to allow a swimmer or rescuer to hold it after an upset.

Depending on where he lives, the most difficult task facing the canoeist learning to paddle closed boats may be in finding experienced C-1 paddlers from whom to learn. Much of his boating will probably be done with groups consisting mainly of kayakers, who are not likely to be able to give him tips on his reverse strokes or roll. Races are one of the best places to meet good paddlers, and if you are willing to donate some of your time to help with the work associated with running races, you will probably find experienced boaters willing to help you with your technique.

Two helmets that may be used for white-water paddling. LEFT. A rock-climbing helmet that gives excellent protection. This type of helmet is a bit heavy, and many paddlers prefer a somewhat lighter one such as the one on the right, reasoning that impacts in white-water paddling are not really severe. Helmets are essential for white-water paddling in closed boats. Both helmets have holes that allow water to escape quickly after a roll.

LEARNING TO ROLL

The Eskimo roll is not at all difficult to do, but it is difficult to learn. Once you have learned it well, you won't forget the roll, although you need to practice at the beginning of each season to polish the timing and be sure of your technique in difficult situations. Physical strength is not really a factor either, once the roll has been learned. A competent closed boater can turn his boat over and over, executing dozens of rolls in a sequence. The only really hard thing about a roll in flat water is learning how it is done.

The difficulties in learning are threefold: intellectual, psychological, and physical. Intellectually, it is not easy to visualize and comprehend just what is going on in the roll. The directions are confused by the fact that the boater rolling up after a capsize begins from an upside-down position under the water, and it is hard to understand the orientation of the paddle, the body, and the boat, particularly since the observer is normally above water, whereas the roller is below. An experienced canoeist also rolls up rather quickly, so the sequence of movements is hard to see. When the beginner gets underwater, however, he tends to rush at the wrong times, and things seem to take much longer than they did when he was observing a practiced boater.

Psychologically, the main problem experienced by the beginner is the tendency to become alarmed, so that he cannot attempt the motions in a methodical way. Anxiety may also prevent him from maintaining an awareness of exactly what he is doing, which is important in analyzing mistakes.

The roll is a physical skill, and the greatest difficulty in learning the technique is teaching the muscles the sequence of movements involved. Even if one understands perfectly how to roll, it does not follow that one will actually be able to do it. This is well demonstrated by the fact that many people take longer to learn on their second side than they did on the first. Clearly, once one has learned to roll up one way, one understands how to do it; the difficulty in learning to roll up the other way is strictly in teaching the sequence to the body.

With all this said, any paddler who wants to should be able to learn the roll, with a little patience and perseverance. Ideally, one should try to find a good closed boat paddler for an instructor. One who already knows how to roll a canoe will usually be able to make learning much easier, because he can demonstrate the proper technique and point out most of your errors along the way. An instructor will generally have ideas of his own about the best way to teach rolling, and if you are lucky enough to find such a person, let him prescribe the sequence.

Even if you are teaching yourself to roll, it is better to have a friend to help. Another person can assist in a number of ways. He can see what you are doing even when you cannot and can often tell what you are doing wrong. An assistant can also help with a number of the preliminary exercises and help you up on your abortive attempts to right the canoe, thus eliminating the need to get out of the boat, empty it, and get back in every time you miss a roll.

The first step in learning to roll is to familiarize yourself thoroughly with the canoe. The bracing system must be adjusted so that you can both lock yourself into the boat with a solid grip and easily get out when you relax your legs. The seats and braces in various canoes will be different, but typically there will be a seat at the back of the cockpit or a contoured beam running through it to sit on, adjustable thigh straps that give good lateral control as long as they are held with the legs, and toe blocks behind or under the seat. If the canoe was outfitted to fit a particular person, some of these may need to be changed. The bracing system can be checked and adjusted in your backyard. The spray skirt should fit snugly around your waist and the elastic should stretch tightly around the coaming, but not so tightly that it is difficult to get on or off. There should be a loop or ball at the front that can be grabbed to snap the skirt off the boat. If you want to get out of the boat quickly, the skirt stays on you and is pulled off the boat. Practice getting the skirt on and off the coaming.

The seat and bracing system in a white-water canoe must fit perfectly to allow the paddler not only to control the boat but also to escape easily in an emergency. This is one type of commercial seat in the bow of a C-2. Note the lip of the coaming over which the elastic of a spray skirt stretches.

Once everything in the canoe is properly fitted, you are ready to learn to roll. The best scheme is to learn in a swimming pool during the winter months. A pool is a comfortable place to work and it is much easier to find an instructor between boating seasons. Many canoe and kayak clubs have arrangements for winter practice sessions and classes in swimming pools. If a pool is not available, any lake or quiet stretch of river with a depth of three feet will do, but unless the water is warm you and your helper will need wet suits.

Before starting actual practice in rolling, it is important to convince yourself that you can easily get out of the boat whenever you wish and to get used to hanging upside down in the water. Get in, attach the spray skirt, and tip the canoe over. Wait until you have turned all the way over, count to ten slowly, pull the spray skirt off the coaming, and push yourself easily out of the canoe. Move the boat to shore or the side before righting it, so that water will not get into the cockpit.

Repeat this exercise a few times until you are satisfied that you will not be trapped underwater and are familiar with the feeling of hanging in the water. If a face mask is available, it is helpful to be able to see. Some prefer to wear nose clips during rolling practice to keep water out of the nostrils.

Once you are comfortable with the wet exit from the canoe, get in again and tip the boat over, but this time after counting ten, bend forward, grasp the boat with your hands, and extend your head up on one side to breathe, duck under again, and then reach up and breathe on the other side of the boat. Again, practice until you are comfortable. This is particularly useful if you are practicing alone, as you will be able to breathe and then make another attempt after failing with a roll.

The first step in learning the actual roll is to develop the hip and torso action. During a roll, the canoe must be rolled most of the way out of the water before the body is lifted out. The natural stability of the hull then assists the paddler in coming up. The beginner's natural impulse is to bring his head up first, then his body, and finally to roll the boat out, but the order must be exactly reversed. Work on the hip action along the side of the pool or next to some other support you can hold. Your partner can provide the support if none is available. Practice tipping the boat over and rolling it back up with your hips. Then drop your body below the surface and tip the canoe all the way over. Roll the boat back up with your hips before pulling your body up. Roll the hull of the boat up by pulling with your inside knee and pushing with the outside. Finally, turn all the way over, wait a bit, and roll the canoe back up, using the side to pull on. As you pull your body up, lean forward onto the deck so that your center of gravity is lowered and the righting action of the canoe helps pull your body up. The motion should be fluid and should require very little effort. Work on this on both sides for some time, and don't try to switch the paddle until you have perfected the torso movements.

The roll shown in the drawings on pages 241–44 is only one of several, although it seems to be the most powerful. If you have an instructor who prefers another method, however, learn his way first. The roll is in two parts, because the paddle is rotated 180 degrees in the middle of the roll. The roll finishes with a low brace directly out from the side of the canoe as far as one can reach. It is well to start practice with this stage. Have your partner stand beside you for help when you miss, but rely on him as little as possible. Lean over on the brace and right yourself. Keep leaning farther out and righting yourself with the brace until you fail and fall back into the water, then try again. Keep practicing this stage until you can push back up after getting your head completely in the water.

If you have an instructor, you should now have him demonstrate the roll several times at this point, watching from different vantage points. Watch from underwater, if you have a mask or goggles. Then get in the canoe, hold the paddle as shown in the drawings, capsize, and let the instructor move your paddle through the correct motions, carefully feeling the whole sequence yourself. Then try the roll with your helper or instructor assisting you at the end, but only to the extent that you really need assistance. Keep working, and try to figure out your mistakes after each failure. The correct sequence is shown in the drawings.

The most common mistakes are:

1. Not angling the blade correctly; it should plane somewhat during the sweep out.

2. Sweeping the blade too far or not far enough before starting to pull up on it; it should be perpendicular to the canoe and still on the surface when pulling is started.

3. Not waiting underwater long enough and not positioning the paddle properly before starting the sweep.

4. Pausing between the two stages while the paddle is being rotated, which must be done quickly so that there is a smooth transition from pulling up on the paddle to pushing down on it. If the canoe settles back between the stages, the roll will fail.

5. Not leaning forward to lower the center of gravity, or trying to raise the body from the water first.

Once you have accomplished the roll, it is important to keep practicing and consolidate it on the first side before assuming it is learned. A few successful rolls do not drill the muscles correctly. The paddle should be near the surface at the end of each roll. If it is deeply buried in the water, the roll is only marginally successful. When you can do a dozen rolls in a row with no failures, start learning on the other side, and expect to take just as long learning that.

After learning both sides, continue to practice. Paddle hard across the pool and back a couple of times, then capsize. Try starting with the paddle in all sorts of awkward positions. Then float the paddle beside the boat, turn over the other way, grab the paddle, and roll. To be able to do a reliable roll in white-water you need to learn really thoroughly in the comfortable water of the pool.

The sequence shown here is for a complete roll beginning with falling in the water to the left and ending with the paddle on the right side of the canoe. A roll beginning with a fall to the right is a mirror-image execution. One can also roll up on the same side as the capsize if this is convenient. Once the roll is learned on both sides, this is not complicated.

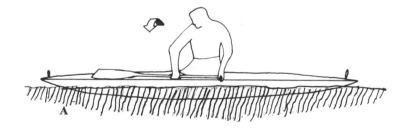

A. The proper position of the paddle for rolling. At the beginning, arrange this before capsizing, although later on it is important to practice rolling without preparing in advance. The paddle should be laid along the deck with the torso twisted so that the power face of the paddle is up, on the opposite side of the deck from the paddling side. Capsize toward the paddle.

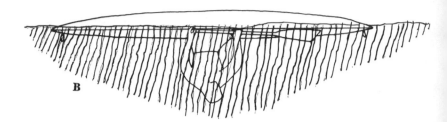

B. Looking from the other side, this is the position identical to **A,** except that the boater has turned upside down. It is important to pause long enough to be sure one has turned completely over and that the blade angle is correct, with the outside edge angled slightly up.

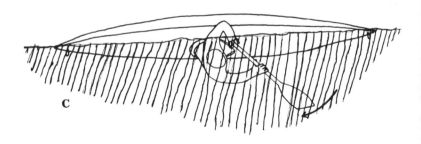

C. The paddler now sweeps the paddle around in an arc as far out as possible. The angled blade planes along near the surface of the water, partially lifting the canoeist's body, and the boater starts to turn the canoe up with the hips. The sweep continues until the paddle is sticking out just perpendicular to the canoe, still near the surface. The paddler begins to pull himself up on the paddle, continuing to rotate the hull out of the water.

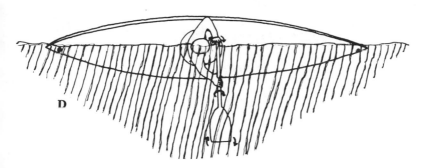

D. As soon as the paddle has sunk a little in the water and the canoeist's body is high enough to make it possible, the canoeist turns the paddle on its shaft 180 degrees, the thumb of the grip hand turning up and away from the face so that the paddle ends in the low brace position straight out from the boat, as shown in E.

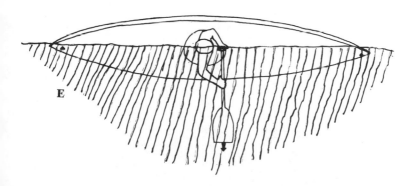

E. It is critical that the switch be made as soon as possible and without any significant pause. Loss of momentum at this stage is a common reason for failure. Hip action is paramount at this point, because if the boater instinctively tries to raise the body out of the water first, the roll will fail. The boat must be turned up first and the body bent forward so that the righting action of the hull will then help to bring the body up.

F. The canoe is almost upright as the body breaks completely out of the water. The paddler continues to push down on the water with a low brace, which should still be high in the water. If the paddle is deeply buried, the roll is marginal and will not work in difficult situations. A sculling action can be used at this stage to save a poor roll, however.

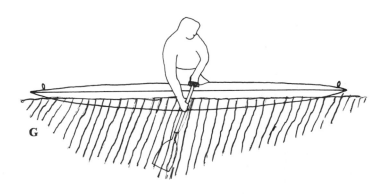

G. The canoeist ends with the paddle in a low brace on the opposite side of the boat from the deck on which it was laid at the start.

ROLLING IN WHITE-WATER

When you get out in a river after learning to roll, be sure to practice some more. Remember that what you are drilling for is the ability to roll back up after you have lost control in heavy white-water. This requires that you have complete faith in your ability to roll up, so that you won't bail out after one failure. Practice will give you the confidence you need.

In white-water the currents themselves are rarely neutral; they will either help your rolling effort or hinder it. Always take time to orient yourself if possible, and try to roll up toward the downstream side of the boat. The current will help you up in this direction, whereas it will be very difficult to roll to the upstream side. It may be necessary to wait a few seconds or switch the paddle to the other side to use the current to advantage. Even if a roll is not successful, you will always come partway up. Take a breath before you go down again, then take time to reorient the paddle correctly and try again. If you have gone into a large hole and capsized, it is often best to hold off for a while before attempting to roll. By this time you will probably have washed through the hole. The key to rolling in white-water is a cool head, and the best way to keep one is to have practiced enough beforehand to have complete faith in your roll. Many people who have practiced insufficiently are already out of their boats before they have turned all the way over. Stay in and keep trying.

PADDLING THE C-2

The two-man closed canoe is probably the most superb of all white-water craft. It is outstanding in speed, maneuverability, and power. A well-coordinated team can do truly amazing things with one, but that is the rub—teamwork is essential. Paddlers unfamiliar with each other can run rapids that are moderate for their level of skill, but to realize the potential of the C-2 the bow and stern have to paddle as a team.

A typical, commercially made C-2 for slalom and recreational white-water paddling. The cockpits are near the ends and there is plenty of rocker. Other types also have a center cockpit.

A downriver C-2 in the water. The cockpits in a downriver boat are closer together than those in the slalom boat on the bank. A downriver boat is difficult to paddle, and its speed can only be utilized effectively by skillful canoeists.

The C-2 is as much an exercise in personal relations as it is in paddling skill. To weld together an effective team in a two-person canoe, the first step is to swallow your words as you come up from a dunking after your partner has missed his brace. If you must say something, say it while still underwater.

All the basic paddling techniques in the C-2 are the same as in an open boat in white-water, except that they must be refined, since the C-2 is more responsive but less forgiving. When a brace is needed it must be wholehearted; half measures will not do.

A C-2 team approaches a gate in a slalom race. A well-matched team can make the C-2 the finest of all white-water craft.

The trim of the C-2 is critical with many boat designs. On touring trips this can be adjusted by shifting the duffel, but with a regular paddling team the seats and bracing should normally be shifted enough so that the boat rides with level trim after both paddlers are in. New C-2s often come with the seats not yet placed for this reason.

Downriver C-2s, which are made for racing at maximum speed down white-water courses, not for pleasure paddling, are beyond the scope of this book, but it is worth noting here that the cockpits are often offset, each toward one side of the canoe. Seats and braces have to be placed so that the canoe is correctly balanced from side to side as well as fore and aft.

Rolling the C-2 would be considerably easier than rolling the C-1 except for the problem of coordinating efforts between the paddlers. The most common method is to agree that one paddler will switch sides. As soon as that paddler is ready, he knocks his paddle against the canoe in a prearranged signal such as three knocks, then both paddlers start the roll in a rhythm that they have practiced in advance.

Different C-2 teams have different practices regarding switching sides. It is generally a bad idea to switch in the middle of difficulties with a C-2, since possible confusion is added to the element of time out of balance. There is always a brace available on either side of the canoe, even if it is not ideally placed, so there is less reason to switch than in the C-1. Some teams switch frequently for relief and to set themselves up in the best position for a particular maneuver, however. For example, when approaching an eddy into which they wish to turn, they may switch so that the bow can use a high draw into the eddy. This will be particularly advantageous when trying to get to a small eddy in a fast current. Others prefer the security of having paddles always at the ready and the advantage of never misunderstanding the sides on which each will paddle; they work out a fixed-side technique where each paddler always paddles on the same side, putting up with the occasional need to use a weaker stroke.

CHAPTER 10

PLANNING CANOE TRIPS

Planning a paddling trip can be a chore, but it can also be the source of much of the pleasure of the whole experience. The same keen anticipation that is felt as one approaches a river bend, wondering what is around the corner, keeping an eye on the landing spots just in case, is also an integral part of planning a cruise, particularly a long one in an unfamiliar area. At the beginning, the imagination is excited by a name, a photograph, a conversation, a blank spot on the map.

Some trips are begun with a fairly complete file of information: a detailed article, descriptions obtained from a friend, or data from a guidebook. Others start with the sketchiest idea and have to be laboriously researched. Gathering detailed information is the first and most important step in actually planning any trip.

One has to find out as much as possible about distances, water levels, rapids, falls, and such on river trips, and about portages and terrain around lakes. Weather and administrative rules have to be checked out, and transportation must be arranged. The party must be chosen, with the trip and the party carefully matched against each other with a cool eye. A trip that is too easy or too hard will be disappointing at least and possibly disastrous. Romantic flights of fancy about running rapids with a loaded canoe on a wilderness river twice as hard as anything you have ever run are fine, provided they are squelched at the appropriate time, before the trip goes beyond the dreaming stage. One of the functions of thorough trip planning is to temper one's fantasies with realistic calculation.

There are a lot of sources of information on canoeing trips. If you are short of time or don't like digging for information, stick to the obvious and easily available ones: guidebooks, articles you've run across in canoeing magazines, government brochures about specific trips, or cruises that have been taken and enjoyed by friends at your level of ability. If you are willing to do a little research, then there are a myriad of sources to which you can turn.

SOURCES OF INFORMATION

The most basic reservoir of data of the kind needed for trip planning is in the maps prepared by the U.S. Geological Survey. Anyone taking on the responsibility of planning trips should become thoroughly familiar with the skills necessary to read topographic maps. At a minimum, the person who gathers the basic information to be used in putting together a cruise is accepting responsibility for the happiness and well-being of his friends and is quite often also taking charge of their lives. Serious wilderness trips that are beyond the capacity of the participants can rapidly degenerate into struggles for survival.

Topographic maps can tell a great deal about a route: how fast a river drops and whether the descent is relatively continuous or occurs mainly at a few big falls; what the prospects are for a portage around rapids that may prove unrunnable; how difficult it would be to walk out in case of trouble; the complications that may be encountered in locating a portage route between two lakes, and the likelihood of finding good camping spots along a particular section of shoreline.

The best way to become an effective map reader, for these purposes and others, is to make a habit of carrying topo maps along on the day trips you take and use them. Whenever you have the chance, take a look at the map, try to locate your position on it, and relate the details shown on the map to the terrain you see around you. Occasionally take a few hours to strike across country to hit a road at a particular spot. Practice will teach you what you can and cannot learn from simply looking at a map. It will allow you to get a far more accurate idea of the nature of places you have never seen, as well as a healthy respect for the limitations of what can be garnered from map reading alone.

Topographic maps are available from the addresses mentioned in Chapter 5. An index map for each state, which shows the positions of all the maps of that state issued by the U.S.G.S., is available free of charge. These index maps diagram the regular series maps on the front and list special maps, often including particular lake and river systems, on the opposite side. Pay attention to survey dates. Unless they are quite recent, you should also obtain more recent maps of the area from other sources, such as the U.S. Forest Service or state and county agencies, that are current in their data on dams and roads.

For lakes, particularly in the far north, one of the most important pieces of information is the date the ice goes out. The dream trip you have been planning for years had better not be planned for the first two weeks in June if ice-out sometimes is as late as the first of July. Local chambers of commerce, fishing lodges, flying services, and the like are good possibilities to get this sort of data, as are forestry services, fish and game departments, and tourist bureaus. In desperation you can write to the nearest postmaster or mistress in a really remote area.

River flow data are collected and recorded for most rivers in the United States and Canada. In the United States one can find out where gauging stations are and the frequency of collection of data from them in the *Index to Surface Water Section,* which is available from the Office of Water Data Coordination, United States Geological Survey, Washington, D.C. 20242. Specific information on past flow levels of particular rivers is filed by state and can be obtained from the Water Resources Division of the U.S.G.S. for that state. The address of the particular office can be obtained from the address just mentioned. Equivalent information for Canada can be found in the *Surface Water Data Reference Index,* available from the Water Survey of Canada, Department of the Environment, Ottawa, Ontario. Flow level data can be had from the appropriate provincial offices.

Map information on recently prepared topographic sheets is usually fairly accurate, although you must make allowances for the fact that maps of wilderness areas are done mainly from aerial surveys. The major errors of the past, when surface surveyors often had to guess at watersheds, have pretty well disappeared. There are limits on the data that can be gained from the air, however, as well as occasional mistakes in the maps themselves, and the cruise planner has to allow for the possibility of inaccuracies.

Other sources of information should be evaluated even more carefully. Guidebooks and articles in magazines range in quality from near perfection to very low levels. The same is true of verbal information. It is important to evaluate all such sources critically. Are they detailed, or general? How long was the cruise taken before the piece was written or the conversation held? Is the description based on memory, or on notes made at the time? Is the information firsthand or is it actually second- or thirdhand? How good a paddler is the person making the evaluation, and does he understand your level of experience? What kind of craft were being paddled on the trip described, and what kind are you taking? What was the time of year and the water level, if the trip was a river run, and what are they likely to be when you plan on going? Remember that descriptions may vary tremendously in quality even within a guidebook, since the sources may not be the same.

People or guidebooks that give detailed information on finding portages, on put-ins and take-outs, on the difficulty of rapids and points from which to look them over or the likelihood of dangerous wind on a particular pass between lakes, on the level of experience needed to make a trip safely, and on the type of craft that are suitable are usually more reliable than those that are vague on such points. It is easy to forget a particular difficult portage or dangerous rapid a few years after a trip is over. Memory of one pleasant day's paddling may gloss over the three days that a party spent miserably tracking back and forth through marsh and bog, looking for a portage between two lakes. If the single rapid being discussed was run by expert paddlers in C-1s and kayaks it may prove disastrous for paddlers of moderate ability in open canoes. You need to view all the information gathered with a jaundiced eye and carefully review it. When possible, compare several descriptions. You will often find that various accounts of the same trip sound as though they describe completely different ones.

Written guides vary a great deal in availability as well as quality. A number are stocked in bookstores and canoeing shops, but often only in those near the area covered, which does not help trip planners who live halfway across the country. The American Canoe Association (address on page 208) carries a number of guides, but many locally published ones are hard to find. Sometimes a letter to a local canoe club affiliated with either the ACA or the American Whitewater Affiliation (P. O. Box 321, Concord, New Hampshire 03301), will elicit reliable information on local rivers. Back issues of the various canoeing magazines and club journals are also useful but usually hard to obtain.

Many state and provincial tourist bureaus and departments have brochures, maps, and booklets on canoeing in their areas. These range in quality from excellent publications that are detailed and useful to others that are poor and quite misleading. Some of the Canadian railroads provide access to superb canoeing and have good information about it, so if the means of getting to your chosen river or lake is by railroad, write to see whether the company can help. Canadian trains will usually let you off and pick you up in the middle of the bush. U.S. railroads are not helpful in this way; except for the Alaska Railroad, their trains will not stop to let a canoeist out, anyhow.

A final mention should be made of historical accounts of canoe journeys. A good library will have dozens of these gathering dust up in the stacks, some of which provide excellent ideas for trips and superb information about them. Clearly, one has to do further research on the impact that civilization has had on the waterways, but the results are sometimes surprising. As one would expect, most of those classic waterways have been dammed, diverted into nonexistence, or polluted beyond recognition, but some of the ones in the North are actually wilder than they were a century ago, when the gold rushes brought tens of thousands of people up the rivers. The modern sojourner can have his history and wilderness too, perhaps in the form of a wrecked paddleboat with not a soul for a hundred miles. There's gold on them there library shelves!

TIMETABLES

One of the most common mistakes in planning canoe trips is to underestimate the time the cruise will take. There are so many fine lakes to paddle and rivers to run that one naturally tries to squeeze as much into a short vacation as possible. The most common result of this error is that the trip is far less enjoyable than one in which half the distance is covered. A trip that is slow enough permits occasional rest days if they are wanted, allows time for exploring side canyons, fishing, or lying around camp, and generally makes the experience more pleasant. If the person planning the cruise bites off more than the party can chew, the result is likely to be paddling into the late hours trying to keep to the schedule, passing up desirable side trips, and rushing to meet a final deadline imposed by the need to get back to work or to avoid having a search party sent out.

The distance that can be covered in a day will depend on the party, their canoes, and the nature of the trip. A group that customarily does twenty-five miles of paddling on a day trip without working too hard or putting in too long a day can probably do the same on a comparable stretch of paddling on a long cruise. The important word is *comparable,* however, and the less one knows of the exact conditions on the trip being undertaken, the more time has to be allowed for error. Driving, loading, and unloading time seems to balance out roughly with the time taken to set up and break camp and pack and unpack the duffel in the canoes. Many variables affect the trip timetable, some of them predictable in advance and some not. A headwind on a big lake can cut progress to a quarter of what it was or stop it altogether if the velocity is high. A lower rate of runoff on a river may cut progress considerably or may speed things up if a number of rapids are made easier. A difficult portage may consume days. Even a short portage is likely to kill an hour or two by the time all the delays it causes are taken into account.

SHUTTLES

The simplest type of canoe trip to plan is one that begins and ends in the same place, so that you can simply drive to the put-in, leaving the cars there until you return. Most cruises are not so simple, however, and the shuttle often requires more thought and advance preparation than any other part of the trip. The exact plan depends heavily on the particular circumstances, but it should be thought out fairly carefully.

Large groups generally have the easiest time with shuttle arrangements, particularly with trips that are not too far from home, so that there is less reason to concentrate on taking the minimum number of vehicles. Many clubs own trailers to simplify the shuttling.

A typical shuttle plan is for everyone to drive to the put-in, where the canoes and most of the members of the party are left. While those remaining at the put-in get everything organized, the drivers take the cars to the take-out, and one car brings all the drivers back. At the end of the trip, this car must be picked up. The exact arrangement of trips back and forth cannot be laid out since they will vary, but it can be quite significant if the distance by road between the put-in and take-out is, say, three hundred miles. A badly planned shuttle can consume several days of the trip as well as many dollars' worth of gas.

There are many techniques for handling shuttle problems. For example, one person who can get away a bit earlier may be able to drive a big car that can carry all the canoes or tow a trailer to the take-out, taking a motorcycle or bicycle along to get him to the put-in, or being followed by someone else who can give him a ride. His canoe is taken by another car. The other cars are then left at the put-in and the shuttle car drags everything back. One person or several, depending on group size, may be able to hitchhike or take a bus for half the shuttle, either at the beginning of the trip or the end.

On long trips it is frequently simplest to pay a local person to drive the shuttle for you. This usually saves a great deal of time, and on some trips the reduced use of fuel may even make this the cheapest means of handling the shuttle. Again, details vary with the situation, but arrangements are typically made in advance by letter or phone, and the shuttle driver is picked up on the way to the put-in. The canoeists can then start as soon as they are unpacked, and the shuttle driver takes the car to the take-out point either immediately or on an agreed date. The shuttle driver either arranges to be picked up by someone or, if an exact rendezvous time can be arranged, meets the boaters at the end of their run and rides back with them. On trips where the access roads are long, a situation common in canoe country, major fuel savings are possible if the driver lives in a town that is on the way. In this situation you can pick up your driver, go to the put-in, and have the car brought to your take-out at a prearranged time so that the car does not have to be driven back and forth along the access roads.

For example, if six people with two cars and three canoes are making a river trip where the access roads, each 150 miles long, begin in the same town, they would probably have to spend a couple of days doing the shuttle. If all the canoes, equipment, and people could be put in (and on) one car, then the shuttle could be done with a total of 1,200 vehicle miles, the same as if a shuttle were hired, but this would still require at least a day of extra time for the canoeists to go to the take-out first and leave a car there. If not everything can be carried by one car, the boaters would have to drive both cars to the put-in first, then both to the take-out, leaving one; then the other would have to be driven back to the put-in. After getting off the river, the car there will have to be driven back to the put-in to pick up the other, and at least one will have to go back to the take-out again to pick up the people and gear still there. Both cars may have to make this trip if enough had to be left. This results in either 2,100 or 2,400 vehicle miles. The cost of 900 or 1,200 extra vehicle miles is certainly enough to pay a good portion of the fee charged by most shuttle drivers, and often it will amount to considerably more than the total.

At some roadheads it is worthwhile to arrange for the shuttle driver to take the car home for most of the time you will spend on your trip, to avoid the possibility of vandalism. This is not usually a problem, but there are exceptions. Be sure your shuttle drivers are reliable, particularly if you are arranging a rendezvous. Make advance contingency plans with shuttle drivers so that everyone understands what will be done in case someone does not arrive at the appointed place and hour due to delay of the river party, washed-out roads, or similar unforeseen circumstances.

Be careful to plan gasoline carefully in shuttles. The example mentioned above should give an idea of the sort of mileage that can be driven in some shuttles. A trip out for gas in the middle can greatly increase mileage and time, and running out of gas on a remote road can cost so much time that the trip has to be aborted.

Shuttle cars should be in good mechanical condition, particularly if the party is on a tight time schedule. A dead battery can be costly in time. If you choose to take a clunker, at least be sure everyone knows and accepts the risk, so that you can laugh about your problems together, rather than having people angry at one another.

THE PARTY

Choosing the people to go on a trip is often the most important aspect of planning. One weak member or one strong person who wants to go twice as fast as everyone else can ruin a cruise. Good parties can be either quite evenly matched or quite disparate in abilities, provided everyone has at least the minimum skill, strength, and endurance required, and provided the nature of the trek and the attitudes of the party about it are mutually understood and shared. Groups with a wide range of levels of skill will have fun together only if the strong members do not feel they are being held back by people who have no business on the trip and weak ones do not perceive themselves as being unfairly pushed beyond their capacities.

The trick is to make sure you have a common understanding of goals at the beginning. If the trip is going to be a marathon bash, then the members should be of roughly equal ability and everyone should know what it will be like. If it is to be a leisurely family excursion, don't take someone along who will be miserable if he is not paddling hard from dawn to dusk.

Make sure your party is up to the trip. Paddling ability on water close to the road is not the only criterion. On long trips at least some of the group need to have a good understanding of wilderness travel. Cool heads and good leadership are as important on multiday trips as is technical paddling ability. First-aid knowledge, ability to deal with emergency situations, and a capacity for unobtrusively keeping others out of trouble are more important than muscular strength. An ability to paddle a rapid is less useful to the group than an understanding of when it would be better to portage.

Long after the memory of a particular stretch of lake or individual rapid has faded, recollection of the companionship experienced on a good canoe trip will remain. The friendship and experiences of and with other people are the finest and most enduring of canoeing pleasures. A compatible party is thus the most important choice of all.

CHAPTER 11

BUILDING A CANOE

There are two basic methods that are reasonably suitable for the home builder who wants to make a canoe. The more difficult and time consuming uses a wood strip construction covered with fiberglass and resin. This method produces some of the most beautiful canoes ever made, and strip-fiberglass canoes are also fairly durable. The stripping technique is to cut a number of forms that are the shape of cross sections of the inside of the finished canoe. These forms, usually cut from plywood, are fastened securely at the proper distances along a solid beam. Thin strips of wood are then attached to the forms. These strips bend over the forms to make the hull of the canoe. To produce a fine canoe, the strips must be closely fitted. The outside of the hull is then sanded, covered with fiberglass, and saturated with resin. The surface is then finished. When it has cured, the beam and forms can be removed and the inside of the canoe finished in the same manner. The seats, thwarts, decks, and other accessories can then be installed.

Curing times of resins are dependent on the temperature, humidity, and mixture. It is a good idea to do a few sample coupons of fiberglass scraps and resin before starting any project, to get a feeling for these factors. With epoxies, mixtures are usually fixed, and to speed a cure you must create warmer temperatures. With polyesters and vinyl esters, additional catalyst may be added to speed cures at cooler temperatures. When in doubt, add less catalyst and wait for a cure, rather than risk having the resin start to harden when you are in the middle of working.

Strip-fiberglass canoes are time consuming to build, particularly for the beginner, but the technique is highly recommended to those willing to go to the trouble necessary to make one of these beautiful canoes. This method has several advantages besides aesthetic ones. No mold is necessary, so a strip canoe can be built from either several available plans or from the builder's own design. The builder is not limited by available molds, and the finished product, although it makes use of modern materials, has a beauty that can be achieved only by fine handcrafting.

Those interested in building strip-fiberglass canoes should obtain either David Hazen's book *The Stripper's Guide to Canoe Building* or the *USCA Strip-Construction Manual,* available from Jim Mack, the treasurer of the United States Canoe Association, 606 Ross Street, Middletown, Ohio 45042. Hazen's book includes plans for several beautiful boats and there are some different types available from the USCA.

Standard fiberglass construction is considerably easier and therefore more practical for the average builder. Basically, the technique consists of laying fiberglass cloth in a prepared mold, saturating it with resin, and allowing the resin-impregnated fiberglass to cure into a fairly rigid hull. The hull is then trimmed and finished, and gunwales, thwarts, seats, decks, and flotation next fastened in place. Roughly half the work consists of molding the hull, the other half in finishing and outfitting the canoe.

Often the major effort involved in building a canoe is finding a suitable mold and materials. The two main sources of molds are clubs and companies that sell fiberglass and resin. Making a mold is a third possibility, but not a practical one for the first-time builder. Contacting canoe clubs in your area is a good way to start, many such clubs having their own molds or members who do. When this is the case they probably also have a cooperative arrangement for buying materials. You will need to spend some time talking with experienced builders in the club to be sure you understand exactly the procedures used in molding the hull. This sort of conference will probably be required before you are permitted to use a mold anyway, but you should insist on it. A mold is expensive and time consuming to make, and a small error on your part could ruin it. Furthermore, since you will probably have the use of it for only a limited time, it is important to have everything prepared in advance.

When dealing with a company that rents or loans molds to people who purchase materials from them, it may help to talk with a knowledgeable salesperson, but it is also worthwhile to take home and study a copy of the directions that the company provides before paying any money.

MATERIALS

The materials used for fiberglass construction are modern, high-technology synthetics, and a complete discussion of them would require several books. The average builder will have little choice but to rely on others for selection, using a few rule-of-thumb guidelines to judge what he is getting. Fiberglass construction uses flexible fibers to form a matrix that is stiffened and bonded by a resin that hardens as a result of a chemical reaction. The fibers are normally formed into a cloth that is laid in the mold and then wetted with the resin. There are many types of cloth and resin available, and quite a few are used for building canoes, but the builder's choice will probably be quite limited because of supply problems and the difficulty of buying small lots of these materials.

For reasonable strength, flexibility, and weight, all the cloth in the layup of the canoe hull should be woven. Mat, which is a feltlike material made from relatively short fibers pressed together in a random pattern, absorbs too much resin, has a nonuniform thickness, and gives weak reinforcement. A canoe made with mat is heavy, brittle, and weak. Mat is sometimes useful for attaching accessories because it bends around corners easily, but it should be used sparingly even for this purpose. Cloth to be used for hand layup of canoes should not be too heavy (generally not more than ten ounces per square yard) or too tightly woven or it will be difficult to work with.

Unless you have researched the subject, it is best to buy cloth and resin from the same source, with assurances that the whole system is compatible. Cloth often must have particular surfacing treatment to bond properly with a resin. Incorrectly matched combinations may later result in delamination of your canoe.

When buying from a company that loans molds, you will often be able to purchase a kit that contains all the necessary materials. This is a good way to start, provided the quality is good, because you are assured of properly matched components, efficient cutting, and the like. It is a good idea to check with someone who has built one of the company's kits beforehand, however, to find out problems in advance. Also be sure to check all the contents before leaving to be sure nothing is missing. You should understand every stage of the building process before buying the materials, or you may find yourself with a short-term loan of a mold but without a suitable place to build or some necessary tool.

The standard cloth for canoe building is regular fiberglass (E-glass) in a weight of ten ounces per square yard. Four or five layers are used to produce a hull of normal weight, although it is possible to use lighter layups with adequate reinforcement. Five layers of ten-ounce cloth are recommended for beginners. Eight layers of six-ounce E-glass or four layers of twelve-ounce would be roughly equivalent.

If other types of cloth are used, one should carefully check both the compatibility with the resin system and the experience that others have had with the combination. Some builders use a layer of polypropylene or nylon cloth to replace a layer of fiberglass. These materials help hold damaged areas together but will decrease rigidity. S-glass is a type of fiberglass that is considerably stronger than E-glass, but it is more expensive, much harder to obtain, and may be difficult to match with the resin systems being used. Kevlar (a trade name of Dupont) is an extremely strong material that can be used to make light canoes, but it is expensive, trickier to work with than fiberglass, and difficult to obtain, so beginners would be well advised to make their first canoes with fiberglass rather than Kevlar. The two major types of resins used for building canoes are polyesters and epoxies. There are different varieties of each, though the polyesters normally used for boat building are more standardized than the epoxies. Properly used, epoxies will make stronger boats for a given amount of weight than polyesters. The epoxies that are most suitable for making canoes are more dangerous to work with and are trickier to use, though, so beginners should generally stick to polyesters for their first efforts.

SAFETY

The materials used in making canoes are commonly used for many industrial applications and are not particularly dangerous if safety precautions are taken, but it is important to respect these materials. Fumes from the resin systems are toxic. Particles of glass from fiberglass cloth are irritating to the skin, and contact with uncured resin components can cause dermatological problems. It is important to work in a well-ventilated area, wear a respirator when working with uncured resin or using motorized sanders or saws on fiberglass, wear gloves and protective clothing when needed, work in a place that will not permit fumes to get into living quarters, and above all to work cleanly. Although building a canoe is not particularly difficult, both good results and safety depend on careful attention to detail and neat, methodical working habits. If you find it hard to work this way, it would be better to buy a finished canoe.

Protect your skin with disposable coverall-type clothing whenever it might come into contact with resin. Careful working will make coveralls unnecessary most of the time, but wear old clothes that can be thrown out, and have a number of pairs of disposable plastic gloves handy. Minor contact with resin components is not serious, but to avoid developing allergic reactions it is best to be reasonably careful and to use soap and water to remove any resin that gets on the skin. Keep the surroundings clean by spreading out newspaper to catch drips and replacing paper that gets resin on it as soon as possible. Large numbers of drips lying around guarantee tracking and spreading.

When working with resin, you should wear a respirator that removes harmful vapors, although many people do not use one. There is no sense in taking chances with highly active organic compounds such as those used in resin systems.

Particles of fiberglass inevitably get on the skin and into clothes when one is building a boat. Wear clothes that protect most of the body, and segregate them from other clothing. It is best to ignore itching from fiberglass particles, since scratching makes things worse. Don't rub your face or eyes with arms or hands when working with glass. A tight-fitting plastic bag is often useful to keep things out of your hair. Shower after working and change clothes, and you will have few problems with the glass. Wear a respirator or dust mask when sanding or working with so-called thixotropic agents that are sometimes added to resin to make it cling better to the sides of the mold. Solvents that will work on resin systems are usually more dangerous than the resins themselves, so it is best to stick to soap and water.

PREPARATION

The first step in building is to find a place to work. A garage or a covered porch may be fine, but this will depend on such details as the weather. Unheated areas are suitable only when temperatures are balmy. Lighting and ventilation must be adequate, and it is not a good idea to work where fumes will make their way into living quarters. The ideal is a well-ventilated place that can be kept at a temperature of around seventy degrees Fahrenheit and that is not subject to falling leaves, blowing dust, flying insects, bird droppings, and other undesirable additions to the layup of the canoe.

In the shop you should have some sturdy supports for the mold that will hold it so that the top is about waist level and there is easy access to all sides. Sawhorses with blocks or cradles attached, a table with cradles fixed to it, or a frame built onto a large beam might be used. The intervals at which supports are necessary depend on the rigidity of the mold, but be sure it is well enough braced to prevent distortion. Once work has started, you will need to be able to get to any part of the mold. Some good things to have available are a drill, screwdrivers, a saber saw, a linoleum knife, scissors for cutting fiberglass (they should be of reasonable quality but will dull quickly), old scissors for cutting resin-soaked fiberglass, a sander or sanding attachment for the drill, assorted sandpaper for both the sander and handwork, newspapers, clean-up supplies, disposable gloves (available at medical supply houses and elsewhere), wax paper and plastic food wrap (not Saran Wrap, which has a different chemical composition and will bond to the resin) for surface coverings to which the resin will not stick, a respirator, movable lights, large and small paper containers for mixing resin, stirring sticks, a container to measure catalyst for the resin (should be available where you get the resin—range of about 1–20 cc's), and tools for applying and working resin. For this last purpose, cheap paintbrushes of various sizes are handy, as are metal rollers and squeegees five inches square and smaller, which can be made from dish drain mats and similar products or purchased at houses supplying auto body shops. A foam paintbrush is good for applying PVA (polyvinyl alcohol) to the mold, and soft, clean cloths are needed for waxing it.

If you are buying a kit, some of the items mentioned above may be supplied, but check this in advance. If you are buying materials separately, you will need to figure the amount of materials to be used and purchase them before picking up the mold. If a pattern is available, use it to calculate the amount of material needed, but if there is none it is worthwhile to cut one yourself from a piece of plastic sheeting, so that waste of fiberglass cloth is minimized. Unless the cloth is at least sixty inches wide, in most cases it will not be wide enough to cut full-sized patterns from it. With narrower cloth it will be necessary to cut a number of pieces that will lie across the mold for each layer of cloth. These should be cut with a six-inch overlap at each junction, and the overlaps in successive layers should not all be on top of one another. Cloth requirements will vary with width and with the particular shape and size of the canoe. As an example, a 16½-foot canoe might require thirty or thirty-five yards of sixty-inch cloth and five or six gallons of resin. Kits should supply adequate resin; otherwise, try to buy with an agreement that you may return unopened containers within a certain length of time so that you will not be caught short while working at one o'clock some morning. Generous allowances are five gallons for small canoes, six for intermediate ones, and seven for large canoes.

THE MOLD

Before picking up a mold, inspect it carefully and talk with the owner about its condition, the terms of use, and any instructions and recommendations he may have. Ask questions; it is important to understand any instructions clearly. If there are imperfections in the mold, they may require some time for you to repair, and a reduction in the fee is in order. A deposit may be required, in which case it is important to be agreed on the conditions for its return.

Most wise mold owners will have quite explicit instructions on preparation of the mold and may sell preparation materials. Since different release materials may not be compatible, use the ones provided or recommended by the owner.

A really good mold should be perfectly smooth on the inside. Before using the mold, repair any rough spots where pieces have been pulled away in bad releases; otherwise, the next release (yours) will be worse. A mold that is scratched at all has to be polished or refinished, and this requires a good deal of work. Don't walk into such a project unless you know what you are doing.

Small imperfections can be filled in with paraffin and smoothed before the rest of the mold preparation. This method is not permanent and will have to be repeated by the next user.

The mold should also be quite rigid. If it deflects when one end is lifted, it will have to be cradled and braced at a number of points to avoid having a warped canoe. The mold will be heavy, so when you go to pick it up, use a car that has a really sturdy rack. Transport it with the inside surface covered with clean blankets to be sure of avoiding damage. If the mold is polyester, don't let it come in contact with a hot car roof, or you may put a dent in it that will be irreparable. Have a helper, since the mold will probably require two people to handle it.

Once you have the mold in your own working area, make the pattern for cutting cloth if you have not already done so, unless you have a kit with precut cloth. Once the pattern is cut, you can begin preparing the mold if you are ready to work. Cloth can be cut while mold wax is drying. If you don't want to do two things at the same time, cut the cloth first, on an absolutely clean surface. A large worktable is ideal, but a floor that has been carefully cleaned or covered with newspapers will do. Roll up each piece of cloth, cover it with newspaper, and label the piece. Follow a standard convention; I would suggest rolling each piece up, starting at the stern, so that the end of the cloth that will be in the bow of the canoe is at the outside of each roll. This is particularly important if the boat is not symmetrical. If you have any doubts about fit, check the pieces at this point, before beginning work on the boat. The fiberglass must be kept dry, clean, and uncontaminated.

Wipe the mold carefully with a soft clean cloth, and be sure there are no scratches before starting to prepare the surface. If the shop needs cleaning, do this before beginning work on the mold, since the job will have to be redone if dirt gets into the surfacing materials.

At least three coats of mold-release wax should be put on the entire inside surface of the mold. Adjust the lighting before you begin working, to be sure that you will be able to see well—it is important not to miss any spots. If the condition of the mold is less than perfect put on more wax, but don't expect to get a good release if there are more than minor imperfections. Each coat should be applied in a thin layer, allowed to dry, and polished lightly. Hard polishing simply rubs most of the wax off.

After the surface of the mold is waxed, carefully apply a thin layer of PVA over the whole area. A three-inch foam brush is perfect for the job, but a soft cloth will do. The ideal application is a thin, smooth coat with no breaks. Try to avoid having to go back over sections already done, but do not miss any spots. Once the PVA dries, which may require fifteen minutes to a couple of hours, the mold is ready. Take care not to scratch the film or get any moisture on it—PVA is water soluble.

THE RESIN SYSTEM

Before starting to lay up the hull, have all the tools for working the resin ready: brushes, rollers, and squeegees. Be sure you understand what you will be doing and that you have enough time and the right conditions. Once the process of laying up has started, it should be finished in one session if at all possible. Any one layer of fiberglass *must* be completely wetted out before the resin begins to cure, or the boat will be lost.

Lay each layer of cloth in the mold and saturate it with resin, carefully working out any air bubbles and pockets and using as little resin as possible. The cloth must be saturated: sections with air bubbles, "resin-starved" areas that show white, will weaken the canoe. However, more resin than necessary makes the boat heavy and brittle. The next layer should be laid in while the first is still tacky. If one layer is allowed to cure fully before the next is put in, the first must be thoroughly sanded to a rough surface to get a good bond or else the hull is likely to delaminate at some time.

It is well to measure components of the resin system for at least several layers in advance. If pigment is to be applied it should be mixed with two gallons or so of resin, which should be used in the first two or three layers in the boat. The more common coloring method is to color brightly a "gel coat," an outer surfacing layer of resin that is painted on the mold before putting in the first layer of glass. If you have a kit including a colored gel coat you will have no choice, but this method shows scratches much more quickly. Do not use pigments unless you are sure they are compatible with the particular resin system you are using. If you are using an epoxy system, you will probably have to preweigh several resin batches. Good scales are generally required. Such systems are very sensitive to temperature. The standard polyester systems have a little more latitude, since they are activated with a catalyst; within limits, larger amounts of catalyst will speed the hardening of the resin and will offset the effects of lower temperatures. Add the catalyst with a volume measurement, following directions carefully according to temperature. Start with two-quart batches. Proportions are not listed here, because the catalyst MEKP (methyl ethyl ketone peroxide) comes in different concentrations. You should receive mixing instructions when you buy the resin. For a start, use proportions that give about a one-hour "gel time," the time before the resin begins to become extremely viscous as it begins to set up. Work at a temperature of about seventy or seventy-five degrees, with the resin at room temperature. Be extremely careful, especially when handling the catalyst; it is the most dangerous part of the system.

Most builders begin with a gel coat to provide a smooth layer on the outside of the canoe. A lighter boat can be made without this coat, but more care will have to be taken to saturate the first layer of cloth very well. A colored gel coat also protects other layers from the degrading effects of ultraviolet rays. You can paint the gel coat on with a brush, taking care not to damage the PVA coat on the mold. Keep the coat thin or it will add weight and flake off easily. If the same resin is being used for the gel coat as for the layup, you can judge its consistency at this point. If the resin runs down the sides of the mold and pools at the bottom so badly that a reasonable layer cannot be achieved, it needs to have added a thixotropic agent such as cab-o-sil, as you will have the same problem in the main layup.

LAYING UP THE HULL

Once the gel coat has been applied, but before it hardens, lay in the first (outer) layer of cloth. Be sure the edges come above the edges of the mold. Work out all wrinkles carefully, starting in the center and working toward the sides. Be sure the cloth is pushed all the way down in the ends and in the keel, if there is one. Mix up a batch of resin and pour a line of it down the center of the boat. Work from the center up the sides, allowing the resin to saturate a section of cloth completely before squeegeeing the resin up farther. Trying to speed the process by pushing resin up before it has saturated one section will simply trap air under the surface of the cloth, which will be difficult to remove.

As soon as a section of cloth is fully saturated, use a roller or squeegee to push the excess resin farther up the side, in order to saturate that area in turn. Work slowly, taking care to push all trapped air out to the side. Squeeze out as much excess resin as possible, but if the cloth begins to look white again instead of dark, you are pushing out too much resin and air is getting back into the matrix of the cloth. Do not pull the cloth so hard that it stretches to make an air space next to the mold. This is a danger, particularly at sharp bending points, such as the keel and the ends of the canoe.

Once a layer is complete, lay the cloth in carefully for the next layer. If a mistake is made during this process, peel it out carefully so that the finished layer is not pulled up. Repeat the process until the entire hull is complete. Extra scraps may be put in between layers, along the stems at each end, for extra strength. If a keel or ribs are to be put in for rigidity, it is well to insert them before the last layer sets up so that sanding does not have to be done. Sections of one-inch dowel can be used for this purpose, with several pieces of heavy cloth laid over each one and saturated with resin to hold them in.

If wrinkles develop in the cloth while you are laying it in, try to work them out with a squeegee, working the fabric back on either side of the wrinkle. In cases where this does not work, use old scissors to cut through the center of the wrinkle and then overlap one side with the other.

CUTTING OFF EXCESS CLOTH

With polyester boats it is easiest to trim off the projecting cloth after the boat has begun to cure but before it has really hardened. When this stage is reached, the projecting material can be carefully cut away with a linoleum knife. Cut from inside the mold so that the material is pressed against it and work very carefully, being sure not to damage the flange of the mold. If the boat has been allowed to harden, wait until it has been removed from the mold before trimming. Scribe a line with the linoleum knife and do the cutting with a saber saw. Never use the saw while the hull is still in the mold. Boats using Kevlar cloth or epoxy resins will have to be trimmed with a saw after curing.

The boat should be well protected from dirt and moisture until it is cured. The room should be kept warm. Heat will speed the cure, as will sunlight, but care should be taken not to use excessive heat with polyester boats. Allow the boat to cure well before removing it from the mold. It can be wrecked if you are in too much of a hurry. Twenty-four hours at about seventy degrees Fahrenheit is reasonable.

REMOVING THE HULL FROM THE MOLD

The art to "popping" the boat is really in the preparation of the mold. A bad release is an indication of sloppy application or poorly chosen release materials. If you experience any trouble, it is a good idea to get in touch with the mold owner and solicit his help.

Releasing the boat is normally fairly uncomplicated. Start at the center of one side and use fingers or a small wooden wedge to separate the boat from the mold, leaving a wide enough space so that you can insert your fingers. Don't use metal tools for this, since they will damage the mold. If the edges have not been trimmed you can simply grab the projecting material. Go over to the other side of the mold, grab the section of the hull you have pried loose from the other side, and gently pull it over a few inches. Work down from the center in each direction, pulling the sides loose, but don't try to haul the boat out by main force. Then repeat with the other side. Keep working the hull loose until it finally pops out.

If you have a hard release, work patiently, trying to minimize damage. Wooden wedges can be used with care; if given time, water poured into the spaces will help by dissolving the layer of PVA. Remember that it is easier to build another boat than another mold.

FINISHING THE CANOE

There are many methods of finishing a fiberglass canoe. Gunwales may be made of aluminum or molded in one piece with thwarts and seats. The method shown here uses mahogany gunwales. Four strips are needed, nominally one-inch square and long enough to run the entire length of the top of one of the sides, which will be greater than the length of the canoe. Any hardwood can be used, but avoid softwoods for the gunwales.

Decide how high you want the ends of the canoe before installing the gunwales. Some molds leave the canoe with an excessively high bow and stern, which can be improved by scribing them and cutting off the unwanted height with a saber saw. Ends that curve up too rapidly are also likely to cause the gunwales to split, so they may have to be ended a foot or so back from high curving ends.

Sand three sides of each of the gunwale pieces. The unsanded sides are installed facing up so that the top of the side and the tops of the two gunwales on each side of the boat can be sanded flush and finished together.

Measure the centerline of the canoe and mark its position on each side. Fit the inside gunwale to one side by trial and error; enough material has to be cut off so that the gunwale will just fit along the inside edge of one side. Cut another gunwale to the same length and bevel

Installing mahogany gunwales. Once the strips have been sanded and cut roughly to length, one section at a time is clamped along the upper edge of one of the canoe sides. Each side requires two strips, one on the inside and one on the outside. The trickiest part is near the bow and stern, where the ends must be trimmed to fit and bent more severely. Here the far-side gunwale has already been attached and the near side is clamped for drilling.

After each section is clamped and drilled, screws are installed to hold the gunwales in place.

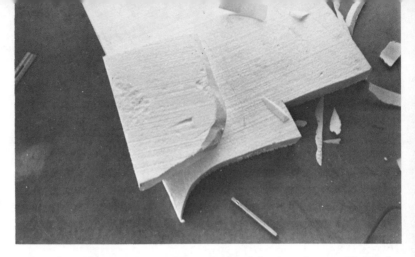

A Styrofoam sheet can be cut into a series of fitted sections to fill flotation chambers at the ends of the canoe. A saber saw with a razor blade attachment works well for the cutting. Begin by making the pieces too large and trim them down to fit.

One end of the canoe after the gunwales have been installed and trimmed and a plywood triangle put in place for a deck. Fiberglass brackets for the seat have been installed, and Styrofoam flotation is being fitted.

the ends of each so that their ends will mate with each other. (Remember when cutting the bevels that the unfinished sides face up.) The outside gunwales should be cut approximately to length, but they can project several inches at this stage.

Mark the center of each gunwale, then clamp one set of gunwales at the center to one side of the canoe. Drill countersunk screw holes at approximately 6-inch intervals along the gunwales, and install 1¼-inch plated, stainless, or brass screws. Alternate the screws, first from the outside gunwale going in, then from the inside out. Do a couple of feet toward one end and a few feet toward the other end, moving the clamps as necessary to hold the gunwales along the curve. As more curve is required toward the ends, use 4-inch intervals between screws.

Flotation and decks can also be handled in several ways, one good method being to make decks and flotation chambers from plywood, which can then be covered with fiberglass. Styrofoam inserts in the chamber will ensure retention of most of the flotation, even in case a hole is broken in the hull. Cut isosceles triangles from quarter-inch plywood, eighteen inches long and of the correct width to fit exactly into the ends of the canoe, in the angle formed immediately under the gunwales. These decks will lend rigidity to the sides of the canoe after installation, as well as hold in flotation. Brace these triangles in underneath the gunwales at each end of the canoe. Cut sections from a two-inch sheet of Styrofoam, available from lumberyards, to fit into the ends. One convenient method is to make cardboard patterns that fit the canoe cross section at two-inch intervals and trace these patterns on the Styrofoam, doing detailed trimming afterward. Once the Styrofoam pieces are cut, snip out a triangle of fiberglass cloth to just fit the top of the plywood triangle (use two layers if the cloth is lighter than ten ounces per square yard). Saturate the cloth with resin and brace the deck in under the gunwales with the foam. Allow the resin to cure. Now cut a piece of plywood to form a wall under the deck to hold the Styrofoam and brace the deck, trimming it to fit closely. Cut a few pieces of fiberglass to fit over this bulkhead with a two-inch overlap, saturate the glass with resin, and seal in the bulkhead.

Now, at each end of the canoe install grab loops, to which painters can be attached when they are wanted. You can use quarter-inch or five-eighths-inch rope, or one-inch webbing. Synthetics that will not rot are strongest and should be used, preferably marine rope, which is weakened less by sunlight than are some other types. Drill the holes of correct size through the gunwales as far forward as possible, leaving room for knotting inside. Install the grab loops.

The ends of the canoe should be covered with small end caps made with about five layers of fiberglass scraps to protect the ends of the gunwales when the canoe is turned over on the ground. Cut triangles to fit the ends, wrapping them around the gunwales and extending back about four inches, then lay them up with resin.

Satisfactory but rather heavy seats can be constructed from hardwood boards; or scrap boards can serve as templates and a wooden frame be made for a webbing seat, which can then be filled with nylon or polypropylene webbing. Cut the ends of the boards being used either for seats or patterns to fit the sides of the canoe. The front of the stern seat should be approximately forty inches from the stern of the canoe and the front of the bow seat between fifty and fifty-five inches from the bow. These placements are approximate and may be adjusted for canoe design, size, and the like. If the canoe will regularly be paddled by a light person in the bow and a heavy one in the stern, for example, the bow seat may be moved forward somewhat to balance the boat. Block the seats experimentally until the correct height is achieved. They should be as low as possible consistent with the feet fitting under easily in the kneeling position. Once the correct position is found, mark the positions with a marking pen on the sides of the canoe. Sand down the areas below each of the seats until glass fibers are exposed, or the bond of the brackets to be installed will be weak.

Cover the ends of each of the seats with wax paper and tape it in place. Set the canoe upside down on stands high enough so that you can work comfortably under it. Block the seats into position from below with wood scraps, and then lay up fiberglass brackets, using fiberglass scraps, to form right angles on top of the upside-down seats.

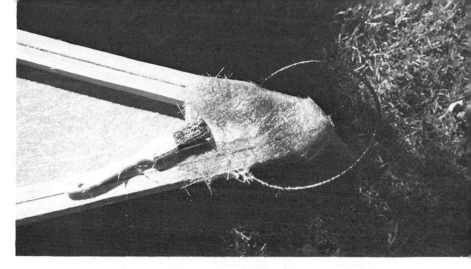

An end cap of fiberglass is put on to protect the ends of the gunwales, using fiberglass wetted out with resin and a brush. A grab loop has already been installed through holes bored in the gunwales. The grab loops shown are made of a special high-strength synthetic. Thicker material should normally be used.

Once the seats have been fitted to the ends of the canoe, the ends of each seat should be covered with wax paper and the seats blocked into the upside-down canoe. The brackets can then be laid up without sticking to the seats. If they are made of good wood, boards like this can be used for seats, or a lighter frame seat can be made using the board as a template.

These should be at least four or five inches wide, should project from the sides of the canoe three or four inches, and should extend five or six inches down the sides of the canoe. After these have cured, drill the boards and brackets, install machine screws with eyebolts, and either finish the boards as seats or make frame and webbing ones.

Thwarts are easily made from one-by-two-inch hardwood boards with the edges sanded round and shaped with a plane to lighten them if desired. These are bolted to the gunwales.

Finish the canoe by sanding down all rough spots in the fiberglass layup and painting the inside of the canoe, bulkheads, decks, and end-caps with epoxy or polyester paint or surfacing resin. Sand the tops of the gunwales and sides and give the gunwales, thwarts, and seats several coats of good quality marine varnish.

CHAPTER 12

MAKING ACCESSORIES FOR CANOEING

There are quite a number of accessories for canoeing that can easily be made at home for a fraction of the cost of commercially available equipment. Other items are more difficult for the individual builder and should be attempted only by those who particularly enjoy such work or who have specialized equipment or skills. Detailed instructions are given in this chapter for some items and others are discussed briefly.

PADDLES

Not too long ago, one could save a good deal of money by making one's own paddles, besides having the pleasure of using a very personal piece of equipment in canoeing. However, most canoeists these days prefer either fiberglass and aluminum paddles or really high-quality ones made with laminated wood, perhaps covered with fiberglass. It is difficult to make really good fiberglass paddles that have the virtues of strength, light weight, and durability without presses and special molds, although some possible techniques remain to be explored. Those who want an adequate but inexpensive paddle would probably be better advised to purchase one of the paddles made with ABS plastic blades.

Home craftsmen willing to take the time can certainly produce fine laminated wood paddles, but their manufacture is quite time consuming, satisfying though it may be. Those who would like to obtain reasonably good quality wood paddles with a little less effort and expense can purchase one of the kits advertised in canoeing magazines.

POLES

An aluminum pole is easy to make very inexpensively. The only complication is in obtaining materials, but an hour or so on the telephone should locate them. Find a yard that supplies small lots of aluminum to local machine shops and manufacturers. You need a twelve-foot length of aluminum tubing 1⅛ inches in diameter with walls .058 inches thick. It should be drawn tubing of 6061 alloy tempered to T-6 hardness. Poles made of this material have proved themselves in national competition after development by champion poler Syl Beletz.

Roughen the inside surfaces of the tubing at each end for several inches with a round file so that plugs can be glued in and bond well. Cut two scraps of Styrofoam into plugs about four inches long to fit into the ends of the tubing. Coat these with epoxy resin and push them into the ends of the pole, making sure the ends are sealed so that the pole cannot sink. To make the ends more durable, cut some scraps of fiberglass into circles of the same diameter as the inside of the tube, saturate them with resin, and cover the Styrofoam with them.

Most polers prefer to paint their poles, for aesthetics, visibility, a quick visual reference when poling to help locate the hands on the pole, and to keep their hands from getting covered with aluminum oxide. The best base is an anodized covering on the pole, and if a company in your area does anodizing, you may be able to have your pole run through with something else for a reasonable charge. Otherwise, paint the pole with some paint made for metals and plan on frequent retouching.

Polers have different preferences for marking out distances on the pole. One way is to paint a series of colored stripes at three-foot intervals over the basic paint job. Paint a center stripe of one color, two stripes of another color three feet in each direction down the pole, and so on to the ends.

BAILERS

It is handy to have large sponges tied within convenient reach of both bow and stern paddlers. (Buy the biggest ones you can find.) Make a hole through the center of the sponge and tie it to the canoe with string. Remember not to use too strong a string, in case it gets tangled around your leg in a spill.

At least the stern should also have a good-sized bailer that can be used for dipping out deeper bilge in a hurry. You can make a good one by cutting off the lower end of a bleach bottle or a similar plastic gallon jug with a large handle at the top, as shown in the photograph.

A bailer made from a bleach bottle with the bottom cut off.

TARP-TUBE TENT

This is an easy shelter to make that is quite useful and versatile for canoe camping. It can be pitched as a tube tent for one or two people by fastening the ends together and then stringing it up between trees or rocks, thus forming a simple floored tent open at both ends. It can be pitched over the canoe or with other supports to form a roomy shelter for several people or a cooking fly for stand-up space in the rain.

Materials needed:

Twelve yards coated nylon material, 44 inches wide; urethane-coated taffeta weighing 3 ounces per square yard is about right;

11 feet Velcro tape, three-quarter-inch wide (separates into two tapes, one with hooks and the other with pile);

25 grommets, number 0 or 1, with setting tool and hole punch;

6 snaps with a setting tool; any reasonably large size will do; polyester thread, needles, seam sealer, and (preferably) access to a sewing machine.

Directions: This shelter is basically a large tarpaulin, twelve feet long and a little under eleven feet wide, with grommets along the sides so that it can easily be pitched or fastened in a number of ways, and with mating Velcro tape strips and snaps along the shorter sides, which permit the tarp to be joined into a tube and pitched with a line stretched between two supports as a tube tent.

Cut the fabric into three twelve-foot lengths. Sew them together, as shown in the drawing, using felled seams, then hem the tarp all the way around, making a one-inch hem along the twelve-foot sides and a two-inch hem along the shorter sides. When fitting the pieces together initially, be sure the coated sides of the fabric all end on the same side of the tarp.

Sew the strips of Velcro along the sides of the tarp with the two-inch hem. The edge of the Velcro should be one inch back from the edge of the tarp. The hook tape should be on one side of the tarp and the pile tape on the other so that when the tarp is wrapped into a tube the two will mate.

Install the six snaps at regular intervals along the Velcro tape to make alignment easy and prevent the Velcro from being pulled apart.

Install grommets at two-foot intervals along the edge of the tarp to provide convenient tie points.

THIGH STRAPS

Thigh straps installed in an open canoe can greatly improve control of the canoe in white-water. A method is shown here for installing them in a fiberglass canoe. In an aluminum one the method is basically the same, except that the brackets are made from bent aluminum and riveted to the canoe rather than being laid up with fiberglass.

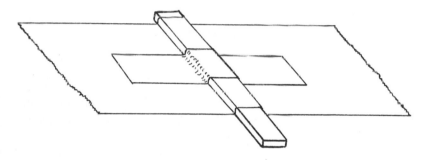

Detail of laying up fiberglass for a thigh-strap bracket.

The drawing above shows the basic method for laying up a bracket to hold the straps. Two brackets are needed for each set of straps installed. One set should be installed at each station that will be used for paddling in white-water. The brackets can either be laid up separately or a wider piece of fiberglass can be laid up and then cut into a number of brackets with a saber saw.

The person who will normally be using a particular set of thigh straps should kneel in the canoe to mark out the best position for the brackets. Normally, they should be placed to run across the canoe with the inside edges an inch or an inch and a half from the keel line, but the outside edges should not project so far that they will be under the knees and cause discomfort. In some cases it may be necessary to

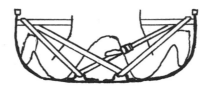

Lacing thigh straps in a canoe.

place them diagonally or even parallel to the keel line to keep them out of the way. The front edges of the brackets should come about three inches behind the knee caps. Once the position is determined, mark it in the canoe. Sand the bottoms of the brackets and a surrounding area where each will be placed on the bottom of the canoe. In both cases, sand down until glass fibers are exposed, since a strong bond will not be achieved otherwise. Paint the sanded areas of the brackets and the canoe with resin, put the brackets in place, and lay some scraps of fiberglass over each end of the brackets and saturate them with resin.

The upper fastening points for the straps will depend on the way the canoe is made. If a seat hung on framework or bars is used, the straps can usually pass around a tube or bar. A solid wood seat can have slots cut into it. Slots in the gunwales or additional brackets installed on the sides of the canoe just below the gunwales and behind the edge of the seat can also be used.

It is also worthwhile to glue in semipermanent knee pads to go with the thigh straps. They are comfortable, do not get lost, and straps for them can't get tangled with the thigh straps. Use ethafoam, Ensolite, Thermobar, or some other closed-cell foam about a half-inch thick and glue it to the canoe with contact cement.

The lengths of the straps themselves will vary with the arrangement of the canoe, but allow about ten feet of 1½-inch webbing for each strap. The ends should be joined with a ladder buckle for adjustability and strung as shown.

GLOSSARY

INDEX

GLOSSARY

ABS. A material used for making very durable canoes. ABS is an abbreviation for acrylonitrile butadiene styrene, but the material actually used for manufacturing canoes is a sandwich of ABS, foam, and vinyl that varies somewhat with the manufacturer. The material is heated and pressed into a mold during manufacture.

BAR. A deposit of sand or gravel. In rivers, bars are formed where the current slows down and thus can no longer carry as much sediment. Typically, bars are found below bends on the inside, at places where the river widens, or where the gradient suddenly is reduced. In rivers carrying heavy loads of detritus, bars may shift constantly. When the water is low, a bar may block most of the river.

BEAM. The width of a boat at its widest point, normally amidships in a canoe.

BIG WATER. Water flowing rapidly in a river carrying a large volume. Big water implies special hydraulic phenomena associated with heavy turbulence, very dangerous for inexperienced boaters and normally unsuited for open boats. Very large and powerful holes, frothy eddies with shifting eddy lines, whirlpools, and similar difficulties are typical of big water.

BOULDER GARDEN. A white-water section of a river in which there is no clear channel because of the large number of exposed rocks; requires a great deal of maneuvering to negotiate.

BOW. The forward end of a boat. Since the front and rear are symmetrical in most canoes, the arrangement of the seats and thwarts determines which end is the bow: the seat or thwart in the bow is farther from the tip of the canoe than the seat or thwart in the stern.

BRACE. A noun or verb describing strokes in which the canoeist leans on the paddle, using the resistance of the water to maintain balance. Braces are the foundation of modern white-water paddling technique. In a *high brace* the forearms are both raised and the paddler braces on the same side of the paddle as that which pushes against the water in a forward stroke. In a *low brace* the forearms are lowered and the opposite side of the paddle is used to brace.

BROACH. To turn sideways across the current. To broach against a rock is to crash into it broadside approximately at the center of the canoe so that the current tends to pin the boat against the rock.

C-1, C-2. Designations used in competition for one-person and two-person canoes, respectively. Since international-style competition in the United States is mainly in white-water races, these abbreviations are often used to refer to the closed boats used in these races, particularly the slalom.

CARRY. See PORTAGE.

CHANNEL. The path followed by a major fraction of the water flowing down a river, where the water is deepest and the current fastest. There may be several channels at a given place in a river.

CHUTE. A narrow, steep slot through which one of the main channels of a river flows.

CLOSED BOAT. A canoe that has a rounded deck connecting directly to the hull and forming an integral structure with it, with only a small opening or openings for the paddler(s). Closed boats are designed for paddling in turbulent water without the danger of swamping. The spaces around each paddler are sealed off with a device called a spray skirt to prevent the entry of any water. Even in case of capsizing, a skilled paddler can right the boat with an Eskimo roll.

COAMING. The rim around the cockpit of a closed boat into which the elasticized edge of a spray skirt fits.

COCKPIT. The opening in the deck of a closed boat in which the paddler kneels.

DECK. The horizontal surface running between the sides of a boat. In standard canoes decks are the small triangles covering the angle between the sides at each end of the canoe. In closed boats, decks are the curved top halves that join with the hulls below to form continuous curved structures.

DECKED CANOE. See CLOSED BOAT.

DOWNRIVER CANOE. A canoe designed specifically for downriver racing, in which the object is to negotiate several miles of white-water at maximum speed. Such craft are unstable and difficult to maneuver except in the hands of experts.

DRAFT. The depth to which a boat sinks in the water at its lowest point, a figure that naturally varies with the load it is carrying. Canoes generally have a very shallow draft.

DROP. A place where a river descends steeply between more level sections.

EDDY. An area in a river where the water moves in the direction opposite to the main current. Eddies form behind obstructions in the current, around bends, and at places where the channel suddenly widens. Eddies make good places for the canoeist to stop and look at the river below, and their current reversals can be used to maneuver the canoe. Mastering them is the key to white-water paddling.

EDDY LINE. The boundary along the edge of an eddy where the main current and the reverse current meet. The eddy line is often quite sharp and may be very turbulent. Crossing strong eddy lines successfully demands considerable practice.

EDDY TURN. A technique for moving into an eddy from the main current or back out again into the current. The canoe is leaned into the turn to resist the capsizing force of the current shift, using a paddle in the current the boat is entering as a pivot.

ENDER. A spectacular maneuver performed in a closed boat in which one end of the canoe is driven down into the subsurface current in a hole and the whole boat turns end over end. Enders are done on purpose by good paddlers playing in rapids and are sometimes performed unintentionally by novices.

ENTRY ANGLE. The angle formed by the bow of a canoe at the waterline. A small or sharp entry angle requires the water displaced to be accelerated more slowly, so the canoe will be easier to drive forward and will thus go faster. A large or broad entry angle requires the water to be pushed aside more rapidly, so the canoe will be slower and require more effort to paddle.

ESKIMO ROLL. A maneuver used by closed boaters to right a capsized canoe by sweeping the paddle(s) out to an angle perpendicular to the side of the canoe and levering the canoe up.

FALLS. A drop where the water cascades very steeply over a ledge or group of submerged rocks. It may or may not be runnable, depending on the exact configuration, water level, types of canoes being used, and skill of the paddlers.

FEATHER. To rotate the paddle ninety degrees as it is brought forward through the air between strokes so that the blade is parallel to the surface of the water. Feathering reduces wind resistance and allows the paddle to be recovered closer to the surface of the water.

FLOTATION. Buoyant material or sealed air chambers attached to a canoe or incorporated in its structure to make it float. Canoes being paddled in turbulent white-water are usually provided with extra flotation so they will float high and be subject to less damage if they capsize.

FREEBOARD. The height of the side of a loaded canoe standing above the waterline at the lowest point, normally amidships. For canoeing in calm water the rule of thumb is that there should be at least six inches of freeboard to provide a reasonable margin of safety.

GRAB LOOP. A loop of rope or webbing attached to the bow or stern of a boat to provide a grip for portaging, rescuing, or swimming with the canoe. Paddlers of closed boats generally prefer grab loops to painters.

GUNWALE. The stiff, wear-absorbing strips attached along the upper edges of the sides of the canoe. Traditionally, gunwales are made of hardwood, but many other materials may be used, including cast upper pieces that comprise gunwales, seats, and thwarts. With traditional construction the inside strips are called inwales, the outside ones, outwales.

HAYSTACK. A large STANDING WAVE. Its steep sides and foamy top make it resemble a haystack. It is difficult to ride haystacks in an open canoe without shipping water.

HEAVY WATER. White-water that exhibits turbulent hydraulics because of powerful currents. Heavy water describes boiling eddies, transient whirlpools moving along a canyon or down an eddy line, very large and dangerous holes, and violent eddy lines in which the water from the main current tends to sheet over the boundary, making it powerful, wide, and indistinct.

HOLE (SOUSE HOLE). A low spot that may form in a river when fast-moving water travels over an obstacle or steep drop that is not too deeply submerged. The main current dives down on the far side of the obstruction so that a very steep standing wave forms downstream from the depression, and the surface current often runs back down into the hole. This reverse current on the surface, combined with the steepness of the wave, may trap floating objects such as canoes and swimmers for a time. Usually, they wash out after a short while. The single downstream wave with a surface current flowing back into the hole is a REVERSAL. Holes can be dangerous, especially for open boats, but they also provide some of the most interesting play spots for closed boats.

HULL. The lower part of a boat, the section normally in the water. The lower half of the boat in fiberglass white-water canoes.

KEEL. A projecting fin running from bow to stern along the outside centerline of a boat, designed to provide directional stability, to protect the bottom from scrapes, and to prevent the boat from slipping sideways through the water. Keels on canoes are always shallow, generally no deeper than an inch and a half, and are often omitted altogether except on aluminum craft, for which they serve the additional purpose of joining the two halves. *Shoe keels* are very shallow keels. *Bilge keels,* extra keels placed to either side to provide additional protection against scraping, are rarely used on canoes made from tough modern materials.

KEEPER. See STOPPER.

LINE. The nautical term for a rope. To line a canoe through rapids means to float it through without passengers, using lines to guide it.

MARATHON. A flat-water race over some distance involving open canoes with standard specifications. The race is a point-to-point one involving no maneuvering except that demanded by the nature of the course, but there may be portages. The term is borrowed from the long-distance foot race of the same name.

OPEN BOAT. A standard canoe with no permanent covering over the inside of the boat, although removable spray covers of fabric, fiberglass, or plywood may be attached for white-water use. The term distinguishes conventional canoes from white-water closed boats on which the hull and deck form a single curved structure with openings large enough only for the paddlers to get in and out.

PAINTER. A line attached to the bow or stern of a canoe, ranging from ten to twenty-five feet long, to simplify lining, rescue, and landing operations. Most open-boat paddlers attach a painter to each end of the boat, securing it under a length of shock cord or something else on the deck so that it cannot wrap around the leg of a swimmer or catch in rocks accidentally. Closed-boat paddlers tend to prefer grab loops alone, without painters attached, because the Eskimo roll makes rescues less necessary. Closed boats are also less likely to swamp or broach badly, because of their construction, and the danger of having a painter wrap around a swimmer's leg is far greater in the turbulent water in which closed boats are paddled.

PILLOW. A cushion of water formed by the current of a river bouncing against the upstream side of an obstacle. A pillow helps deflect the hull away from the obstruction and gives the paddler advance warning of its position.

PITCH. A distinct and usually short section of rapids between two quiet sections of river or two resting spots.

PLAY SPOT. A place in rapids especially suited to maneuvering back and forth, generally a chute with eddies on either side and with safe water below so that canoeists can safely risk capsizing.

POOL-AND-DROP. A term used to describe a river that alternates between steep rapids and long, quiet sections so that the average gradient does not give a true indication of the difficulty.

PORTAGE. To carry a canoe and equipment around a set of rapids or across land between lakes. Used as a noun, portage can describe the act of carrying or the ground over which a canoe must be carried.

RAPID(S). A section of river in which the water is rough because of a combination of a steep gradient and obstructions in the channel.

REVERSAL. A standing wave having a backward-running surface current on the upstream side, with the main current diving below the surface. Reversals are found below some holes and may trap floating objects, including canoes and swimmers, in the holes. See also STOPPER.

RIFFLE. A relatively inconsequential rapid with small waves.

ROCKER. The upward curve of the bottom of a hull along the keel line toward each end of the canoe. A canoe with a level keel line is said to have no rocker, whereas one that curves up several inches toward each end is said to have pronounced rocker. A canoe with significant rocker will be more maneuverable than one with a straight bottom but will not be as easy to paddle on flat water.

ROLLER. A large, breaking reversal wave.

RUDDER. A stroke in which the paddle is inserted in the water while the canoe is moving, to deflect its direction, like a rudder on a ship or sailboat.

SCOUT. To inspect a rapid before running, lining, or portaging it.

SLALOM. A race, derived from the skier's slalom race, in which the object is to paddle a canoe through a number of gates (sets of two poles through which the canoes and paddlers must pass) in the proper sequence and manner. A slalom is usually set up over white-water and is a test of maneuvering skill. One's score is the number of seconds required to run the course added to penalty points assessed for mistakes in negotiating the gates.

SLEEPER. A rock just below the surface with no prominent wave disclosing its location.

SPRAY COVER. A covering for an open canoe that seals the boat off from the entry of sloshing water. Used for paddling in white-water or in very large waves. It may be made from fabric, plywood, or fiberglass and usually has elasticized tunnels that fit around the paddlers' waists.

SPRAY SKIRT. A tunnel made from coated fabric or neoprene rubber that seals the gap between the coaming of a closed boat and the waist of the paddler.

STANDING WAVE. A stationary wave in a river, which dissipates the energy of the rushing water below a drop. A chute or deeply buried obstacle will usually have a series of gradually diminishing standing waves downriver of it, though a shallowly covered rock typically has only one. So named because the wave stays in the same place while the water moves on downstream. By contrast, waves on lakes and oceans move while the water remains in place.

STEM. The curved endpiece on either the bow or stern of a canoe. A separate unit in wood-and-canvas or aluminum construction but not in molded canoes.

STERN. The rear end of a boat. See BOW.

STOPPER. A REVERSAL wave that extends for some distance across a river, especially one unbroken over the entire channel, which tends to trap floating objects. Stoppers occur because the main current dives below the surface and the water on the back of the standing wave runs back down into the trough. They typically form below dams, and even very small ones can be extremely hazardous.

SWAMP. To fill up with water, as when a large wave comes over the side. A swamped canoe is unstable, difficult to paddle, and in a river is readily damaged by rocks.

SWEEP. A forward or backward stroke in which the paddle is swept in an arc to turn the canoe.

SWEEPER. A fallen tree that extends over a channel of the river at or a little above the surface. The current flows underneath, and the branches often form a seine in the water. Sweepers are one of the true hazards of river running. While the current is deflected from a rock and will push a canoe away from a collision, the force of the water can carry unwary boaters under a sweeper, drag them from their canoe, and perhaps trap them underwater. In addition, sweepers may fall or wash into familiar stretches of rivers that paddlers unthinkingly run without first scouting.

TECHNICAL. A term that describes white-water that is complex, filled with obstacles, and has no clear channel so that a lot of precise maneuvering is required, though the water is not necessarily turbulent or powerful.

THIGH STRAPS. Straps, usually adjustable and made of nylon webbing, fitted to go over the legs of a kneeling paddler to allow firm gripping of the canoe.

THWART. A crosspiece running between the upper edges of the sides of a canoe, generally between the gunwales. Thwarts serve to make the structure of the canoe rigid and are often used as supports for the buttocks of a kneeling paddler. Thwart placement is therefore often chosen to be compatible with particular paddling positions. A center thwart may also be used for portaging the canoe.

TRACKING. The characteristic of holding a straight course. A long canoe with little rocker and with a keel or V-shaped hull tends to track well, whereas a short canoe with a rounded or flat bottom and pronounced rocker will track poorly. Tracking also refers to the action of dragging a canoe upstream using bow and stern lines.

YOKE. A support carved or molded to fit the shoulders, to aid in portaging a canoe. A yoke may be permanently affixed to the canoe or may be designed to be attached to the center thwart or gunwales when needed.

INDEX